Parenting Bright Kids With Autism

Parenting Bright Kids With Autism discusses the frustrations, the diagnoses, the challenges, and the joys as parents help their gifted children with autism spectrum disorders (ASD) thrive in school and at home. This book:

- ◆ Helps families navigate twice-exceptional life by translating best practice into helpful advice.
- ◆ Guides parents who are trying to reach out, find information, and develop their child's talents.
- ◆ Helps parents acknowledge and get help for, but not focus on, areas of challenge.
- ◆ Is written by a professor of special education who is also a mother of a gifted child with high-functioning autism.
- ◆ Is a revision of the popular *Children With High-Functioning Autism*.

Topics range from understanding the first signs of autism and the diagnosis, finding a support network, and filling out necessary paperwork, to determining the various types of therapies available and planning for adulthood. The book also discusses issues that these kids may face as they become teenagers and enter college. With the advice and encouragement provided in this book, parents will receive valuable insight into this new world of caring for a gifted child with autism.

Claire E. Hughes-Lynch, Ph.D., is Professor of Elementary and Special Education at the College of Coastal Georgia, USA. A Fulbright Scholar to Greece, she has taught in twice-exceptional programs and lives her life in twos—two cats, two dogs, two children (but one husband) across two countries.

Parenting Bright Kids With Autism

Helping Twice-Exceptional Children With Asperger's and High-Functioning Autism

Claire E. Hughes-Lynch

Routledge
Taylor & Francis Group

NEW YORK AND LONDON

Cover image: © Shutterstock

First published 2022
by Routledge
605 Third Avenue, New York, NY 10158

and by Routledge
4 Park Square, Milton Park, Abingdon, Oxon, OX14 4RN

Routledge is an imprint of the Taylor & Francis Group, an informa business

© 2022 Taylor & Francis

Library of Congress Cataloging-in-Publication Data
Names: Hughes-Lynch, Claire E., 1967-author.
Title: Parenting bright kids with autism: helping twice-exceptional children with asperger's and high-functioning autism/Claire E. Hughes-Lynch, Ph.D.
Description: New York, NY: Routledge, 2022. | Includes bibliographical references.
Identifiers: LCCN 2021043119 (print) | LCCN 2021043120 (ebook) | ISBN 9781646320639 (paperback) | ISBN 9781003237006 (ebook)
Subjects: LCSH: Autism in children–Popular works. | Autistic children.
Classification: LCC RJ506.A9 H823 2022 (print) | LCC RJ506.A9 (ebook) | DDC 618.92/85882–dc23
LC record available at https://lccn.loc.gov/2021043119
LC ebook record available at https://lccn.loc.gov/2021043120

ISBN: 978-1-64632-063-9 (pbk)
ISBN: 978-1-003-23700-6 (ebk)

DOI: 10.4324/9781003237006

Typeset in Palatino
by Deanta Global Publishing Services, Chennai, India

Contents

Preface

Construction Zone: What Is New and Different in This Book?

Changes in Children: Elizabeth and Ray Grew Up

In the first edition of this book, *Children With High-Functioning Autism*, I told stories about my children in my voice. By sharing my story, I hoped to help others. I still want to help families impacted by autism, but the story is now bigger than just mine. Ten years have passed, and my children are the authors of their own stories now. In this book, I will include their voices when they give permission, but I have amended some stories, shared other families' stories, and broadened the scope. I realized along the way that *voice* is an incredibly important concept because recognizing voice begins the recognition of a person. I have also done a lot of reading in the past ten years, and I recognize how my experience of autism is that of a mother, a teacher, and an advocate, but I cannot speak for someone who has autism. I can only speak as someone who has been impacted by autism, and I can only speak to families who are trying to navigate these waters. At the end of this book, there is a list of some essential resources, and I would highly recommend the books written by people with autism themselves. They are the real experts. As Maya Angelou said, "Now that I know better, I do better" (Oprah, 2011).

Changes in Definitions: DSM-5 and 2eCOP

Since the original book was written, the fifth edition of the *Diagnostic and Statistical Manual of Mental Disorders* (DSM-5) was released, and with it came many changes in autism diagnostic language (American Psychiatric Association, 2013). Gone are the categories. Gone are the differences between pervasive developmental disorder-not otherwise specified (PDD-NOS) and Asperger's syndrome. The *DSM-5* subsumed multiple types of autistic-like conditions, such as Asperger's, PDD-NOS, and childhood disintegrative disorder into code 299.00 under the category *autism spectrum disorder,* often abbreviated as ASD. Although the term *Asperger's* has been merged into ASD, there is still a rather sizeable group of people who use the term—not in a diagnostic manner, but in a descriptive manner—to distinguish those who struggle with appropriate usage of language from those who struggle with more global language processing (Autism Society, n.d.). Elizabeth shared with me recently that she distinctly remembers when our dog died when she was five, and she had no idea what to say to me when I was crying. She still flashes back to that helpless feeling of not knowing what to say when someone is crying. Finding the words at emotionally charged moments is an issue different than not having words at all.

The *DSM-5* now uses two criteria for autism: (1) persistent deficits in social communication and social interaction, and (2) restricted, repetitive patterns of behavior, interests, or activities (APA, 2013) that interact with each other. See Figure 0.1.

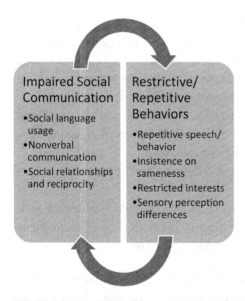

Impaired Social Communication
- Social language usage
- Nonverbal communication
- Social relationships and reciprocity

Restrictive/ Repetitive Behaviors
- Repetitive speech/ behavior
- Insistence on samenesss
- Restricted interests
- Sensory perception differences

FIGURE 0.1 Autism Criteria from the DSM-5 (APA, 2013)

The first criterion of ASD defines three communication deficits that appear in multiple contexts, meaning that they cannot occur in only one place or around one person. Examples of communication deficits can include challenges with back-and-forth conversation, failure to initiate or respond to communication, and/or a reduced sharing of interests or emotions. For parents, this can mean that their child might only talk about one topic when they are anxious. A mother I know shared that she knew her young adult son was stressed when he asked her if a date went badly because he couldn't explain cephalopods well enough. Examples also include issues with nonverbal communication, such as a lack of gestures, facial expressions, and/or eye contact. Although avoiding eye contact is supposed to be one of the hallmarks of autism, I find the *autism gaze* to be more significant, where autistic individuals might be able to make eye contact, but their facial emotional responses are different (Gillespie-Lynch et al., 2013). There is often a "flatness" of expression around the eyes, or a different way of looking. Lastly, the communication aspect of ASD can also be found in the problematic use of language, such as cracking jokes at inappropriate times or difficulty "code switching" and changing vocabulary for different audiences.

The second criterion of ASD states that two of four possible aspects of "restrictive or repetitive behavior" must be present, either at the current time or in the past. These restrictions include:

1. Repetitive movements and use of objects or speech, such as lining up toys, repeated phrases, or physical movements;
2. Insistence on sameness, rituals, or routines, such as the need to eat the same food every day, scripts for greetings, and distress when the routines are not followed;
3. Highly restricted or fixated interests that are abnormal in intensity or focus; and
4. Hypo- or hyperreactions to sensory input or interest in sensory input from the environment, such as lack of awareness of pain or fascination with lights or movement.

The *DSM-5* clarified that ASD is not a "have/don't have" diagnosis, but that it varies according to levels of severity. There is no blood test for autism. The severity of the autism is defined as the ability to function in a given environment. Levels of support needed range from Level 1, which is a mild level of support, to Level 3, which is substantial support (APA, 2013). Support systems in a school might range from a 1:1 paraprofessional, to provision of the day's schedule on the board. Although types of support are highly situational, the emphasis is on the fit between the individual and the demands of the environment. This flexible model of support emphasizes the social model of disability, in which the presence and severity of a disability is not diagnosed by a doctor but is determined by those within the environment based on the social and behavioral demands and the individual's need for assistance to meet those demands (Shakespeare & Watson, 2001). This definition shifts the focus from "How much autism does someone have?" to "How much support does someone need?"

Around the time of the *DSM-5* changes in autism identification, the Twice-Exceptional National Community of Practice (2eCoP) shared its definition of twice-exceptionality that described how people could be gifted and have a disability at the same time (Council for Exceptional Children—The Association for the Gifted, 2021, para. 1). This definition states that:

Twice-exceptional (2e) individuals evidence exceptional ability and disability, which results in a unique set of circumstances. Their exceptional ability may dominate, hiding their disability; their disability may dominate, hiding their exceptional ability; each may mask the other so that neither is recognized nor addressed. Additionally, twice-exceptional individuals come from—and are impacted—by neurological, linguistic, socio-economic, individual, and cultural diversity.

2e students are capable, and may perform below, at or above grade level. They may require additional considerations in the following:

◆ **Identification**: Specialized methods of identification that consider the possible interaction of the exceptionalities

◆ **Instruction**: Enriched/advanced educational opportunities and pedagogies that develop the child's interests, gifts and talents while also meeting the child's other learning needs

◆ **Support Services**: Simultaneous supports that ensure the child's academic success and social-emotional well-being, such as specialized accommodations and interventions

Working successfully with this unique population requires specialized academic training and ongoing professional learning.

These two definitional shifts are part of a shift in focus of schools and professionals away from diagnosing what is wrong with a person to determining what could be improved in the environment. At the same time, in the past ten years, there has been a significant change in our culture; we are now looking at practices and determining how we can be more inclusive and welcoming of all people. Although the battle for services, recognition, and appreciation is still one that families of bright children with autism have to face, there are a lot of other families fighting similar battles.

Changes in Scientific Findings

Perhaps one of the biggest changes in scientific findings is that the rate of autism continues to increase. When the first edition of this book was written in 2010, autism was being diagnosed at the rate of 1 in 110 children—an already stunning number compared to the 1 in 10,000 in the 1980s and the 1 in 500 children in the 1990s. Currently, the Centers for Disease Control (Maenner et al., 2020) estimate that 1 in 54 children are diagnosed with autism before they are eight years old. I will discuss the changing prevalence and possible causes in Chapter 2, but the science and the awareness continues to grow.

A major area of growth in scientific understanding is in the role of genetics. A large-scale study (Satterstrom et al., 2020)

of more than 35,000 people around the globe identified differences in more than 102 genes, with 53 of those significantly tied to autism. The higher the intellectual abilities of the individual, the more autistic impact those 53 genes had on their functioning. Findings like these have led to the collaboration at the University of Iowa between the Belin-Blank Center for Gifted Education and Talent Development and the Iowa Neuroscience Institute to further examine this neurological relationship between giftedness, twice-exceptionality, and autism.

Ironically, while scientific knowledge of autism has increased in the last ten years, the perception of the link between autism and immunizations has polarized into two different groups. The scientific findings of the lack of a link between autism and immunizations have remained consistent over the last decade, even with numerous additional research studies. Autism is (still) not caused by immunizations. This has been found over and over again by government agencies around the world (CDC, 2020; National Institute of Neurological Disorders and Stroke, 2015); large studies in the United States (Jain et al., 2015), the United Kingdom (Kaye et al., 2001), and Denmark (Hviid et al., 2019); many organizational studies (American Academy of Pediatrics, 2018); and large metanalyses of all of the data (Taylor et al., 2014). Three components of scientific data have attempted to demolish this link:

1. None of these studies have been able to replicate the original flawed and unethically determined "results."
2. Numerous heavy metals, including mercury, have been removed from immunizations since 2000, and yet the rate of autism continues to increase.
3. There is a similar rate of autism found among unimmunized groups.

However, with the rise of social media, there has been a rise in "immunization-hesitant" families. Although only 16% of surveyed families who had children with autism considered immunizations a factor in their child's autism (Fombonne et al., 2020), more than 77% of the families who are hesitant to immunize are so because of a fear of autism (Statista Research Department, 2016). Interestingly enough, the families with an autistic child who believed there was a link to their child's immunizations tended to be from poverty and poorly educated (Fombonne et al., 2020), while the families who were more hesitant about vaccines tended to come from more highly educated areas, with affluent areas around New York City and Austin, TX, leading the way (LaVito, 2019).

It should also be noted that there is not only a factual issue with the connection between autism and immunizations, but also growing ethical and public health issues. Children who are not immunized run the risk of dying from preventable diseases. There is a serious ethical inference that families would prefer the risk of death to the risk of autism (Picciuto, 2021). Although the possibility of dying from autism is zero, the possibility of dying from measles is small but possible; 2 out of 1,000 patients die in the United States, and globally the World Health Organization (2019) estimated that more than 140,000 children died of measles in 2018. "Measles anywhere is a threat to children everywhere," stated Henrietta Fore, UNICEF's executive director (World Health Organization, 2019, p. 19).

Rise of Awareness/Social Media

Another significant change in the last ten years has been the rise of awareness of autism. The character Sheldon on *The Big Bang Theory*, in particular, has well established the image of a bright person with probable autism who has loveable quirks while maintaining a job and a circle of friends. Although the experience of many families may not be as rosy or amusing, the perception of autism has shifted significantly because of this popular media character. Other popular media portrayals, such as the novel and the play *The Curious Incident of the Dog in the Night-Time* or the television show *The Good Doctor*, also demonstrate the links between autism and intelligence and functioning.

In addition to changes in media portrayal, there has been the rise of social media, which allows families and individuals with autism to find each other and provide support. There has been an influx of autism-friendly sites and groups that allow people to share their experiences and even begin to question the "standard" views of autism. There are several Facebook groups, including "Finding Poppies" and "Parents of Twice-Exceptional Students," that share and support the various challenges that face families and individuals who are smart but have other issues. Social media in the last decade has emerged as a significant force in the mobilization and knowledge distribution of what it means to be bright with autism. This impact of social media has also fueled some "neuromyths," such as antivaccination rhetoric and learning styles, while in other cases, it has helped mobilize social movements, such as neurodiversity.

Rise of Neurodiversity and the Social Model of Intervention

Originating in the biological concept that a species' strength and survival are based on the diversity of the species, the neurodiversity movement takes an activist role that human diversity is to be celebrated and accommodated rather than "cured." Steve Silberman (2015) stated that:

> [T]he notion that conditions like autism, dyslexia, and attention-deficit/hyperactivity disorder (ADHD) should be regarded as naturally occurring cognitive variations with distinctive strengths that have contributed to the evolution of technology and culture rather than mere checklists of deficits and dysfunctions.
>
> (p. 6)

There are several "battles" that this group fights in order to receive respect, including issues of "curing," imagery, and phraseology.

One of the major battles that neurodiversity fights is the issue of "curing" autism. For many years, the stated goal of Autism Speaks, one of the major autism charities and advocacy organizations, was to "cure" autism. Autistic people, justifiably, don't feel that they need "curing"—what needs "curing" are societal barriers and attitudes that do not accept who they are. One autistic friend of mine said, when discussing the issue of immunizations, that it was unbelievable to him that even if vaccinations *did* cause autism (which they don't), *people would rather choose death by measles or mumps than to be autistic*. His perspective shifted mine rather dramatically. Although Autism Speaks changed their mission in 2016 to remove the word "cure" from their goals, the damage in perception had been done.

Imagery used to promote the awareness and acceptance of autism is a significant area of issue. For years, the image of the puzzle piece has been used, primarily by Autism Speaks, as a metaphor for the "puzzle" of autism and the concept of "solving" it. Clearly, the neurodiversity movement does not perceive autism as something that needs "solving" and rejects the puzzle piece, preferring to ask: if autism is so puzzling, why don't people try to get to know people with autism? Similarly, the color blue has often been used to represent autism. "Light It Up Blue" is a call to action for the month of April, and many places, such as the Empire State Building and the White House, used blue lights to demonstrate their support for autism. There are numerous problems with this imagery that the neurodiversity movement rejects. The color blue was initially chosen because of the overrepresentation of boys among those diagnosed with autism and the impression that autism is a "boy disease." In addition, these organizations seek to raise money to "cure" autism in much the same way that cancer or juvenile diabetes should be cured.

Recently, the blue puzzle piece now has a trace of pink at the bottom, and the language has shifted to "April for Autism Awareness" or "Autism Acceptance." In 2016, Autism Speaks, after pressure from advocacy groups, changed their mission to "advocate with" the autism community. However, they only have two autistic people on their board of directors and very few people with autism in leadership positions making decisions. There has been significant damage done. The divisions among the autism organizations are deep and highlight the anger that autistic people feel when people without autism are making decisions. "Nothing About Us Without Us" is the rallying cry of the Autistic Self Advocacy Network, revealing an increased demand for self-determination, and numerous neurodiversity movement organizations have adopted the infinity symbol in a rainbow motif to emphasize the concept of *spectrum*, not as a series of shades, but as a range of differences.

A significant ongoing battle is in the use of phraseology. Is autism a *condition* or a *disorder*? As Robert Dudas et al. (2017) noted,

> We prefer the term ASC (Autism Spectrum Condition) rather than ASD (Autism Spectrum Disorder) because it is less stigmatizing. Also, ASC is more consistent with the fact that these individuals have not only disabilities requiring a medical diagnosis, but also areas of cognitive strength.
>
> (p. 1)

Simon Baron-Cohen (2010), a well-known British autism researcher, noted that without the term "disorder," there is no inferred medical issue, and American insurance companies would be unlikely to pay for treatment and interventions. His study of American autistic college students found that when they perceived autism to be *different*, they were more focused on career aspirations than those who perceived autism as a *disability*. However, it is unknown to what degree the level of support impacts people's perceptions.

Another phraseology issue is how we refer to people who have autism. Called *people-first language*, the phrase *people with autism* emphasizes the humanity of the person first and their area of disability second. People are not defined in their personhood by their disability; it just happens to be a characteristic that they have. We commonly refer to *students with learning disabilities* or *students with ADHD*. Such a practice appears at face value to be very respectful. But in a powerful essay "Why I Dislike Person-First Language," Jim Sinclair (2013) stated that he *is* autistic, just as he *is* generous; you would never say a *person with generosity*. He also noted that placing autism last implies that is something that can be separated from the person, like a coat. He felt instead that his autism shapes who he is—as part of his identity; autism is him and he is autistic. He noted that saying *person with autism*:

suggests that autism is something bad—so bad that it isn't even consistent with being a person. No one objects to using adjectives to refer to characteristics of a person that are considered positive or neutral. We talk about left-handed people, not people with left-handedness.

(para. 4)

Lydia Brown (2011) further stated:

when we say, "Autistic person," we recognize, affirm, and validate an individual's identity as an Autistic person. We recognize the value and worth of that individual as an Autistic person—that being Autistic is not a condition absolutely irreconcilable with regarding people as inherently valuable and worth something.

(para. 1)

She went on to say, "To those of you who use 'person with autism,' I will always respect your Constitutional right to express yourself however you like, but I urge you to reconsider the consequences of using such language" (Brown, 2011, para. 21). Perceptions cannot shift without language used to shift them.

In addition to the shifting language around autism in the last ten years, there has been shifting language around the terms *gifted* and *twice-exceptional*. June Maker first described children who had disabilities but were also gifted as *gifted-handicapped* in 1977, a term that was changed to *twice-exceptional* in the 1980s by Dr. James Gallagher (Coleman et al., 2005). The term was then shortened to *2e* in the mid-2000s (Baum, 2019), perhaps to separate it from *exceptional child education* or special education. In the more than 40 years since it has been in existence, the term *twice-exceptional* has become relatively commonly used throughout the field of gifted education and, although it is not specifically used in the Individuals With Disabilities Education Act (1990), several memos from the U.S. Department of Education (2010, 2013, 2015) do use the term.

Even the term *gifted* has been in flux during the last decade. In a 2011 article, Rena Subotnik et al. stated that although *gifted* implied a potential for high achievement contained within a person, the concept of *talent development* emphasized the process of nurturing someone's capacity and the need to remove barriers from their trajectory. Both the fields of gifted education and autism are deemphasizing the medical model of individual identification and moving toward the social model of environmental intervention. In other words, we are moving away from a perspective of focusing on the fixed nature of an individual (i.e., "The child *is* gifted/autistic") and toward a more dynamic, developmental viewpoint (i.e., "What can we do to help children grow and develop from where they are?").

Hence, the title of this book: *Parenting Bright Kids With Autism*. I didn't want to exclude children who, for whatever reasons, did not have a label of giftedness. *Bright* is an imperfect way of capturing those children who are above their age peers in intellectual curiosity and who need more than their typical age peers in academic interventions. I also didn't use the term *twice-exceptional* because autism is only one form of being twice-exceptional. Finally, I strongly debated using the phrase *autistic bright children*. In this book, I recognize that I am writing from the viewpoint of someone who does not carry a diagnosis of autism and my "job" is to respect the viewpoint of the people with whom I am interacting. My own children do not currently identify with the autistic population, and that is their prerogative. Depending on the demands of the environment, they may have reactions that might be considered symptomatic of having autism, but they are experiencing an ongoing understanding of themselves. Identity is incredibly complex, and people's choices should be respected. I am also an educator who works with teachers to develop strategies and methods to help children with disabilities and their families learn and grow. For these reasons, I often use the phrase *children/people with autism* because of my background, but I have taken efforts to change my language within this book when appropriate. I know that my efforts will not please everyone, and I ask that you see this book as transitional—in the process of moving from one paradigm to another.

References

American Academy of Pediatrics. (2018). *Vaccine safety: Examine the evidence*. https://www.healthychildren.org/English/safety-prevention/immunizations/Pages/Vaccine-Studies-Examine-the-Evidence.aspx

American Psychiatric Association (APA). (2013). *Diagnostic and statistical manual of mental disorders* (5th ed.). https://doi.org/10.1176/appi.books.9780890425596

Autism Society. (n.d.). *Asperger's resources*. https://www.autism-society.org/what-is/aspergers-syndrome

Baum, S. (2019, October). *2e history* [Keynote presentation]. Bridges Academy Annual Conference, Los Angeles, CA, United States.

Baron-Cohen, S. (2010). Autism: Difference or disorder? *The Neurotypical Site*. https://www.theneurotypical.com/autism_difference_or_disorder.html

Brown, L. (2011). The significance of semantics: Person-first language: Why it matters. https://www.autistichoya.com/2011/08/significance-of-semantics-person-first.html

Centers for Disease Control (CDC). (2020). *Vaccines do not cause autism*. https://www.cdc.gov/vaccinesafety/concerns/autism.html

Coleman, M. R., Harradine, C., & King, E. W. (2005). Meeting the needs of students who are twice exceptional. *Teaching Exceptional Children*, *38*(1), 5–6.

Council for Exceptional Children—The Association for the Gifted (2021). Definition of 2e. Board draft. Personal memo.

Dudas, R. B., Lovejoy, C., Cassidy, S., Allison, C., Smith, P., & Baron-Cohen, S. (2017). The overlap between autism spectrum conditions and borderline personality disorder. *PLOS ONE*, *12*(9), e018447. https://doi.org/10.1371/journal.pone.0184447

Fombonne, E., Goin-Kochel, R. P., O'Roak, B. J., & SPARK Consortium. (2020). Beliefs in vaccine as causes of autism among SPARK cohort caregivers. *Vaccine*, *38*(7), 1794–1803. https://doi.org/10.1016/j.vaccine.2019.12.026

Gillespie-Lynch, K., Elias, R., Escudero, P., Hutman, T., & Johnson, S. P. (2013). Atypical gaze following in autism: A comparison of three potential mechanisms. *Journal of Autism and Developmental Disorders*, *43*(12), 2779–2792. https://doi.org/10.1007/s10803-013-1818-7

Hviid, A., Hansen, J. V., Frisch, M., & Melbye, M. (2019). Measles, mumps, rubella vaccine and autism: A nationwide cohort study. *Annals of Internal Medicine, 170*(8), 513–520. https://doi.org/10.7326/M18-2101

Individuals With Disabilities Education Act, 20 U.S.C. §1401 *et seq.* (1990). https://sites.ed.gov/idea/statuteregulations

Jain, A., Marshall, J., Buikema, A., Bancroft, T., Kelly, J. P., & Newschaffer, C. J. (2015). Autism occurrence by MMR vaccine status among US children with older siblings with and without autism. *JAMA, 313*(15), 1534–1540. https://doi.org/10.1001/jama.2015.3077

Kaye, J. A., Melero-Montes, M. d. M., & Jick, H. (2001). Mumps, measles and rubella vaccine and the incidence of autism recorded by general practitioners: A time trend analysis. *The British Medical Journal, 322*(7288), 460–463. https://doi.org/10.1136/bmj.322.7284.460

LaVito, A. (2019, March 29). Here's where parents are refusing to get their children vaccinated. *CNBC Health and Science.* https://www.cnbc.com/2019/03/28/heres-where-parents-are-refusing-to-get-their-children-vaccinated.html

Maenner, M. J., Shaw, K. A., Baio, J., Washington, A., Patrick, M., DiRienzo, M., Christensen, D. L., Wiggins, L. D., Pettygrove, S., Andrews, J. G., Lopez, M., Hudson, A., Baroud, T., Schwenk, Y., White, T., Rosenberg, C. R., Lee, L.-C., Harrington, R. A., Huston, M., Hewitt, A., Esler, A., … Dietz, P. M. (2020). Prevalence of autism spectrum disorder among children aged 8 years—Autism and developmental disabilities monitoring network, 11 sites, United States, 2016. *MMWR Surveillance Summaries, 69*(4), 1–12. https://doi.org/10.15585/mmwr.ss6904a1

National Institute of Neurological Disorders and Stroke. (2015). *Autism spectrum disorder fact sheet* (Publication No. 15-1877). https://www.ninds.nih.gov/Disorders/Patient-Caregiver-Education/Fact-Sheets/Autism-Spectrum-Disorder-Fact-Sheet

Oprah (2011). *The powerful lesson Maya Angelou taught Oprah.* https://www.oprah.com/oprahs-lifeclass/the-powerful-lesson-maya-angelou-taught-oprah-video

Picciuto, E. (2021, January 19). Twisted anti-vaxxer parents choose fatal diseases over autism. *The Daily Beast.* https://www.thedailybeast.com/twisted-anti-vaxxer-parents-choose-fatal-diseases-over-autism

Satterstrom, F. K., Kosmicki, J. A., Wang., J., Breen, M. S., DeRubeis, S., An, J.-Y., Peng, M., Collina, R., J. Grove, Klei, L., Stevens, C., Reichert, J.,

Mulhern, M. S., Artomov, M., Gerges, S., Sheppard, B., Xu, X., Bhaduri, A., Norman, U., Brand, H., ... Buxbaum, J. D. (2020). Large-scaled exome sequencing study implicates both developmental and functional changes in the neurobiology of autism. *Cell, 180*(3), 568–584. https://doi.org/10.1016/j.cell.2019.12.036

Shakespeare, T., & Watson, N. (2001). The social model of disability: An outdated ideology? In S. N. Barnartt & B. M. Altman (Eds.), *Exploring theories and expanding methodologies: Where we are and where we need to go* (Vol. 2, pp. 9–28). Emerald Group.

Silberman, S. (2015). *NeuroTribes: The legacy of autism and the future of neurodiversity.* Penguin.

Sinclair, J. (2013, October). Why I dislike person-first language. *Autonomy, the Critical Journal of Interdisciplinary Autism Studies, 1*(2). http://www.larry-arnold.net/Autonomy/index.php/autonomy/article/view/OP1/html_1

Statista Research Department. (2016). *Most common reasons given to U.S. health care professionals by families refusing vaccines or requesting alternative schedules as of 2016.* https://www.statista.com/statistics/665592/reasons-families-refused-vaccinations-health-care-professionals-us

Subotnik, R. F., Olszewski-Kubilius, P., & Worrell, F. C. (2011). Rethinking giftedness and gifted education: A proposed direction forward based on psychological science. *Psychological Science in the Public Interest, 12*(1), 3–54. https://doi.org/10.1177/1529100611418056

Taylor, L. E., Swerdfeger, A. L., & Eslick, G. D. (2014). Vaccines are not associated with autism: An evidence-based meta-analysis of case control and cohort studies. *Vaccine, 32*(29), 3623–3629. https://doi.org/10.1016/j.vaccine.2014.04.085

U.S. Department of Education. (2010). *OSEP Policy Memo, January 13, 2010. Evaluation Procedures.*

U.S. Department of Education. (2013). *OSEP Policy Memo, December 20, 2013, Letter to Delisle.*

U.S. Department of Education. (2015). *OSEP Policy Memo, April 17, 2015 State Directors of Special Education.*

World Health Organization. (2019, December 5). *More than 140,000 die from measles as cases surge worldwide.* https://www.who.int/news-room/detail/05-12-2019-more-than-140-000-die-from-measles-as-cases-surge-worldwide

1

Starting the Journey

From the Beginning and Even Before

An Unplanned Journey Between Holland and Italy. Switzerland?

It's important to know that no one chooses autism—you, your child, and your family were drafted. You need to remember this when teachers, other parents, and total strangers feel free to tell you that you're using autism as an excuse for (name your issue here: misbehavior, laundry piling up, financial failure, your lack of showering…). Just like being drafted and being shipped off to another country, autism will change your whole life—your plans, your dreams, your family structure, and even your relationship with your local grocery store. Everything will be different than you expected, but not always in a bad way. Just different.

This book was inspired by the essay "Welcome to Holland" by Emily Perl Kingsley (1987). I love this essay and present it to my college students when teaching Introduction to Disabilities, but I never really appreciated its wisdom until I sat crying as I reread it one night. I realized that there was a lot of information about "Italy," or children with typical development, and "Holland," or children who had disabilities, but very little about children who were in-between and different—children who exhibited some, but not all of the characteristics, and who had

DOI: 10.4324/9781003237006-1

some really significant strengths that were both a result of and impacted by differences. There wasn't much information about children from "Switzerland" who aren't quite typical and who aren't quite gifted, but who don't have classic disabilities—children like my child, who was smart and diagnosed with autism. And so, the idea for this book was created.

WELCOME TO HOLLAND[1]

by Emily Perl Kingsley

I am often asked to describe the experience of raising a child with a disability—to try to help people who have not shared that unique experience to understand it, to imagine how it would feel. It's like this…

When you're going to have a baby, it's like planning a fabulous vacation trip—to Italy. You buy a bunch of guide books and make your wonderful plans. The Coliseum. The Michelangelo David. The gondolas in Venice. You may learn some handy phrases in Italian. It's all very exciting.

After months of eager anticipation, the day finally arrives. You pack your bags and off you go. Several hours later, the plane lands. The stewardess comes in and says, "Welcome to Holland."

"Holland?!?" you say. "What do you mean Holland?? I signed up for Italy! I'm supposed to be in Italy. All my life I've dreamed of going to Italy."

But there's been a change in the flight plan. They've landed in Holland and there you must stay.

The important thing is that they haven't taken you to a horrible, disgusting, filthy place, full of pestilence, famine, and disease. It's just a different place.

So you must go out and buy new guide books. And you must learn a whole new language. And you will meet a whole new group of people you would never have met.

It's just a *different* place. It's slower-paced than Italy, less flashy than Italy. But after you've been there for a while and you catch your breath, you look around…and you begin to notice that Holland has windmills…and Holland has tulips. Holland even has Rembrandts.

But everyone you know is busy coming and going from Italy…and they're all bragging about what a wonderful time they had there. And for the rest of your life, you will say "Yes, that's where I was supposed to go. That's what I had planned."

And the pain of that will never, ever, ever, ever go away… because the loss of that dream is a very, very significant loss.

But…if you spend your life mourning the fact that you didn't get to Italy, you may never be free to enjoy the very special, the very lovely things…about Holland.

Throughout this book, the metaphor of traveling and maps will be used frequently. I found that there were lots of coping guides, lots of informative books, some "cures," and reams and reams of technical books. Most importantly, there were a small and growing number of first-person books written by families and individuals with autism. I am hoping that in this book you find a familiar voice of someone who refused to let other people's perceptions of autism win over her, her family, and her child— someone who refused to get overwhelmed, but found that there was hope, growth, and a really wonderful journey through it all. Switzerland, like Holland and Italy, has its own beauty!

Maps and Autism

"Welcome to Holland" originally was written for a child with intellectual disabilities. However, it is an analogy to which I could deeply relate: you think you're going somewhere, and suddenly you're not there. Parenting a child with autism is like entering the world of *The Wizard of Oz*: you think you're just like all of your friends, and you think you're on the way with a clearly defined map, but then you start getting strange signs that things are not the same as all of the baby books would have you believe. I had read Vicki Iovine's (2007) *The Girlfriends' Guide to Pregnancy* and laughed so hard I was sobbing. (Seriously, my husband was concerned about me. Perhaps it was an overreaction to hormones...) However, I truly bawled when I read *The Girlfriends' Guide to Toddlers*. That wasn't what I was seeing in my children. I didn't get to laugh at funny things my oldest child was saying. I had the child who wouldn't leave the swings. I had the child who screamed at the idea of taking a bubble bath. I had the child who stared in fear at a camera lens.

But I also had the child who could complete 100-piece puzzles at age two. I had the child who at ten months could understand when I told her that rocks broke apart to become sand and who could use that knowledge to bring herself back from the brink of overwhelming fear. I had the child who pulsed in his baby seat to *The Muppets'* song "Mahna Mahna" in perfect rhythm and used the multiplication tables to calm himself down—over and over again. Autistic behaviors, yes, but gifted, nonetheless.

Autism is so odd because, to use the Holland analogy, for a while, you are in Italy. The language spoken is Italian. But in small pieces, the language changes. The people change. The activities change. The landscape changes. It reminded me for a while of one of those *Star Trek* episodes where a part of a character was in one world and the other part was in another. Yet, having a smart child with autism isn't quite the Holland of "regular" autism. There are some real strengths, and there are aspects of autism, but how much of each? Professionals are often reluctant to diagnose anything. It's perhaps like being in Switzerland—a little bit of Italy, and closer to Holland than some of the other people in Italy, but not so close that you feel welcomed by the Dutch. Autism is more like Schweizerdeutsch, the spoken variant that is part Swiss, part German, with erratic spellings, usage, and pronunciations. Switzerland can be very confusing.

There are several different metaphors about autism that people use. In her book *The Autism Trail Guide: Postcards From the Road Less Traveled*, Ellen Notbohm (2007) noted how having a child with autism is like being on a strange trip; you have to communicate with others that you've arrived safely and that you want to share your experiences. In contrast, Karyn Seroussi (2002) called autism "The Jabberwock" and talked about defeating the disease that causes autistic behaviors. Still others, like Nancy Popkin (2017), see autism as a flexible Hula-Hoop surrounding a person that expands and contracts depending on the person's attention, stress, and environment. To some, autism is a scary, external thing; to others, it's a process and a journey. To others, it is a difference in how people operate and perceive the world.

That's autism: something to be worked with and accepted while at the same time trying to understand the journey. It's a process, a condition, and a person. It reminds me a bit of trying to capture the dual nature of light. Scientists have found that when they provide a substance to react to, light clearly acts as a particle. When they provide a slit, it appears to be a wave. Being smart and autistic at the same time is something our children are. For me, living on the coast of Georgia, my children's form of autism is like the marsh, where the salt water and fresh water combine to form a vastly unique and fragile ecosystem. It's a really fine line between "quirky" and "problematic," a gap between "talented" and "not quite right," and somewhere between "cute" and "hmmmm."

Mapmaker: Who Am I to Write This Book?

There are lots of books about autism out there written by people with doctorates, parents of people with autism, and people with autism. This book happens to be written by a mother with a Ph.D. in special education and gifted education who has two children, both on the spectrum in different ways and who had different labels at different times. This book is also written by someone who can look back and see aspects of autism and ADHD in my husband's and my growing up. I'm writing this book because I read like a mad woman when I was going through my daughter's initial diagnosis and treatments. I was completely overwhelmed by information. There are so many sources of information available and so many viewpoints and arguments that I would turn off the computer in frustration after reading for hours, only to turn it on again the next morning to order the next book or peruse another webpage—trying to find someone or something to help. Some books really spoke to me, some were a waste of my time, and some were, in my opinion, downright dangerous.

I am the mother of a daughter, Elizabeth, who was identified with general developmental delay (GDD) at age two, identified with autism (autism spectrum disorder; ASD) at age three, and identified as gifted at the age of seven; and a son, Raymond, who was diagnosed with generalized anxiety disorder, not otherwise specified (GAD-NOS) and Tourette syndrome at age six, and also identified as gifted at age seven. (*Note.* For their own privacy, I have changed their names, as well as those of the other children discussed in the book.) Both of them had their special education labels dropped in middle school because they were not "failing" enough for additional help and because the labels no longer served their needs. Because most of the lessons our family learned were through the experiences we had with our daughter because of her identification, much of this book is based on our journey through the maze of her diagnosis, treatments, and future outlooks. However, when necessary, I also will focus on my son's issues. He has never been formally diagnosed with autism but has had labels that are "cousins" to autism. I've learned that this is not uncommon—siblings often will share characteristics but have different labels.

However, in the irony of the universe, I received a doctorate in both special education and gifted education before I ever had children, and I am also a college professor in both of these areas. I should have been prepared for all of this, right? Wrong! I was familiar with the map of an educator, which is a vastly different map than that of a parent. This book is the middle ground of both parts of my life: my professional knowledge combined with, and at times, in conflict with, my personal role of "Mommy/Mom."

I have been taught through my training to focus on children's abilities. Twice-exceptional (2e) children, who have both gifts and disabilities, are a particular passion of mine professionally. I have always loved working with children who have amazing insights and problem-solving abilities but can't read for some reason. I loved the intellectual challenge of trying to figure out what would work with a twice-exceptional student—what reading strategy to use, what question to ask, and the like. What can I find to help *this* child develop their abilities rather than be stymied by areas of challenge? But *this* child was now *my* child, and I had no professional knowledge of autism. I used to laugh ironically with my husband, "Give me a child who can reason but not read, and I'm all over that. But I have a child who can't talk!" Talking is a strength of mine, to put it mildly. I drove my parents crazy talking. I got in trouble at school for talking. I went into a profession where I talk for a living! And *I* had a child who couldn't talk. Ah, the irony!

My own professional pride was a major "oughtism" that I encountered. I, of all people, with a Ph.D. in special education *ought* to know what to do. And I had not a clue. I now share a presentation with teachers called "The Other Side of the Table." I have been at countless Individualized Education Program (IEP) meetings as a teacher or advocate, translating terms, concepts, and processes to parents. I have reassured them that I will do my best to help their child read, behave, make friends, and so on. I have always (after the first scary year of teaching) felt capable of doing so—knowing that there were lots of things to try, I would keep trying, and hopefully, something would work. But I also knew that children are so highly individual that sometimes it can take longer to find a strategy and that solution can change. My job was not to give up on the family or the child, but to keep trying. I knew that as a teacher.

Then, as a parent, I sat on the other side of the table, and I realized how little I knew about speech, autism, and early intervention processes, and how much I was depending on the education professionals across from me to love my child, to help my child, and to know exactly what to do. I wanted them to tell me that they've seen lots of children like mine and all of them have been helped. I wanted them to see that, yes, Elizabeth fixated on geography and could point to most of the states in the country, but this was not a problem; this was a strength. Perhaps Elizabeth would be a geographer one day and we could nod sagely and say, "It all started when she was two." I needed those professionals to see my daughter not as a problem to be solved, but a wonderful collection of abilities to be developed and grown. I needed Elizabeth to know everything I didn't. I sat on the other side of the table and cried for someone to help my little girl because I didn't know how.

I finally stopped crying when I read a marvelous book called *The Boy Who Loved Windows* by Patricia Stacey (2003). She is a phenomenal writer, and her story read like she was talking directly to me. She wrote of how her therapist said that one of the ways that parents of children with disabilities cope is by finding another child who has symptoms worse than their child's. Patricia's was the "bottom" of the group—no child was worse off than hers. "My God!" I thought, "This works! Her child *is* worse off than mine!" But, you see, her child got better. By the end of the book, which I read in one long night, her son was talking, interacting, asking questions, and learning—all of those things I worked on as a teacher developing talents. If *her* son could get better, maybe my daughter could, too! Her book was the first hope I had that maybe my family was on a path where Elizabeth could get better and be more of who she is—who she truly is. I had found my map.

Read books. Visits blogs. Find someone whose story inspires you, lifts you out of your angst and distress, and helps you believe that your child will grow into who they were always going to be.

Second Thoughts: How'd We End Up Here?

If you're reading this book, you're probably researching autism, trying to get a handle on this *thing*, this *condition*, this *disability*. You've read countless books and webpages about autism that don't quite paint the full picture of your child; they don't quite capture your child's incredible abilities that autism sometimes hides and sometimes makes clearer. You've read about autism and Asperger's syndrome, but you still aren't sure what to tell your parents, your in-laws, or your child's teacher. You're almost certainly wondering what you can do and worrying about what you have done.

Second thoughts are like regrets: you can't have 'em because you can't fix 'em. You are making the best decisions you can right now with the information you have. Just like on any journey, you might wind up in a place that you're not really thrilled with. You might look at your house (a mess), your marriage/partnership (a mess), your relationships with others (a mess), and your child (oh, such a mess), and want to start over. You will probably obsess a bit: "If only I had..." The reality is that you did the best you could, and now you have to continue to do the best you can and get yourself through this mess, one piece at a time. Some advice my mother once gave me was, "You want this fixed *right now*, and it's just not going to happen. It will take time, and you have to give it that time."

No second thoughts also means that you don't give up, believing yourself to be a victim of circumstances, doctors, therapists, God, bad genes, or something else. As Rachel, a friend of mine and a mother of a child with Level 1 ASD, formerly known as Asperger's, said,

> It can be extremely frustrating to deal with this disorder, but as much as a parent did not ask for a child with these issues...the child did not ask to be like this either. Ben describes his confusion as "birds in his head." We as parents need to take a step back, take a deep breath, and realize that the child is not intending to create chaos, he is just trying to cope with it. The more we understand this disorder and let the child know that we understand how he is feeling, the better off he will be.

As in any trip, you are certainly allowed to cry when you wonder, "How on earth did I get here?" Now it is time to go and build yourself a map to get through it.

"Wait and See" Is Apparently a Medical Strategy

On March 6, 2001, our family began. Our daughter, Elizabeth was born at 5:25 in the afternoon after 12 hours of labor. She was a much-wanted child we had been trying to conceive for more than a year. Because of fibroids and other issues, it had been difficult.

I remember crying, realizing that it seems so easy to conceive in your teens and 20s, but here I was in my 30s, and all of those years of desperately trying *not* to get pregnant were coming back to haunt me. We cried and celebrated that day in July when the stick showed two lines of pink.

Often mothers of children with autism will report that they had a feeling of something "not quite right" even while they were pregnant. Autism is highly genetic, with more than 102 genes possibly being involved (Satterstrom et al., 2020). I loved being pregnant, and I was always aware of another life force within me. I truly believed in God after being pregnant because of that connection to life and a sense of growing. However, 12 weeks into my pregnancy, we had a scare when an ultrasound found a fiber wrapped around her little tiny fetus head. Our obstetrician told us that we would have to "wait and see," and many prayers later, no sign of the fiber was present at 20 weeks. But there were fibroid tumors in my uterus that were *huge* and growing, and the poor baby was curled around them. The challenge of the pregnancy made me so relieved that she was "normal" at birth that I never questioned some of her odd antics as a baby. She was pink and beautiful and all potential.

Her birth story is different than that of many children with autism because it was the pregnancy that was stressful, not the actual birth. Ray's birth is more typical of a birth reported by mothers of children with autism. His labor was about an hour from 0–10 dilation, with only two hours of active contractions. In the birth process, the muscles of the birth canal contracted so fiercely, he was born with a significant cephalohematoma or cone. Lots of babies are born cone-headed, but the lump on Ray was almost as big as the rest of his head. It was quite disturbing. The doctors told us to watch the lump and that it could take up to a year to go down. There was a good deal of "Well, we'll have to wait and see. It should be fine," which was just vague enough to worry us. To our great relief, it had rounded off after about four months, but the pressure of those contractions pushed significantly on his brain.

Both children also were quite jaundiced and did not receive treatment in a timely manner. We were released from the hospital one day after birth, and we were told that they might be a little jaundiced and to put them in the sun. Not a real problem finding sun in Southwest Florida! So, we bathed our little darlings in sunshine until their first appointments at one week. In both cases, the pediatrician found significantly elevated jaundice levels that were "coming down," indicating higher levels before that would have required the bilirubin lights. Even in the case of my son, where we were looking for problems, we were told, "We will just have to wait and see," by the hospital and told later by our pediatrician that we had gone into the danger zone. Jaundice can carry the possibility of brain damage—not often, but it can.

Ray also had a terrible fall onto a concrete floor where he hit the front of his head when he was seven months old. He did not pass out, and the x-ray came back OK, but again I heard the cheery doctor voice of "He should be fine. Just wait and see."

Do we have MRI data that our children have brain trauma? No. But there is the underlying fear and niggling concern of what happened and "if only" thinking. I still sense that some of their issues were triggered by some form of brain pressure or injury—both in utero and afterward. In addition, there is a common theme of head trauma or high fevers noted among children later identified with autism. There is even a condition called PANDAS, short for "pediatric autoimmune neuropsychiatric disorders associated with streptococcal infections," that seemed to fit some of the profiles associated with my children, in which autoimmune reactions trigger autism and obsessive compulsive disorders. My son dealt with multiple bouts of pneumonia and strep before he was one year old. He was treated with antibiotics and we were told to "wait and see."

RACHEL'S STORY

My pregnancy with Ben was as normal as could be. Blood pressure, weight gain, growth rate: all good. Then came delivery day. After ten hours of unmedicated intense labor, I finally resolved that this was not going to happen without medication. I took the epidural and things calmed down, at least until it came time to push. I was ready to go and so was Ben. After just a few times, the nurse's face turned to grave concern, and she told me to stop immediately. Was I doing it wrong? Apparently my tailbone was digging into his forehead each time I pushed, and his heartrate kept dropping in half. An emergency C-section had to be done and the nurse had to then push him back up through the birth canal. We have heard from other parents that they too experienced a traumatic birth and that frontal lobe trauma is a common factor.

Ben also had to have surgery to correct a hydrocele in his scrotum when he was four months old. He was taken back to surgery with a smile on his face and woke up a few hours later a different baby. We were told that he would not even remember the surgery and be back to the happy baby we had in no time. It was a few weeks before we started thinking that something had gone wrong during the surgery because our happy baby was not back. He seemed more introverted and irritated. Neither of us had experience in raising babies, so we just kept trying our best to do the right thing. We later heard from a psychologist that it is unusual that we were not permitted to be with him while he was undergoing anesthesia, and I regret that I couldn't be with him during the surgery to protect him. We will never know if something did go wrong.

Hindsight Is 20/20

Autistic characteristics can be sneaky. I can look back now and say, "Ahhhh, so that was her being autistic." I have backgrounds in both gifted education and special education, and my gifted education experience means I tend to look at kids from a strengths-based perspective. I see things that could be the germ of a talent or activities that show promise of great thinking. Even with a special education background, I tend not to look at things from a deficit view. One of the most significant challenges of working with two different sets of professionals is that one might see a behavior as characteristic of a deficit, while the other sees the behavior as evidence of a strength.

For example, as an infant, Ray would get the cutest expression on his face when he was startled. His eyes would get round, his mouth would open, and arms would fly out at the slightest change in his environment. We were intrigued at this and said, "Wow! What an alert child we have!" and I would spend some time soothing him. It's a startle reflex that infants have and adults still have to some degree. It's more than surprise—it's an instinct that infants use to let themselves know that something has changed, and it activates their "fight or flight" adrenaline rush. Heart rates accelerate, pupils dilate, and the body tenses up, ready for action. All infants have it, but infants who later develop autism often have a very sensitive startle reaction. In other words, they don't normalize very quickly—the world is a very nerve-wracking place that causes high anxiety.

Another example: when she was nine months old, my daughter would bang on the dryer and then listen to the differences as she banged on the washing machine. Then, she would repeat her actions. Repeat. Repeat. For about 30 minutes. Isn't that cute? We were convinced she would either be a drummer or a repairwoman. She spent an hour at a time listening to the different sounds of the bangs. She still has this skill of distinguishing little details and analyzing how things are alike and different. Hidden picture games are no fun for her because she just points right at the missing objects. I had to explain to her once that this is hard for most of us, and it's fun for us because it's a challenge. She just shrugged. Now, of course, I know that it's her autistic abilities combined with an eye for detail, but at the time, we were very impressed with her ability to concentrate and discriminate.

As a baby, Elizabeth insisted very definitely on being held facing outward. She would cry and strain her head around trying to see around me when I held her facing me. So, I happily turned her around so that her back was to me and she was free to observe the world around her. I was pleased to have such a curious and exploratory child. Because of an old back injury,

I couldn't carry her in one of those front sling-style packs, so I ended up with the baby on my hip, watching the world from a slightly tipped angle at times. However, putting her down was a real challenge.

Elizabeth hated tummy time—not just resisted it, but *hated* it. I was a good mommy of the early 2000s who laid her child down on her back to avoid sudden infant death syndrome (SIDS). We were deeply grateful that we lived in Florida so that the whole issue of blankets was not a concern. She would go into her little onesies, lie down on the big crib mattress, and play contentedly, often soothed by the mobile. But get her up and put her down on the floor face down, and she would turn into this monster of a child who would shriek uncontrollably for hours. At first, I thought that she would cry herself to sleep, but no such luck. For the first five months of her life, Elizabeth experienced this Jekyll-and-Hyde transformation every time we turned her over onto her stomach. Tummy Time became Torture Time—for everyone. I tried the nifty mat with the colors and activities. I tried no mat. I tried a soft texture. I tried the cold tile floor. In all cases, we had unrelenting crying.

Once she learned to roll herself over, around five months old, we would put Elizabeth on her little mat and she would immediately roll herself over onto her back to play with her toes. All of the baby books said not to worry about this—that the baby's head will round out when she can hold her head up. But our baby spent so much time on her back looking out at the world that her actual head shape was altered. Needless to say, Elizabeth still has a flat spot on the back of her head. When I'm rubbing her head, I am always reminded of the western Native American babies who were carried on flat boards, or "papoose boards," and had flat heads. Flat heads used to be a significant cultural trait encouraged among some Native American populations in the West, and White men and other tribes were called "round heads" when the cultures collided. There's even a Flathead Reservation and a Flathead River in Montana named after this practice. However, I know that for us, her flat head is a symptom and symbol of her autism—hidden, but faintly perceptible.

RACHEL'S STORY

Even at an early age, Ben was driven by color. He had to have a specific colored cup, plate, utensils...everything. He arranged his cars in order of color and the most significant recollection of his need to organize by color was an activity cube that had colored pegs and slots to put them in. He was only six or seven months old when we found the cube with all of the pegs arranged in the slots by color. It was actually our first realization that this child was a bit different.

Around the age of two he began to assign colors to family and friends. Based on your relationship to him, you were assigned a color. Mom = yellow, Dad = blue, brother Charlie = green, both grandfathers were red, and ironically his one grandfather's girlfriend was assigned orange, which is the combination of authoritative yellow (Mom) and fun red (grandfathers). The same was applied to his fun aunt.

Once he began understanding family relationships, he no longer used colors to comprehend the relationship of a person to himself, but during that time it was fun to see what colors he would assign people. At the time we just thought it was just another quirky thing that he did.

There comes a time when you begin to realize that something really isn't normal or even "cute" anymore. I remember Elizabeth playing in the bathtub, happy and content as she watched the water run through her fingers. She was sitting in one of those bath seats that kept her sitting up while I could wash her and her hair. She loved bath time, until the washing part. She would submit to my washing her hair, which she didn't like but didn't stress out about too much. Then, the water would rinse off the soap and she would go ballistic. I remember being very proud of myself when I finally realized that she was afraid of the rainbows of the soap bubbles reflecting on the surface of the water. She was nine months old and scared of rainbows in the water.

Hair washing and haircuts are frequent issues among children with autism. My friend Tina would cut her son's hair while he slept over the course of several days. "Badly," she emphasized, "but at least he didn't have hair in his eyes anymore." We were determined that we would win the haircut battle with my son, and it took three adults to hold him down in the stylist's chair one memorable day when he was two. I was determined that I would not be giving in to my strong-willed child's demands and that he would not be spoiled. He was *not* going to win this battle, but afterward, when we had tipped the stylist more than the haircut itself cost, I realized that this was something more than mere resistance.

Babies with autism will often lock into sensory stimuli that scare or intrigue them. In our case, I realized after the fact that her love of different sounds, fear of water reflections, hatred of tummy time, and abhorrence of sand were part of the sensory-seeking and avoidance facets of autism. That sensory input was too much for her to handle. And such sensitivities are highly individual to each child. I have a friend whose son hates green—but only a particular shade of it. Dark green—fine. But light, bright green—no go. One memorable dinner at our house a plate of peas was presented to him (along with a hamburger and French fries—I *was* trying to be a good hostess!), resulting in the beginning of a meltdown, whereupon my friend and the child had to leave immediately. Such immediate leavings often are a symptom of the recognition that you don't get to live the same life that other parents seem to get to live.

Similarly, babies with autism often hate being touched. When Elizabeth was an infant, I bought a book about baby massage— how it's so good for developing nervous systems, how it can calm them down, and how it's a wonderful soothing process right before bed. Not for us. Elizabeth loved to be held, but not rubbed in any way. She turned over for the first time as I was trying to calm her down by rubbing her back—she squirmed so much away from it, she flipped herself over. She was so surprised but soon mastered the art of flipping! Many, many parents tell about how their child hated, or passively withstood, being hugged, touched, or otherwise shown affection. In her 2003 book, *The Boy*

Who Loved Windows, Patricia Stacey noted that it isn't because they have no feelings, but because they are so completely overwhelmed by their feelings of neediness and love, that they avoid the situation that causes such intense emotions. Thus, hugging and loving has to be carefully controlled so that they aren't overwhelmed by the intensity of their emotions.

You quickly learn as a parent to avoid certain situations, certain textures, or certain places. You accept things that you never imagined you would find acceptable. It's frustrating when you realize that your child's issues are controlling your life—and everyone else has something to say about that.

Warning Signs: Doctors, In-Laws, and the Public

Three little words can trigger you to know that *something* is wrong beyond your child being quirky. You will hear them time and again from your mother, your in-laws, and complete strangers at the grocery store—even you will say them once in a while. These three words will be directed either at you or your child, and you will soon learn to wince—hard—at them: "Can't you just…?"

Behave? Say "hello" to our neighbor? Play nicely with the children on the play date? Stop buzzing? Go to sleep? Wear the nice pretty dress for Easter? Make him stop? Tell her to be quiet? Get her off the swings? Clean up those crushed Cheerios?

These words will haunt you at home until you can educate everyone who comes into your house. They will be everywhere in public. My reactions ranged from shrieking back at the judgmental idiot, to apologies, to stone cold silence.

There was the nasty young woman at our local sandwich shop. We had literally just moved that day from New Mexico to Kentucky. We were filthy from driving, meeting the truck, and unloading a whole house's worth of stuff. Everything was in boxes, we were all exhausted, and we had to eat. There was a soup and sandwich shop down the street from us, and because it was a chain, we were used to going there. We were all craving something familiar. So, off we went. While waiting for the food, my husband took our son and daughter into the restroom to wash their hands. I could hear the water play and shrieks from where I was sitting halfway across the restaurant. I knew that they were playing in water to bring themselves to a sensory calm. I couldn't even move I was so tired. I stayed there—knowing that I would deal with it when they came out. And besides, it was his turn. When they came back, the children immediately hid under our table with muffled giggles emerging. They were finally quiet.

A young woman in all of her young cuteness strode up to my table, and in the snottiest manner said, "I have *never* seen such poorly behaved children in my whole life!" and stalked away in righteous indignation. I just watched her go, angry, tired, and beyond irritated that *she* had clearly never been so tired that her eyelashes hurt and that sometimes children needed to find a sense of balance by shrieking.

"Too" Compliant

Although the behaviors often were out of control, there were some things that were not. Elizabeth and Ray never tried to cross streets, poke their fingers in light sockets, or battle for control of cabinets. As toddlers, they stopped at the corners on their scooters and waited for me to catch up. They never went out late and got drunk in high school. I certainly didn't mind this overcompliance, because we often have enough battles to worry about, but it did make me wonder when I watched my friends engage in power struggles with their children. We had power struggles, just not the usual kinds. In her book, Susan Senator (2005) also noted how compliant her child was, unless he was screaming and out of control. When autism has hijacked their reactions, children appear unable to control anything, and when they are momentarily in charge of their autism, they can be "too good." Rules are important to them and breaking the rules means that their world is shutting down. There often is very little middle ground.

And Yet...

Despite the warning signs of autism, there often are signs that can signal significant intelligence. Experts can watch children and say, "Nope, I don't see autism" because the child is making eye contact, listening to you, engaging in imaginative play, or talking—behaviors that may not be found in children with more stereotypic autism. There are often evident attempts to cope and mediate difficulties. These are the challenges that families face: there is "something," but what? Is it giftedness, autism, anxiety, or OCD? These children often defy easy classification and are ultimately amalgams of many different, overlapping issues.

Calling Roadside Assistance: Asking for Help

When raising a child, you worry about when you should start worrying. I remember making "appointments" for worrying: "Well, I'll pay attention to her language in a month; we'll see how she's doing then." When you start suspecting something might be wrong, you will either look for confirmation that you're crazy or check in with the professionals—who will probably tell you you're crazy.

I first started asking the pediatrician about concerns of mine at about 16 months. Elizabeth wasn't talking. She wasn't babbling or even making much noise, other than a pleased hum when she was happy and an ear-piercing shriek when she wasn't. She was, however, very athletic. She could walk at 9 months, climb slides at 11 months, and was trying to swim at a year. The pediatrician listened to my concerns at 16 months and then smiled and said something like, "Oh well, children develop at their own individual rates. She's obviously spent so much energy on physically growing up—she'll catch up."

I was *livid* when a mere eight months later, at two years old, the pediatrician asked very casually, "Does she have 50 to 100 words in her vocabulary?" I just looked at her and said, "She has about five words, and four of them are only words that we can understand." The pediatrician then said, "Oh, that *is* a problem!" In her defense, she was using checklists given to her by the American Association of Pediatricians, and autism was less on the horizon in 2002 than it is now. And my daughter was considered high-functioning—she did not exhibit some of the other characteristics of autism. But I was still angry: I *knew* my daughter, and I *knew* that there was a problem. I found my list of her words the other day:

- Mama;
- *Da*, which could mean "Daddy" or "What's that?" based on the context;
- *Diddle-la*, which was a variation of our dog "Cody Dog" and also meant "home"—we always found that sweet;
- *Ay*, meaning Ray, her brother; and
- *Ee*, meaning Irene, our frequent babysitter.

That was it. Five words. No, she did not have 50 words, and yes, that was a problem.

Note

1 Note. © 1987 by Emily Perl Kingsley. All rights reserved. Reprinted by permission of the author.

References

Individuals With Disabilities Education Act, 20 U.S.C. §1401 *et seq.* (1990). https://sites.ed.gov/idea/statuteregulations

Iovine, V. (2007). *The girlfriends' guide to pregnancy.* Pocket Books.

Kingsley, E. P. (1987). *Welcome to Holland.* https://www.ndss.org/lifespan/a-parents-perspective/

Notbohm, E. (2007). *The autism trail guide: Postcards from the road less traveled.* Future Horizons.

Popkin, N. (2017). *Understanding autism with the hula hoop analogy.* Autism Society of North Carolina. https://www.autismsociety-nc.org/understanding-autism-with-the-hula-hoop-analogy

Satterstrom, F. K., Kosmicki, J. A., Wang., J., Breen, M. S., DeRubeis, S., An, J.-Y., Peng, M., Collina, R., Grove, J., Klei, L., Stevens, C., Reichert, J., Mulhern, M. S., Artomov, M., Gerges, S., Sheppard, B., Xu, X., Bhaduri, A., Norman, U., Brand, H., … Buxbaum, J. D. (2020). Large-scaled exome sequencing study implicates both developmental and functional changes in the neurobiology of autism. *Cell, 180*(3), 568–584. https://doi.org/10.1016/j.cell.2019.12.036

Senator, S. (2005). *Making peace with autism: One family's story of struggle, discovery, and unexpected gifts*. Trumpeter.

Seroussi, K. (2002). *Unraveling the mystery of autism and pervasive developmental disorder: A mother's story of research and recovery*. Broadway Books.

Stacey, P. (2003). *The boy who loved windows: Opening the heart and mind of a child threatened with autism*. Da Capo Press.

2

The Landscape and Its Signage

Autism Causes and Terms

It would be so much easier if there were some clearly identifiable traits of autism, or even only one kind of it. Down syndrome is relatively easy to identify. There is a genetic marker for it—the 21st chromosome is tripled (typically, humans have two copies of this chromosome). There also is a characteristic look among children with Down syndrome. However, even among children with Down syndrome, there are so many levels of development. There are children who never develop language. There are children who grow up to live fairly independently. There are people with Down syndrome who can become professional actors (you *need* to watch *The Peanut Butter Falcon*). It is becoming more clearly understood that although genetics are important to autism, a whole interaction of events take place in order to trigger it. Although evidence is clear that there is a genetic link to autism, it is still identified through observed behavior, not a DNA sequencing test. Thus, depending on how a child acts or behaves and how severe these behaviors might be, there are a variety of labels that might be applied.

Many families will use what I call the "University of Google." This can be supplemented by the "University of Wikipedia" and the various small "colleges" of blogs, books, and organizations' websites. In most of them, you will see terms that keep popping

DOI: 10.4324/9781003237006-2

up—terms that you might have seen before, or you thought you knew, but now apply to a different context. It is like learning a new language: the language of autism. As Beryl Markham (1942/2021), one of the first acclaimed women pilots said, "It was disconcerting to examine your charts before a proposed flight only to find that in many cases the bulk of the terrain over which you had to fly was bluntly marked UNSURVEYED" (p. 31).

These common terms to describe various aspects of autism are described in the following section:

◆ Autism spectrum disorder (ASD);
◆ Levels of support;
◆ Asperger's syndrome (AS).

Autism Spectrum Disorder (ASD)

Autism spectrum disorder is a blanket term—it covers a lot of ground and vague characteristics. My child with autism might act, speak, and interact nothing like your child with autism. You can watch two children with autism in the same place and wonder how on earth these two children could share the same label. There is a phrase I've heard many times: *when you meet one child with autism, you've met one child with autism.* The key word in understanding autism is to understand that it is a *spectrum*, not a *continuum*. A continuum ranges in tone from intense to light like a gradient. A spectrum ranges in color, which means that there are different aspects to it, not just intensity. It isn't a question of whether a child *has* autism, but in what ways does the child *demonstrate* autism? Thus, there really isn't *mild* or *severe* autism—but there are multiple ways that autism can be exhibited.

According to the Centers for Disease Control (2020), individuals with autism spectrum disorder are characterized by impairment in two primary areas of development before the age of three: (1) social communication and social interactions; (2) restricted or repetitive interests or behaviors. Social communication and interactions impairments can include:

- Lack of eye contact;
- Lack of or limited imaginary play;
- Lack of emotion or difficulty responding to other's emotions;
- Difficulty turn taking;
- Limited interest in others.

Restricted or repetitive behaviors can include, but does not always include:

- A strong focus on the pattern or parts of something, not the function;
- Obsessive interests;
- Flapping hands, rocking, or spinning in circles;
- Adherence to specific routines;
- Repetition of words or phrases.

There are also a group of common characteristics that aren't necessarily part of the criteria, including hyperactive or inattentive behavior, delayed language and/or developmental skills, gastrointestinal issues, and extreme emotional reactions. Likewise, cognitive and adaptive functioning can range from gifted to severely impaired. ASD does not describe a delay in development, but rather a difference or deviation in development in the areas of social engagement and behaviors.

Boys are four times more like than girls to be diagnosed. No one really knows the reason for this. There are various theories, from an overexposure to testosterone in the womb to "protection" from the genetic impacts of autism because of the XX chromosome structure and the weakness of the XY structure (Ferri et al., 2018). The role of hormones and genetic structure is unclear. We know that girls are underrepresented, as are children from diverse racial and ethnic backgrounds (CDC, 2019). The reasons for this are wide and range from cultural and gender biases in identification to differing level of medical access.

To add to the challenges of the language of autism, although autism is a spectrum, there are three levels of support for social communication and three levels for behaviors, making the support a continuum. Confused yet? The emphasis on the level of support rather than the "high or low functioning" of an individual means that support can change with changing environments. There is a recognition that in some environment where the child is comfortable, there is less need for support, whereas there may be a greater need for support in different environments. The support for autism can be described as:

♦ **Level 1: Requiring support:** A child's difficulties in back-and-forth communication or social success require support to keep or maintain friends, or their organizational issues or discomfort with flexibility require intervention. Most individuals needing Level 1 support can lead independent lives with minimal support.

♦ **Level 2: Substantial support with limited language or very few social interactions:** A child's behaviors interfere with daily functioning, and there is distress regarding changes in routines.

♦ **Level 3: Very substantial support with very limited verbal or nonverbal communication and rare initiations of engagement:** There is significant distress with changes in routines, and self-harm is an issue. Coping with daily life is very difficult. Medication is often used at this level.

In this book, when I say *bright children with autism*, I mean those children who have the capability of interacting, speaking, and learning general education curriculum and beyond in a general or gifted education classroom environment with the right supports—typically at a level 1 or 2. I am purposefully not using the term *high-functioning autism* because some studies (Alvares et al., 2020; den Houting, 2019) have found that an autistic adult's functioning adaptive behavior, although related to their intelligence scores, is more closely related to their age of identification, with early identification playing a significant role in helping adults become more functional. In other words, the earlier the support is provided, the better the outcome. It's not how smart a kid is that determines their level of functioning; it's the quality of the support that is provided while they are growing up.

Older Terms

These terms are listed because they are often still used in the general population. Your parents or grandparents may be familiar with some of these terms. However, they were all subsumed under the single term *Autism Spectrum Disorders* by the American Psychiatric Association in the DSM in 2013.

Childhood Disintegrative Disorder (CDD)

Also known as Heller's syndrome, this is perhaps the most heartbreaking form of autism and the rarest. According to Dr. Colin Tidy (2021), only 1 in 100,000 people demonstrate CDD. On our road trip with autism, this truly is where you are in Italy, and in a very short space of time, you are lifted into Holland. This term describes children who develop typically, and then around three to four years of age begin to regress—to disintegrate—right before your eyes. Children with this form of autism typically end up with more severe forms: very limited language, very limited social skills, and behaviors that are more stereotypically "autistic" to the general public.

Asperger's Syndrome (AS)

This term is used to describe children who are on the autism spectrum but do not have language delay, although they may have communication differences. However, they do have the social issues and often have the repetitive behaviors and sensory sensitivities of other children with autism. First written about in 1944 in German by Hans Asperger, but not translated into English until the 1980s, Asperger's syndrome was not included in the autism spectrum until 1995, and then was removed again in 2013. Although the term has been subsumed under *autism spectrum disorder*, it is still often used to distinguish autistic children with grammatical spoken language skills but difficulties using appropriate language in social situations, from autistic children with significant language impairments and other needs (Autism Society, n.d.). There is still some resistance to subsuming *Asperger's*, a more positive term with its inference of high-functioning and "geekiness," under the more negative term *autism*. Numerous adults who were identified with Asperger's struggle with their identity as *autistic* with the changes in the language (Smith & Jones, 2020).

Often, children with this milder version of autism aren't identified until late elementary or even middle school, although more severe cases do tend to get identified earlier. And, as I can attest to in my friendship with Sam, there are a large number of functioning adults who weren't identified but clearly have it. Sam could have an amazingly interesting conversation with people one-on-one with fascinating insights into politics, humor, and pop culture. He could quote entire episodes of *Seinfeld* that made friends laugh. But put him at a party, and he would barricade me into a corner to talk about the same subjects one-on-one and not perceive the subtle social cues of shifting feet, the comments of "OK, well, that's interesting, but…," and yawns. These children often grow up to be thought of as "geeks" and other not-so-nice labels. It is important to remember that social difficulties *are* a problem, and ASD does not just represent overlabeling by protective mothers, as some believe. It has been found that the earlier support is provided through early identification, the better the outcomes.

Not Part of Autism Spectrum Disorder
Rett Syndrome
This is a known genetic mutation on the X chromosome that can cause significant "autistic-like" behaviors and almost always occurs in girls. It is very rare, and can be confused with cerebral palsy, because a child's walking gait and movements can be spastic or jerky. Children often will have small heads and have little language ability. They also have seizures and digestive issues. Children with Rett syndrome often will behave in ways similar to children with autism, but there is a known cause for their actions. It is not considered inherited, because it seems to be a genetic mutation that occurs randomly.

Mercury Poisoning
There are children who have been affected by mercury poisoning. The rates of mercury poisoning, while rare, are often the result of access to hazardous waste sites or illegal dumping. Most buildup of mercury in our bodies comes from eating fish that have been exposed to mercury in the water or from breathing in coal vapor

emissions (Willingham, 2017; World Health Organization, 2017). Mercury poisoning often results in numerous issues with children's development, including neurological and kidney functioning. Although there are certain similarities between autism and mercury poisoning, they are not identical. It is also important to note that the rate of mercury poisoning decreased from 2005 to 2012, while the rate of autism increased during this same time period. As our environment becomes more and more polluted, there are going to be more issues related to heavy metal poisonings, but the increase in autism is not directly related to these issues.

Other Maps, Other Countries: Overlapping Disorders

There are lots of other issues that children with autism may have as well. These are called "comorbid disorders," and there appears to be some form of link between these and autism, but researchers haven't found the linkages yet. I tend to think of them all as a vast Venn diagram with overlapping circles of characteristics (see Figure 2.1), with some children having some of the symptoms, and some not.

FIGURE 2.1 Overlapping Circles Representing Symptoms of Autism and Other Disorders

Febrile Seizures/Epilepsy

Children with autism are more likely to have epilepsy, and children with epilepsy are more likely to have autism. We don't know why, even though Leo Kanner, the "father" of autism described the connection in his early papers in the 1940s (Kanner, 1943). There isn't even one type of epilepsy that children with autism are more likely to have—it's across the board. We do know that autistic children with intellectual disorders are more likely to have epilepsy than those with higher intelligence (Venkat, 2016). Many children with autism have seizures in which their brain goes through a small series of electric shocks. Rachel, the mother of a child with autism, experienced this when her child became sick:

> It was a very hot and busy day and I was treating him with Tylenol every 4 hours. His grandmother was holding him while I ran a cool bath for him. Suddenly he began to shake all over, his eyes rolled up into his head, and he went limp. I thought he had died. He was out for more than a few minutes and taken to the hospital. When we got there, his temperature was around 104, and I knew from how he felt earlier that this was cooler. His actual maximum temperature was never determined and therefore, it's unclear as to the damage it may have done.

Doctors are quick to reassure parents that febrile seizures are not life-threatening and can happen many times in a child's life. However, there is such a strong link between brain seizures and autism that I have to believe that there must be some form of cause and effect.

Digestive Issues

There are some very interesting research studies that have found links between autism and the digestive system at a chromosomal level. Many parents can tell you about their child's "leaky gut" in which their child does not develop well physically, nor do they digest food well. Chronic constipation and diarrhea are common issues among children with autism. According to Melinda Moyer (2014), the bacteria and inflammation in the gut appear to make autism symptoms worse. A study that provided a fecal transplant to 18 autistic children found a significant decrease in problematic behaviors (Kang et al., 2019). Phenylketonuria, or PKU, often is confused with autism because of the similar behaviors. Children with PKU are missing a key digestive enzyme that, when left untreated, can lead to problems in brain development. In most states, infants are automatically screened for PKU with blood tests conducted right after birth, but it is important to know if your child was or not. Celiac disease often is suspected in many children with autism as well, and gluten-free diets appear to work well in both groups of individuals with autism and those who have PKU.

Tourette Syndrome

Tourette syndrome is a genetic disorder noticed when the child develops a tic or physical and vocal movements associated with stress. The version that most people think of is the more extreme one, where people shout obscenities and make highly inappropriate remarks. In reality, there are lots of children and adults with Tourette syndrome who do nothing more than clear their throats and blink their eyes when they're anxious. However, tics can fall under repetitive behaviors, so there are many children who meet criteria for both autism and Tourette syndrome, and there appears to be a certain amount of overlap. Up to 22% of autistic children can have tic disorders (Canitano & Vivanti, 2007), and some of the genes associated with Tourette syndrome are the same genes implicated in autism (Wright, 2012). In addition, Tourette syndrome can be influenced by stress and anxiety, conditions that can aggravate autistic behaviors as well.

Anxiety Disorders

Many children with social problems act out when they are placed in situations where they have to talk with other people. According to the National Institute of Mental Health (2017), up to 20% of the general population may have anxiety disorders—a number that increases to 32% among adolescents. Adults and children can get headaches, exhaustion, or muscle spasms. Some people with anxiety disorders have problems maintaining physical balance—an interesting correlation to their inability to maintain mental balance. My son, Ray, has anxiety disorder and Tourette syndrome, and when he is going somewhere new, or something has happened in his life to disrupt his schedule, he will lose his language, avoid eye contact, and be unable to eat. Obsessive-compulsive disorder (OCD) can fall under anxiety disorders as well, so there are overlaps of all kinds of issues.

Sleep Disorders

Many children with autism experience sleep disorders, sleeping little at night, having bedwetting episodes, and being tired throughout the day. Colic among babies is common for an extended period of time and can last for years. Recent studies have found a link between lack of sleep and a large number of disorders, including autism and ADHD. This is true around the world (see Taira, Takase, & Sasaki, 1998).

A friend of mine has had her son participate in many sleep studies, trying to figure out how to get him to sleep well. "I would give anything for a decent night's sleep," she says. "When by some miracle, he does sleep, everything is better—for all of us. The professionals' recommendation? Get more sleep. Have an established sleep routine." I was so annoyed for her! It's a chicken and egg argument. Does autism cause the sleep disorder, or does the lack of sleep aggravate autism? I certainly know that when Elizabeth experiences sleeplessness, her autistic tendencies increase and her language skills markedly decline. We laugh in our family that we can tell when she's tired—she starts talking about herself in the third person ("Elizabeth wants popcorn"). Her pronouns decline dramatically. She falls more often. But we are lucky: she does tend to sleep well, but she needs lots of it.

Language and Learning Disabilities

Having difficulties with language, many children with autism are unable to communicate their needs or questions. They can behave in ways that seem much younger than their actual physical age. Determining the actual intelligence of a child who is unable to communicate with others is challenging. Intellectual disabilities can be found in anywhere from 60%–70% of children with autism (Clarke et al., 2016). The relatively strong ability with language appears to be one of the most significant characteristics of bright children with autism; it is in their social usage of language where autism becomes most noticeable (Faridi & Khosrowabadi, 2017).

Because of the delay in language or inability to understand others' perspectives, reading and comprehension scores can lag significantly behind age peers for some children on the spectrum. Reading comprehension is a typical problem where the child can "word call" (or read words in isolation) but is not able to determine the meaning of the piece or make connections between readings.

Giftedness

Because some children on the spectrum learn to read and do math at very young ages, they can be gifted in many areas. Because of their ability to focus, long attention spans, and deep interest in a subject, many intelligent children with autism also are gifted. Webb et al. (2016) suggested that many experts who are trained in a "deficit model" and are looking for problems will identify children with autism, but they are actually identifying characteristics of giftedness. Ed Amend et al. (2008), before Asperger's was subsumed under ASD, developed the Giftedness/Asperger's Disorder Checklist (GADC©) to help teachers and parents distinguish giftedness from Asperger's syndrome. Characteristics of children with Asperger's and gifted children are described, and a checkmark is placed in the appropriate column. For example, teachers and parents might distinguish between "extensive, advanced vocabulary" to determine giftedness and "advanced use of words with lack of comprehension for all language used" to determine if the child has Asperger's syndrome. What might be considered a symptom of a disability through one lens might be considered a symptom of strength through another.

Autism is typically associated with low IQ scores. However, Bernard Crespi (2016) also found that there is a "high intelligence imbalance" (p. 20) of children with high IQs among the students with Level 1 support needs. Not only are high IQ scores overrepresented among Level 1 autistic children, but ASD is over-represented among the gifted population, particularly among prodigies. Joanne Ruthsatz and Jourdan Urbach (2012) found that eight prodigies in music, art, and math all scored exceedingly high in working memory and had a relatively high autism spectrum quotient. Another study of gifted children found that those with varying IQ subtest scores were more likely to also be identified as autistic than gifted children with "flatter" subtest scores (Boschi et al., 2016). However, the most important factor are the challenges that are faced by a child. Jake Michaelson (2021) noted that as IQ went up among typical children, their degree of interpersonal relationships also increased. Among autistic children, as their IQ increased, their level of interpersonal relationships declined. It is one of the areas in which higher intelligence is not considered a "protective factor," but giftedness can add to issues created by autism.

Weakened Immune Systems

Many children with autism almost appear to have an allergic reaction to their lives; their immune systems are compromised, and they often are unable to fight off colds, allergies, and other illnesses. According to Drs. Meltzer and Van de Water (2017), infections and illnesses appear to be more rampant among children who eventually get diagnosed with autism, and many parents report that their children were given frequent doses of antibiotics when they were babies. Similar to the conditions found in the gut microbes, inflammation is higher among children with autism. It is not clear if the immune system issues are a cause of, or a result of, the autism or linked through genetic relationships.

Speaking the Lingo: Describing Your Concerns

My goal in this section is for you to be able to communicate with professionals and use the appropriate language when you're trying to get someone to listen or help. When you're first aware that something's "just not right," how do you move beyond that vague concern to making a professional listen? Your mother-in-law, your babysitter, your sister—they all know that something is not quite right, but how do you describe it?

Official Language

There's a whole host of official jargon that you will have to plow your way through. When I teach college freshmen to start speaking *educational-ese*, I teach them to think of it like learning another language. Autism involves a whole new set of words to learn, and words you thought you knew the meanings of don't quite mean the same thing in this new journey. This is not even close to an exhaustive list, but it's a starting point for you. For more information, please seek out more specific texts or check with the professionals with whom you work.

Typical and Atypical

These are words to describe what *most* children do at a specific age in a specific time and place. It is important to not think of them as normal and not normal, although most people do. *Normal* implies judgment—something you want your child to be. It is considered *typical* of a four-year-old child who is moving from one city to another to act out and cry while in the grocery store. However, is acting out and crying considered *normal* when the child is in the grocery store? Normal doesn't really take background situations into consideration. With *typical/atypical*, you look for things that aren't really explained by the age or the situation. There are lots of young children who act out, scream, or focus on objects, but for how long, at what age, and what else is going on?

Spectrum

Autism is a spectrum disorder, which means that there are degrees of severity among a whole lot of different characteristics. There are some children who will exhibit mild characteristics, and others with very severe symptoms. Some people will tell you that your child doesn't have autism because they look people in the eye. There are many children who do not qualify for services who exhibit some autistic characteristics, and other children who do qualify who demonstrate very different characteristics from each other. The phrase I often use is *children on the spectrum with varying intensity,* which can include all of the various characteristics of autism across a wide range of functioning.

Characteristics
The use of this term means that children might show a certain behavior, and that many other children with autism have this same type of behavior. But it may not be enough to qualify for a label, or there may be other significant characteristics that are missing. It's a bit like looking at one puzzle piece and saying, "Yes, that looks like it goes to that puzzle, but without the other pieces, it's hard to say." Children may exhibit autistic-like characteristics and not qualify for autism, but they still act differently than their peers.

Criteria
Criteria is the official term for the level of intensity and combination of characteristics that have to be present to qualify for the label (in order to be treated or receive services). Criteria do not imply severity, just that according to an outside authority, the child meets the standards for that label on multiple characteristics. For example, children with social impairments and repetitive behaviors but without language delays might fit the criteria for Level 1 ASD but not Level 2.

Dysfunction
Dysfunction means that something does not work well or the way it's supposed to for others of the same age. Social dysfunction means that children don't socialize the way that other children do. It's a global term that tries to take out the judgmental aspect without going all the way to the term disorder. According to my husband and mother, I have an organizational dysfunction, but it's not a significant problem for me. It may be annoying for my husband, who has to see my bedside table piled with things that I'm doing at the time—a sewing project, three books, several cards in process of writing, random earrings I took off and didn't take back to the jewelry box, and so on—but it's not a real problem in my life. I can find things I need, and my life is not deeply affected. Still, a dysfunction *can* become a disorder or disability if it becomes too significant in a person's life.

Disorder

I love this comment from one mom, who noted that "disorder is not the same as delay." Disorder literally means "not in order," while delay means "in order, but later than expected." Having a disorder implies that the ability that is impaired is creating a significant problem in a person's life. However, disorders are not assumed to be permanent and can sometimes be "cured" given appropriate treatment or developmental growth. It is important to know that treatment for a disorder is not an equation—there is never one right way. There may be many, many strategies and treatments available that may or may not be effective for a particular child, and there may be times when a condition is a problem and times when it is not.

Disability

Disability means that there is a dysfunction that creates significant problems for a child, and it is assumed to be a permanent situation. However, although it may be permanent, there are still strategies and techniques that can help the child learn to cope. Many people have learning disabilities or behavior disabilities, and they can be taught to cope with them. I tell prospective teachers that you can't teach someone to overcome their disability, but you can teach them how to learn *around* it or cope with it. An example of a disability would be someone with artificial limbs. This person can learn to run again with a prosthetic leg but can't ignore the fact that their original leg is missing. Someone with a learning disability can learn to cope and function, but they can't ignore the fact that they learn differently.

Handicap

Handicap is the old term for *disability*, but there is an underlying assumption that the condition cannot get better. My college sweetheart's mother had a handicapped sticker because she had a serious heart condition. That heart condition could not be *taught* to get better.

High-Functioning Versus Low-Functioning/Levels of Support

There are no clear-cut differences between high-functioning and low-functioning children with autism. The informal understanding is that children who are high-functioning have stronger language and problem-solving skills and have slightly below-average to above-average intelligence. Children who are low-functioning tend to have characteristics that are more severe, have lower language abilities, lower intelligence scores, and often other issues as well. Traditionally, Asperger's syndrome and PDD-NOS were considered higher functioning. When I used to describe my daughter as high-functioning, I was trying to imply that she is on or above grade level in most academic subjects, she still struggles with language to some degree, she still has some sensory and social issues, and you might not even know that she had autism if you met her. My friend Tara's nephew has very limited language, just got potty trained at age 11, and is in a self-contained classroom in his school. There are lots of children in between, above, and below these levels; all of them have autism, and yet all of them are unique.

Rather than focusing on "how much autism" is within a person, it is more important to focus on how much support is needed at this time and in this place. There are different levels of support for each of the two characteristics (Autism Speaks, 2021). See Table 2.1.

TABLE 2.1 Levels of Support

Social Communication	
Level 1 Support	Without support, relationships and speech patterns are "odd" and difficult; challenges initiating social engagement and appropriate use of language in social situations.
Level 2 Support	Social impairments are evident even with support systems in place; limited initiation of social engagement.
Level 3 Support	Severe language deficits and little engagement; little to no initiation of communication.
Restricted, Repetitive Behaviors	
Level 1 Support	Difficulties switching between activities; difficulties with organization; difficulty functioning in one or more settings.
Level 2 Support	Difficulty with change and flexibility of interests or thoughts; behaviors are obvious to observers.
Level 3 Support	Extreme difficulty coping with change; great distress and lack of flexibility significantly impacts daily functioning.

There also is a greater chance of children with higher intelligence "recovering" from autism. According to a 2019 study by Dr. Schulman and colleagues, approximately 7% of children diagnosed with autism between the ages of one and three no longer qualified as having autism by the age of nine. However, only 3% had no challenges remaining. Most of those who no longer qualified for autism had anxiety, language processing difficulties, or some other issues. Some parents and methods claim that autism can be "cured," but it would appear from Dr. Schulman's work, as well as work by Dr. Alvares and colleagues (2020), that children with autism who have higher intelligence and who receive intensive early therapy are better able to overcome many of the debilitating issues they face.

Behavioral Terminology

There are essentially five ways you can describe a child's behavior. Use the terms correctly, and you've gained instant credibility from a professional. These also will help you explain to your mother or your grandmother what the difference is between your child's behavior and being "spoiled." The visible difference between a spoiled child and a child on the spectrum is in your responses to the behavior; if you are consistent, are firm, and follow through on natural consequences, then the problem is your child's response to good parenting. Of course, that then places the burden back on you to prove your child's problems, and not be blamed for them, because the tantrums that a child on the spectrum can throw can look an awful lot like the tantrum of a child whose parent is too tired and too unwilling to be the enforcer. Much of the difference lies in what appears to *cause* the problem—is it manipulation of the situation or being overwhelmed by the situation? Is the child engaging in a power struggle with you, or are they searching for power of any kind because they feel so out of control? It often is very difficult to determine the difference and to describe the differences. But if you *know* that you're doing the best you can, ask for help and use the following vocabulary to assist you.

◆ **Characteristics:** What does something look like? Characteristics are a way of describing what a child is doing: what words are being used? What expression is on her face? Lots of kids want to go swimming. When Elizabeth was five and we were at a party, she fixated on the fact that there was a pool there, it was warm, and she wanted to go swimming. Never mind the fact that she had no suit, and no one else was swimming. (We were at my office party.) Every word out of her mouth was about swimming for the whole party until she said, "I can't stop thinking about it!"

◆ **Frequency:** How often does a certain behavior occur? For example, as I was keeping track of her vocabulary, I noted that my daughter said the word "mommy" twice in one day. You'll have to count and keep track of how many times a behavior occurs.

◆ **Latency:** How long after you ask for a certain behavior does a child do it? For example, how long does it take to get them to respond to their name? Typical kids will respond immediately to their name. Our friend Gus sometimes would appear to have to think about what his name meant before he would turn toward us.

◆ **Duration:** How long does a behavior last? My son didn't throw tantrums often: once every four to six months. The frequency of tantrums is low. But when he does... phew! His tantrum record is 3.5 hours. That's 3.5 hours of shrieking, hurling himself about, and repeating the same statement over and over again.

◆ **Intensity:** How loud, soft, hard, big, or small is the behavior? What is the size of the behavior? It's one thing to shut the door. It's a whole other thing to slam the door. Middle school kids are prone to issues of intensity, and when you fuss at them, the response typically is "What? I was just (dropping my books, closing the door, getting out a pencil, setting the table...you name it)." Intensity has to do with degrees. It's typical behavior, that's just, well, more intense.

Potential Detour Signs

So, given all of these overlapping names, types, and other issues and words, what *are* you looking for? What behavior are you trying to describe? Autism and other spectrum disorders are diagnosed when there is a problem in two areas:

◆ Social delay or social communication problems;
◆ Repetitive or restricted behaviors.

Although not often part of the official diagnostic criteria, the following characteristics are often noted among kids with high-functioning autism:

◆ Sensory under- or overstimulation;
◆ Preference for visual information over language or auditory information;
◆ Pathological demand avoidance;
◆ Physical issues;
◆ Discrepant academic abilities.

But what do these *look* like? Not every child is going to exhibit all of these. Many children without autism exhibit some of these characteristics, and many of these characteristics overlap with other exceptionalities, including giftedness. But look at the list *holistically*—is there more than one characteristic that is significant? Do these characteristics cause a problem rather than just being traits? Does your gut instinct tell you something is wrong? Most importantly, do you worry? If you do, it's worth checking out.

There are several characteristics of autism spectrum disorder to look for and to be able to describe to your doctor/therapists. Your child may not exhibit all of them, but you need to be able to describe them, either to say, "No, my child doesn't do this," or "This is what I'm seeing." For more information on spotting characteristics of autism, please also consult a more in-depth source. This section is just an overview of some of the more common issues and is *not* meant to provide comprehensive information.

Language Usage

Language is the most significant characteristic of children on the spectrum. What they say, how they say it, and when they talk can be affected. However, it also is one of the hardest issues to get anyone to help you with. Before the age of two, there are so few words that most children say, so much room for individual differences, and so many myths about how children talk. Some common myths include:

- Boys talk later than girls;
- His dad/our neighbor/Einstein didn't talk until he was three/four/when he was good and ready (many, many variations of this one);
- The ear infections could be an issue;
- They are living in a bilingual environment;
- They're developing in other ways—language will catch up.

Some of these myths are rooted in reality—children *do* develop in highly individual manners. My first child walked at 9 months; my second at 13 months. Both are well within the range of "normal" for that developmental milestone. But, if you have questions or concerns, see a professional. A delay may be just that—a delay that the child will overcome on their own. But a significant delay may need some assistance to overcome. We had a phrase, "Helping isn't going to hurt." Seek out that therapy. Ask for that assistance. It can only help and it might hurt if a child doesn't get it if they needed it.

Language Problems

Language problems can range from delayed, to nonexistent, to blurry, to just strange usage. It's important to recognize that language is not just spoken language, but the whole process of communication—facial expressions, gestures, body language, and reactivity.

Nonverbal language usage is a key trait to verbal language. Many children on the spectrum do not use nonverbal gestures, such as pointing, to communicate. Karyn Seroussi (2002) shared how excited she was that her son was learning how to point, until the therapist said that typical children don't *have* to be taught how to point—they do it automatically.

Echolalia is a frequent issue with kids with autism. They will repeat things that they hear either immediately afterward or quite a while afterward. The key is that they are repeating what someone else has said, not generating unique phraseology on their own. We used my daughter's ability for echolalia to teach her scripts: "When someone says, *How are you, Elizabeth?* you say, *Fine.*" A friend of mine's son, who is lower-functioning, particularly loves Elmo, and will provide you sentences from "Elmo's World" when you try to engage him in conversation.

Echolalia can be sneaky. You might think that children with autism are having a conversation, or even talking to themselves, until you realize that they're feeling the words around in their mouth, almost from an experiential sensory process. At age six, my son was fascinated to learn what the "F" word was. I had told him that I wasn't going to teach him what it was, but when he thought he knew what it was, to come and talk to me about it. On a class field trip, an oh-so-helpful boy in his class taught him the full range of George Carlin's Seven Words. Ray popped into the car that afternoon, full of questions, and asked, "Mommy, is the F word F—?" Ahhh…the end of innocence.

"Yes, Ray it is," I said sadly, realizing my son had made an important vocabulary leap, followed by a full-on parental lecture on why we never *ever* say that word. Ray listened politely. I then heard him whispering the word, rolling it around in his mouth, feeling it out, trying different emphases and tones.

"Huh," he said, disappointedly. "I thought it would be longer."

Words are sensory things. The short bark of the "F word" is short, sharp, and harsh. The rhythm of the word "Savannah" has long been a favorite of mine with its cadence and relaxed mouth muscles. Kids with autism will feel the words in their mouth and sometimes completely ignore the meaning behind them.

Echolalia also is a word-finding strategy, but as Laura Mize and Kate Hensler (2008) noted, it is a positive sign, as it demonstrates that the child is using language for communication purposes—they just have no idea what words to use. Children who do not have a strong grasp of finding or understanding words may reach for what they've heard before or, more likely, learned on television or heard from others close to them. They do not understand the question or cannot find an appropriate response, and so, in an effort to remain engaged, will parrot back something that caught their attention at an earlier time. The frustrating thing is that echolalia really is a desperate strategy of staying engaged, but it ends up cutting off conversation as the other person has nowhere to go.

Interestingly, music seems to play a role in echolalia with its ability to help kids remember words. Many kids with autism will be able to sing back television theme songs or repeat music heard off of the radio. For reasons we don't quite yet understand, music is processed in the brain in a location different than the place where language is processed. Therefore, it can be more accessible at times when words are not available. Studies, such as Maya Marom's (2018), found that echolalia was often used like music to reduce anxiety and to create an emotional communication.

With no musical ability at all, we learned to sing and chant things that Elizabeth and Ray needed to remember on the days that they are not overwhelmed by the "noise" of music. The morning schedule? Posted visually and sung to them: "This is the way we clean our room, clean our room, clean our room…We put clothes away, clothes away, clothes away…We make our bed, make our bed, make our bed…" I would hear them humming it as they (badly) make up their beds. Some issues, such as messy rooms, are just not unique to kids with autism.

Dyspraxia/Apraxia

There are many overlapping terms, but all have to do with muscle coordination; in the case of language, dyspraxia is a condition where the tongue muscles are difficult for the child to move smoothly, and it requires great effort for the child to make clear sounds. Children with autism can hold onto "baby speech" for too long. When Elizabeth was tired or hurt, she would call herself "Ewizabeth." It takes great concentration and energy for these kids to keep their tongues active and toned. L's and R's, difficult sounds even for typical children, can be very challenging for children with autism.

A symptom of dyspraxia, perhaps as a result of possible poor neurological connection, is that the child often will put things in their mouth. It was explained to me by our speech therapist that a baby's first nerve is the shortest and strongest one, from the mouth to the center of the brain. Babies put things into their mouth because that's the first way they learn about things—it's their version of looking at something carefully. They're putting deep pressure on their upper palate, creating a stronger sense of connection and stimulation. Because touch and sight senses develop more slowly, babies really do "know" things first by the way they feel in their mouth. Kids with autism often have scrambled sight and touch senses, so their mouth remains their best way of learning about the world. My friend Tina's son still sucked his thumb at age 13. We always have gum on hand in our house to keep Elizabeth's mouth occupied with a socially acceptable activity. Sucking is both a means of soothing stress as well as exploration and stimulation in all children; it's just that this soothing and exploration continues in children with autism.

According to speech therapist Valerie DeJean (2008), dyspraxia is found in poor muscle tone and poor muscle planning in movements beyond speaking. Hyperflexibility is often an issues with autistic children, and they often can sprain ankles and various joints. We have spent an amazing amount of time in emergency rooms with broken and sprained body parts because my children's bodies did not hold them in place. Children with autism often do not perceive their body as completely as they should and so can have a symptomatic gait or stiff-legged walk. Poor muscle tone can show up in other ways as well. Ray has terrible handwriting because he does not hold a pencil firmly enough. He can stand straight up, but his whole body is sort of "noodle-y." Buttons and zippers can be extremely problematic. Children with autism know how to manipulate them but not their purpose or how to make them achieve their purpose. Brandon's mother complains about how difficult it is to find shoes for her 13-year-old son because he needs them to fasten with Velcro. He does not have the physical dexterity to tie his shoes.

Dyspraxia also relates to these children's ability to perceive things in space relative to other things. For example, they can spin the wheels on a car, but they don't understand how that is representative of a car going down the road. Thus, when asked to "make the car go," they experience frustration. They know how to walk but have difficulty adjusting their gaits when surfaces change. Their relationship to the world around them is different because of their different relationship to their own bodies.

Problems With Pronouns

For some reason, perhaps because pronouns are representative of the thing, not the word for the actual thing itself, children with autism can have problems with first- and second-person pronouns, using "he/she" for "I" or "I" for "you," and confusing gender pronouns with each other. I often hear parents of bright children with language problems complain that their child refers to themselves in the third person or that their child is using the royal *we*. These challenges with pronouns are highlighted in today's world, where one's choices of pronouns are often preferential statements. This societal ambiguity makes pronouns even harder.

Global Versus Specific Terms

Concepts are particularly hard for children with autism. Concepts are vague and include many other skills in them. Because children with autism often don't generalize, they aren't sure what specific skills are being called for when they're asked to do something. Children on the spectrum often don't understand "umbrella terms," or words that mean a series of actions rather than one specific thing. They have challenges making generalizations between one activity and how it might relate to other activities.

I made Elizabeth cry when she was 12 when I called to her to "come clean the kitchen." She just stood and looked at me, and I thought that she was being willful—a very strong possibility. "Clean up the kitchen, Elizabeth!" I repeated.

"What do you mean, mommy?"

"I mean clean the kitchen!"

"I don't understand."

"What don't you understand? I told you to go and clean the kitchen, and I mean *now*!"

Prolific tears then came: "What do you mean by 'clean'? What am I supposed to do?"

Bad mommy moment. I looked down at my daughter who had just taken the "Big Girl" responsibility a few months before of washing the dishes and realized that she didn't know that that was synonymous with "cleaning." I had to take a deep breath and explain that "clean" is a large, vague term for wiping down the counter, rinsing the dishes...all of those small tasks that involve cleaning. Elizabeth often had problems with global terms such as "check your work," "clean your room," "go play," "be nice," "use your manners," and "are you finished?" There are so many parenting admonishments and questions that are too vague for her to understand. She often got in trouble at school for similar things. She lives in a world of specifics.

While bright kids with autism may have difficulty with global terms, they also use vague terms to cover when they are unable to find the specific term. Finding the right word for the right situation often can be a challenge. They use vague words like *stuff* or *that*, or phrases designed to fill in conversational gaps, such as "You know." When asked to tell back stories or events, they have a hard time retelling them.

It is important to note that this need for specificity can sometimes be an area of strength. Often these traits can lead to a deep fascination with computers, math, or the law. After all, computers are extremely precise, and math is the process of quantifying things!

Lack of Imagination

Because imagination is formed when a child can generalize beyond the here and now into a hypothetical realm, children on the spectrum often have a great deal of trouble with imagination. Hypothetical situations, estimating, and other broad thinking activities tend to be very difficult for these children. They often can see things in black and white, and complex issues are very difficult to understand.

My daughter didn't know what to make of it when our local nature center was encouraging children to make fairy houses. She was very confused because she *knew* that fairies did not exist, and yet, here were grownups telling her that they did. She assumed that she was wrong and went around looking for fairies. She wasn't confused between imaginary and real—she just didn't understand what imaginary was.

Hyperlexia and Hypernumeracy

Hyperlexia is a condition where a child develops a precocious ability to read, often along with a fascination with letters and numbers far above their age peers, while hypernumeracy is the ability to count and do math operations far beyond age peers. Gifted children often read at advanced level as a characteristic of their giftedness; however, hyperlexia has a corresponding problem of language usage or verbal understanding of what is being read. Thus, children with hyperlexia have very strong word-calling skills, but often cannot tell you what it is that they've read. It is estimated that 86% of children with hyperlexia or hypernumeracy behaviors also have autism (Ostrolenk et al., 2017).

My family has a history of thinking in visual words. That means that when we talk, we have to *see* it first in our minds. We laugh about how people cannot tell us directions, we have to see it written down. It is a learning preference that is shared with other people, but is a very strong one in my family. Consequently, I read a tremendous amount to Elizabeth and Ray as they were growing up, trying to create emotional and physical connections, as well as developing concepts through books. For example, I bought *The Berenstain Bears Visit the Dentist* to prepare them for their first dentist visit. We understand things when they're in a book, and it helps ease the anxiety produced by the experiencing of it.

Although I wasn't intentionally doing it, using hyperlexia often can be a method of therapy. Reading aloud to a child a book as they read along is a means of allowing them to connect the visual with the auditory, thereby reinforcing the process of language. In *The Mind Tree*, Tito Mukhopadhyay (2000), who is hyperlexic and wrote the book when he was eight years old, shared the insight he got when he finally realized that "the voices related to people and lips" (p. 16).

Pedantic

Many children on the spectrum can have excellent language skills and have fantastic vocabularies. However, they also can have very little emotion in their voice or face when talking and will use "fancy" words when simpler words might be more appropriate. They can be called "little professors" (which I find funny and irritating—my being a professor and all). I can always tell when my husband is stressed—he will start using words that are multisyllabic and precise. I believe that the pedantic language is an attempt to control the chaos that children with ASD feel when they are in a stressful situation and are trying to get a precise understanding of it for themselves, without really paying attention to the needs of their audience.

Social Problems

Certainly, social problems often are caused by and worsened by language problems. When children can't find the words for a given situation and can't communicate their needs and wants, everyone can get frustrated. But there are several characteristic social behaviors of children with autism.

Lack of Obvious Emotion or Flat Affect

Affect is considered to be the visual representation of responsiveness and emotions: the smile, the frown, and eye contact. This is probably one of the most significant characteristics of autism. Children with autism just don't look or act like most people do when emotions are involved.

Gus was an eight-year-old boy I knew with Asperger's syndrome who was obsessed with his cat, Sunny. He wrote stories about Sunny, talked nonstop about Sunny, and would give you detailed information you really didn't want to know about Sunny (I well remember the day that Gus told me all about Sunny throwing up). Then, one Tuesday, Gus started talking about trains. He was telling me about speeds, types, and histories…everything I ever wanted to know and more about trains. I was surprised and amused that within a day's time, Gus could find a new fixation. I told his mother that afternoon, "Looks like Gus got off his obsession with Sunny and moved on to trains."

"Sunny died last night. He got out and was run over by a car. Gus saw it happen," his mom told me, with tears in her eyes.

I was shocked! I had no indication at all that Sunny had died in such a horrific manner, or that Gus had witnessed it. With any other child, I would have expected him to tell me, express sorrow, and be terribly upset. However, Gus gave every impression of not caring at all about it. Because I knew Gus before I knew much about autism, I was rather disturbed at his apparent callousness and lack of connection to this pet that I assumed that he loved. I made the assumption—as many people do—that people with autism do not feel emotion.

The opposite is true in most cases, however. Often, people with autism care so deeply that they don't know how to deal with it. The power of the emotion overwhelms them and they shut it down. What appears to be callousness or negativity actually is a coping mechanism. They may appear not to have emotion, when what they're doing is stuffing down intense emotion that then releases itself in a tantrum, a torrent of tears, or extreme agitation, or hides through a lack of response.

Lack of Eye Contact

Many children with autism can't make eye contact. The anxiety that they feel when they connect eyes with someone can overwhelm them. They would rather focus on a detail about a person—their shirt, their buttons, anything other than the emotional upheaval of sharing eye gaze. And because they don't process language in quite the same way, they often are unresponsive to their own names. It's as if they just don't hear it as a name or as anything related to themselves. Often, a child not responding to their own name is a trigger for many parents to start to believe something is wrong.

Rozella Stewart (2000), from the Indiana Resource Center for Autism, shared the story told to her by a well-educated man with Asperger's syndrome, who stated, "If you insist that I make eye contact with you, when I'm finished I'll be able to tell you how many millimeters your pupils changed while I looked into your eyes" (para. 7). Eye contact is so invasive to their psyche, most people with high-functioning autism cannot do it. And yet because of the communication component needed by typical people, developing eye contact is one of the first, and hardest, things that therapists focus on in behavior and communication goals. Being able to look people in the eye is a key first step of communication.

Inappropriate or Delayed Interactions

Often it seems as though children with autism try to learn the social codes without truly understanding how or why they work. For example, Gus did not understand the concept or need for personal space. He would be so excited about what he was talking about that he would creep closer and closer to you until he was literally inches from you. He would be gesturing wildly, and the person to whom he was talking would be inching away looking very uncomfortable. One day, Gus made me laugh when he implemented a strategy he had obviously been taught. He was chattering about something, probably trains, when he stopped himself and said quietly, "arm's distance," and carefully measured the distance from me using his arm. He then looked at me for approval and was off and chattering again. *He* didn't feel the need to be an arm's distance away from his audience, but he had been taught exactly how far he needed to be in order to make other people comfortable. He was learning the code without completely understanding the reason for it.

Aaron, a four-year-old son of a friend of mine appears to have understood the code for children his own age quite well. He plays games well and has a great sense of imagination. His older sister Anna, who is autistic? Not so much...

One day, Aaron had his best friend, Mallorie, a five-year-old girl, over to play at the park. "Let's play dinosaurs," he enthusiastically suggested.

"Let's play house," she replied.

"Let's play dinosaur house!" he retorted, and within minutes, they were setting up rocks as a Tyrannosaurus rex's house, and he was running about to steal eggs for dinner. She was the dinosaur mama and was cooking the stolen eggs while he busily defended the home with ferocious teeth. Beyond the obvious gender roles they were playing out, I was deeply amused at how Aaron was able to combine two games of play into a game agreeable to all and to truly live his play.

Meanwhile, five-year-old Anna had been swinging and gradually wandered over to the action. "I want to play," she told me.

"So, go play with them, honey. They're good at figuring out things to do."

So, Anna went and stood stock still in the middle of their "kitchen." "Will you play with me?" she said in a plaintive tone.

"Sure!" replied her brother. "You can be Sister Dinosaur!"

"I don't want to play dinosaurs," she whined. Aaron shrugged and zoomed off with arms widespread, turning into a pterodactyl. All dragging arms and droopy eyes, Anna came back to me crying: "They won't play with me!"

Oh, my darling: how do I, as an adult, help her navigate the strange world of five-year-olds? I suggested that she invite them to climb the play structure when she stopped crying. That time it worked, but later? As a 10-year-old? Lord help us, as a 13-year-old? And as a 16-year-old starting to fall in love? Ah me...

Theory of Mind

There is a developmental step called "theory of mind" that develops in most children around age four. They can understand that what they see, think, and feel is not necessarily what other people see, think, and feel.

There is a famous test, devised by Dr. Simon Baron-Cohen (see Baron-Cohen et al., 1985), called the "Sally Anne" test, where you can test to see if children have reached this understanding. Essentially, the child is presented with two dolls named Sally and Anne, a bucket, a basket, and a story that is carried out using the dolls. The child is told that the dolls are playing and that they hide a marble in a basket. Sally then goes for a walk. While she is gone, Anne moves the marble into the bucket. When Sally returns, the child playing with the dolls is asked, "Where does Sally think the marble is?" If the child has theory of mind, the child will understand that even though they know that the marble is in the bucket, Sally would think that the marble is in the basket. If the child does not have theory of mind, they will fully believe that Sally thinks that the marble is where the child knows it was moved. The child will be unable to understand that other people do not know or are not interested in the information or beliefs that they have.

Most children develop theory of mind around age four naturally and cannot be hurried into it. I remember trying to teach my two-year-old son this concept. He was looking at a picture book in his car seat in the backseat while I was driving. "What's that?" he asked, pointing to the book.

"I don't know, Ray. I can't see it," I responded.

"That, *right there!*" he insisted.

"I can't see it, sweetheart. I'm looking forward, you're looking at it. I can't tell you because I can't see it."

He then proceeded to have a complete meltdown because he just knew that I was holding out information on him. It was a learning experience for me about the power of developmental thought and how important it was to be able to understand others' perspectives.

Often, bright autistic people will not be able to fully demonstrate theory of mind. They do not understand that other people are not as fascinated with geology, trains, animals, space, or whatever they currently are involved with. An adult friend of mine on the spectrum was sharing about a date that he had gone on.

He said, "I started talking about cephalopods, and then she said she had to go."

I replied, "I'm so sorry it went badly. Do you think that there was anything you could have done differently?"

He responded, "Started talking about cephalopods earlier so she could know how cool they are, and we could have talked longer about them!"

I encouraged him to reach out to find someone who might be as interested in cephalopods as he is! Bright kids on the spectrum often do not understand why other people behave or feel differently than they do. They are unable to understand other people's reactions to them other than as an intellectual problem. This trait also can be found in gifted children who also can have strong interests and express frustration that other children do not understand or follow their rules. However, most gifted children are advanced in their developmental process and are thinking like children much older than they are, causing them to be frustrated at their peers' inability to think at the same level.

Repetitive Behaviors

This is a pretty broad term for actions that are done over and over again for the purpose of soothing or stimulating. Sometimes these behaviors are easy to recognize: rocking of the body, head banging, and flapping of arms. They can also be verbal: hooting, humming, or whooping. It is *very* important to know that repetitive behaviors are ways that all people deal with stressful situations—both positive stress and negative stress. We all know people who eat or tap pencils, jiggle their legs, chew their fingernails, and twiddle their thumbs. It's not the process of moving that is a characteristic, but both the intensity of the repetitions and the cultural appropriateness of the situation. Many people hum to themselves when they're standing in line or bored. But most do not hum during a business meeting. Many people will clap their hands or shake them when they're excited about something, but most don't flap their whole hands or arms.

Lines

Parents often first notice their child's autistic-like behaviors when the child lines up toys, sorting by color or some criteria unknown to the watching parent. Aaron, a friend's son, would arrange his toy vehicles according to function: road workers first, mass transportation second, cars third, and "other" last. Typical children also will line up cars, but they play with a car as a miniature car in a miniature world, not as a thing that is blue or spins.

Obsessions/Compulsions

Repetitive behaviors also can be collections of things that people keep around themselves or actions that have to be done. A friend of mine collects rocks—not just a few, but roomfuls of rocks, particularly quartz and geodes. He says that the rocks soothe him because he understands their crystalline nature and being surrounded by their various structures gives his life a feeling of structure. Other children may fixate on one topic and try to learn everything there is to know about vacuum cleaners, and then abruptly switch to airplane schedules. Again, for a child who is bright, this is behavior that is similar to characteristics found among gifted children. The difference is the problem that the obsession creates: can the child switch to another topic, or are they locked into only the topic of interest, despite whether another person may or may not be interested?

Stimming

Short for "stimulating," stimming is when a child fixates on a repeated action, deriving great enjoyment and a feeling of peace from the action (Children's Hospital of Philadelphia, 2016). It can be rocking, spinning, flapping, bouncing a ball, masturbating, closing a door, hitting their head, pulling on jump ropes, repeating a phrase…anything that is repetitive, sensorial, and reduces anxiety for the child. The difference between stimming and self-soothing behaviors is small—most people will jiggle pencils, twitch their feet, or fidget with their fingers. Sometimes when children are stimming, they often are oblivious to anything else around them, and it serves to cut them off from social interaction rather than allow them to engage in it. And other times, "stims" allow them to feel free and disconnected and peaceful as a way to self-manage stress and anxiety.

Tito Mukhopadhyay (2000) wrote that at the age of eight, he spun because he felt that his body was a series of disconnected parts. He would see his hand and feel no sense of connection between that and his foot. He spun because he had seen that the fan blades, which were disconnected parts, would form a whole circle when they spun. He felt through the sensation of spinning that he could truly feel his body as a whole. On the other hand, Amanda Baggs (2007), sharing her experiences via YouTube, noted that stimming is how she interacts with the world—how she gets to feel connected to and learn about the world directly without the need for language to intervene. Clearly, stimming is a significant need for children with autism and relates to their jangled neurology. Their stim can be a way to be happy, a way to self-soothe, or a way to disengage. Too often, adults try to stop the stimming without seeking to understand the purpose of the stim.

Other Characteristics, Not Part of the Criteria

There are a whole host of other issues that many children on the autism spectrum seem to experience. There is limited research data on many of these issues, and so they are not part of the diagnosis process. Hard science professionals express doubt that they even exist in the terms that experienced practitioners have created. I found that many of these issues were ones that I noticed, and many other mothers I knew saw them too.

Sensory Integration/Sensory Processing Disorder (SPD)

Many children with various forms of autism experience sensory issues—either reacting too little or too much to different stimuli—and each child is highly individual about what they react to. The list of behaviors can range from odd to very odd. Tina, a friend of mine, shared a few such behaviors exhibited by her child: licking glass, licking the saltshaker, leaping out of the shopping cart to touch the carpeted pillars, chewing fingernails until they bled, spinning in circles, walking in a pattern, crying when the car stopped at red lights, screeching suddenly, having a sensitivity to light, and needing to have the volume at a specific level. The list goes on and on.

RACHEL'S STORY

Did you ever take notice of *The Incredibles* DVD main menu? Probably not…Ben insisted that when the colors flash red, then blue, then purple, and back to red, that we only hit start when the screen flashed purple. All hell would break loose if we did not. If we missed it, we would just wait another round of the colored backgrounds and be ready for purple. Control freak? Maybe to some, but who knows how much this affected him? His all-out tantrum seemed to indicate that it was very important for the movie to start when he needed it to start. Maybe it is compensation for feeling so out of control of so many factors and gaining extreme control of a few things that helps keep him from spinning out of control.

For most people, the process of interpreting and modulating sensory information is automatic. We hear someone talking to us, our brains receive that input and recognize it as a voice talking in a normal tone, and we respond appropriately. Children who have SPD, however, don't experience such interactions in the same way. SPD affects the way their brains interpret the information that comes in; it also affects how they respond to that information with emotional, motor, and other reactions. For example, some children are overresponsive to sensation and feel as if they're being constantly bombarded with sensory information. They may try to eliminate or minimize this perceived sensory overload by avoiding being touched or being particular about clothing. Some children are underresponsive and have an almost insatiable desire for sensory stimulation. They may seek out constant stimulation by taking part in extreme activities, playing music loudly, or moving constantly. They sometimes don't notice pain or objects that are too hot or cold, and may need high-intensity input to get involved in activities. Still others have trouble distinguishing between different types of sensory stimulation.

One of the challenges of a child with high-functioning autism is that receptivity and awareness of fine sensory details is characteristic of giftedness as well. Psychologist Kazimierz Dabrowski (1964) noted that gifted children often expressed what he called *overexcitabilities*. The five overexcitabilities he discussed were psychomotor, sensual, emotional, intellectual, and imaginational. Gifted children often are highly responsive to sensory input as well, a very related and hard-to-distinguish issue from sensory integration issues. Such issues can be problematic and lead to an overrepresentation of gifted children who have SPD, according to the Sensory Processing Disorder Foundation (2021).

When I teach students about SPD, or sensory integration disorder (a term first used by A. Jean Ayres in 1979), I teach them that there are actually seven senses that children with SI often cannot integrate with a sense of comfort. There are the traditional five (sight, taste, touch, smell, and hearing) and two others that researchers define as vestibular and proprioceptive.

Vestibular relates to the child's sense of balance and resides in the inner ear. According to Dr. Kern and associates from the University of Texas Southwestern Medical Center at Dallas (2007), many children on the spectrum have either an excellent or a terrible sense of balance; they tend to the extreme. I have noticed that many children with autism do not get dizzy. They have an underresponsive vestibular system. As a result, spinning tends to calm them down, and they love to swing and spin for great periods of time. My family went to the park two to three times a day only to swing.

Proprioceptive sense is the child's awareness of where they are in space—information received by their body and its relationship to itself. A classic study by Drs. Masterson and Biederman in 1983 found that children with autism have to rely on their sense of being touched firmly to learn new tasks rather than their visual sense. This can translate into either clumsiness or complete body awareness through focused awareness. Many children will "toe walk" or walk on their tiptoes and have an ungainly gait in which they are stiff-legged and seem as if they are barely standing upright. They may try to squeeze themselves into spaces too small for their bodies. They may not conform their body when being hugged or held. They also can have significant issues with stamina.

Elizabeth has superior proprioceptive sense—she almost never fell as a baby and walked at nine months. I don't know if it's a feature of her autism or her own abilities, but Elizabeth is a natural athlete and has always known where she is in space. Selected for competitive gymnastics training when she was four, and on a world championship cheer team in her teens, athletics is her area of strength and social activity. I have very clear memories of being at a mother's group when she was 11 months old. The others were standing around chatting and snuggling their children in their arms, and I was the only mother monitoring her child as she climbed unaided up the six-foot slide. It was not the first time I decided that mother's groups were just not for us.

Sand on her feet? Oh no. Rubbing her back? Only if you wanted to irritate her. Touch and visual things that moved and varied made her extremely agitated. But taste? She was understimulated in the area of taste. Her first food that she did not reject was spicy taco meat. She loves salty, spicy things. She dives right into pickled beets and Indian food. She was the only eight-year-old I knew who liked raw green onion bulbs—banned from me since I can't stand the smell. She is a very adventurous eater and has been open to trying most new foods.

Synesthesia

Some children and parents report that the sensory information process is so confused that the information appears to get "crossed." Some researchers have hypothesized that all children are born with developing sensory neurons, and as they obtain experiences, the neurological linkages "harden" and blue becomes "blue" rather than "tart." However, some people with the genetic tendency will have crossed neurons so that they then taste "tart" in their mouths when they see something blue. Not all people with synesthesia have autism, but there does appear to be a link. In his book, *Born on a Blue Day*, Daniel Tammet (2006), who has autism, stated that to him colors have taste, numbers have shapes, and days have colors. The information is processed in ways that do not make sense to people with typical neurological development.

It often is the sensory issues that are the first sign that something's different in your child...and it's often the sign that gets noticed and remarked upon the most.

Pathological Demand Avoidance (PDA)

Some children can experience such high levels of anxiety that they can avoid anything that causes stress, including tasks in which they want to participate (National Autism Society, 2020). There is a strong resistance and avoidance of ordinary aspects of life, and there tend to be significant mood swings. Children with this profile can appear to be controlling and dominant when they are anxious. While they may crave structure and routine, it is very important that they be part of the creation of the routine because they will struggle against the authority figure who is imposing rules upon them.

PDA can lead to significant behavior problems and difficulty with authority figures. Some strategies that families can use and share with teachers include the use of the following PANDA acronym (PDA Society, 2021):

- ◆ **Pick your battles:** Minimize rules and explain the reasons behind them. Try not to take the negative response personally;
- ◆ **Anxiety management:** Think ahead and work to reduce uncertainty. Give strategies and "back up plans" for more uncertain activities or events;
- ◆ **Negotiate and collaborate:** Keep calm and demonstrate respect;
- ◆ **Disguise and manage demands:** Do things together, provide options that you determine;
- ◆ **Adaptation:** Use humor and distraction and try to provide enough time.

I see PDA with a lot of bright autistic kids. Their intellect allows them to think of possibilities, while their autism provides anxiety and social stress to detract from the experience. One mother described how her son slept through a soccer championship party. He wanted to go, he had been looking forward to going, but the pressure of it got to him and he refused to wake up for it. Other parents describe fights to get their child to go to school, to go to games, or even to eat dinner with friends. Many children will choose colleges that are not at the level of their academics or will withdraw into sleep or virtual reality to avoid social demands. My son Ray goes into deep, dark moods at the slightest hint of negative judgment. I learned to stop my instinctive "No, Ray!" when he was about to do something he shouldn't—reach too high for a glass bowl, walk out into a parking lot without me, or do a problem using addition instead of multiplication—and replace it with a question of "Why is that *not* a good idea?" Turning it into an intellectual exercise allowed him to deal with the pain of negative attention coming his way.

Visual Learners

With their difficulty with social cues and language, children on the spectrum often learn best visually. In fact, Temple Grandin (2006), who has both high-functioning autism and a Ph.D., wrote a book called *Thinking in Pictures*. Far more than the "learning style" theory, when a child is a visual learner, it means that they must use pictures, rather than words, to better convey concepts and ideas. Some forms of technology have capitalized on this. In one particular system, called the Picture Exchange Communication System (PECS), teachers and parents present choices and information to children using pictures rather than written words. Similarly, teachers have been using visual reminders for years for children with autism (e.g., picture schedules, lunch choices, etc.).

There can be some very interesting skills that emerge from this learning ability. Some people, such as my daughter, are very spatial and have a phenomenal ability to read maps or to understand directions. At the age of two, we were running errands before we went to the beach. My husband, who does not have a strong sense of direction, was in the righthand turn lane coming out of the bookstore. Elizabeth started screeching, "Bee…Bee" and frantically gesturing to the left. I turned to her, thinking she had been stung, and realized that she was trying to tell him to turn left rather than right to go to the beach. At the next intersection, I asked her which way to go and she, with a wide grin on her face, pointed in the correct direction.

Our house is decorated with maps. When the kids were growing up, we did not live near family, and so we often traveled around the country to see them. The stress and anxiety of traveling with two young children with high levels of sensitivity was reduced when we could show them on the map where we were and where we were going. It helped reduce anxiety because they could relate to and understand a map. Similarly, many parents with children on the spectrum note that their children understand graphs and charts very well. They like having data nicely organized in such a visual manner. I use maps as an analogy in this book for many reasons.

Puzzles are another popular item among families with autism. Children with autism *love* the repetitive nature of puzzles, the visual "fit" that happens, and the problem-solving process of seeing how things fit together. Sudoku, wooden puzzles, or hidden picture puzzles all are visual games that are attractive to children with autism. Qwirkle was a favorite at our house because of the visual skills needed.

These are children who must watch in order to learn. They cannot be told how to do something; they have to either do it themselves or watch others first. I often think that traditional instruction is like Charlie Brown's teacher to them—babble in a sea of noise. They tend to thrive on lists and very specific, written-down directions.

Reading can be a challenging experience for children who are very visual. Learning to read often can be very difficult because making the language connection between the visual representation of the words, the meaning of the word, and the sound of the word are three different tasks that require a great deal of mental connections. Evidence-based practice suggests that children with autism focus on sight-word instruction because of their strength of visual associations, and reading comprehension (El Zein et al., 2014). Yet, if children with high-functioning autism can learn to read, they often become fantastic at it. In my family, we think in visual words, not sounds. I have many words that I can use, write, and spell because I've seen them, but I can't pronounce them because that's not a visual skill.

Face Blindness
There is one notable exception to this skill of visual learning— the ability to recognize and respond to faces. Faces are certainly visual locations for information, but there is something in the emotional impact of a face that can sometimes render it almost

blind to a child on the spectrum. Persons with face blindness (or prosopagnosia) simply cannot connect faces with names or faces with particular emotions. This is not unique to autism, as many people with autism do not have it and many people with face blindness do not have autism; however, they are issues that often occur together. In a fascinating discussion, Olga Bogdashina (2003) described one man's method to recognize people by their jeans, gait, movements, and hair. He can see a pattern in hair texture and process hairlines. Interestingly, many autistic children are fascinated by people's hair, and many do not recognize their relatives if they wear unfamiliar clothes. People with this disorder can notice small details about a face, such as hairline, scars, and other features that do not really change over time. However, the ever-changing expressions blur the understanding and ability to process their information. It is a condition that my family has to a mild degree and we have learned the fine art of having extended conversations with people when we have no idea who they are or what their name is. Elizabeth was asked to draw pictures of and describe her friends. She drew a picture of her friends, including Morgan (see Figure 2.2; Morgan is the child

FIGURE 2.2 Picture of Elizabeth's Friends

in the center of the top row). She had great details on clothing (note the boots on one friend), but she did not draw faces. Just a circle, a smile and dots for eyes. No curly hair, no color details. To Elizabeth, faces just weren't features that were important.

You can test your own skills at face recognition. I prefer the test at https://facememory.psy.uwa.edu.au/, but there are many others!

Discrepant Academic Abilities

Often, these various learning capabilities create a very uneven learning pattern. Bright autistic children may excel at subjects and instruction that focus on rote memory, analysis, and visual awareness, and do poorly in areas that are highly language or socially based. They may excel at drama but perform poorly in literature. Much of their learning will be highly dependent upon the content, their level of interest, and the method of instruction. But they may look very much like other twice-exceptional children who have significant strengths in some academic areas and very poor skills in others.

Such diverse skills found within a child with high-functioning autism can translate to test scores and cognitive abilities that are highly discrepant. For example, my daughter has a visual processing ability that is in the 95th percentile, but an auditory processing speed that is in the 9th percentile. Such wide fluctuations of scores can serve to flatten a child's overall ability or achievement scores. For example, a very bright child I worked with had an overall IQ score of 126, but a verbal score of 112 and a performance score of 135. Within each of these larger domains, he had equally wildly fluctuating subtest scores. He did not qualify for gifted services in that particular state because his overall score was not high enough, nor did he qualify for special education services because his scores were not low enough. However, many of his individual scores indicated significant strengths and some debilitating challenges. Overall, his achievement was moderate and he made grade-level B's with an occasional A.

Interestingly, according to Bernard Crespi (2016), prevalence rates of autism are higher among gifted populations, and many gifted children are misdiagnosed or overdiagnosed with autism and other labels, because of, or exacerbated by, their giftedness. I would recommend the book *Misdiagnosis and Dual Diagnoses of Gifted Children and Adults* by Dr. Jim Webb and others (2016) as an excellent resource for looking at children with high-functioning autism and other labels.

Describing My Child

The problem with checklists and descriptors is that they still don't capture the wonderful, funny essence of any child, much less mine. I read so many checklists and realized that Elizabeth fit many of them. I kept holding their descriptions up against Elizabeth, much like shopping for clothes—does *this* label fit her? How about this one? Untangling autism from the essential "Elizabeth-ness" sometimes can be problematic. Does she have communication problems, or is she just that way? Does she have significant sensitivities, or is she just a member of our family (who all hate loud noises and like nuts in our ice cream because of the texture)? And what about her strengths? Were these autism at its best or a version of giftedness? She has a very strong spatial ability, phenomenal abilities with puzzles, and unbelievable athletic skills—how could such strengths be characteristic of a terrible label such as autism? All parents deal with tantrums; my mother was full of stories of my crankiness and my severe inability to fall asleep, and I turned out fine...didn't I?

And did she really fit the label? Yes, she had some characteristics, but not all. Was I being paranoid? She was a *girl*—girls weren't supposed to have autism. Here was a child who loved kisses, smiled at me, and made funny faces at herself in the mirror. She reminded me of the nursery rhyme:

> There was a little girl
> Who had a little curl
> Right in the middle of her forehead
> And when she was good
> She was very, very good
> And when she was bad, she was horrid.

I didn't want a label; a label might provide my child with that very future that I was trying to avoid—the ones that so many other mothers on blogs and bulletin boards were living, full of pain and hope for their beloved child. Mothers who celebrated a child's first sentence at age seven. Families who could not travel on airplanes because of the extreme meltdowns. Was I one of *those* mothers? Or was I a mother who was simply unprepared for motherhood? But my family did need help, and so finally we went looking.

References

Alvares, G. A., Bebbington, K., Cleary, D., Evans, K., Glasson, E. J., Mayberry, M. T., Pillar, S., Uljarevic, M., Varcin, K., Wray, J., & Whitehouse, A. J. (2020). The misnomer of "high functioning autism": Intelligence is an imprecise predictor of functional abilities at diagnosis. *Autism, 24*(1), 221–232. https://doi.org/10.1177/1362361319852831

Amend, E. R., Beaver-Gavin, K., Schuler, P., & Beights, R. (2008). *Giftedness/ Asperger's Disorder Checklist (GADC) pre-referral checklist.* Amend Psychological Services.

American Psychiatric Association. (2013). *Diagnostic and statistical manual of mental disorders* (5th ed.). https://doi.org/10.1176/appi.books .9780890425596

Autism Speaks. (2021). *Autism diagnostic criteria: DSM-5.* https://www .autismspeaks.org/autism-diagnosis-criteria-dsm-5

Ayres, A. J. (1979). *Sensory integration and the child.* Western Psychological Services

Baggs, A. (2007). *In my language.* https://www.youtube.com/watch?v =JnylM1hI2jc

Baron-Cohen, S., Leslie, A. M., & Frith, U. (1985). Does the autistic child have a "theory of mind"? *Cognition, 21*(1), 37–46. https://doi.org/10.1016 /0010-0277(85)90022-8

Bogdashina, O. (2003). *Sensory perceptual issues in autism and Asperger Syndrome: Different sensory experiences: Different perceptual worlds.* Jessica Kingsley Publishing.

Boschi, A., Planche, P., Hemimou, C., Demily, C., & Vaivre-Douret, L. (2016). From high intellectual potential to Asperger Syndrome: Evidence for differences and a fundamental overlap—A systematic review. *Frontiers in Psychology*, *7*, 1605. https://doi.org/10.3389/fpsyg.2016 .01605

Canitano, R., & Vivanti, G. (2007). Tics and Tourette syndrome in autism spectrum disorders. *Autism*, *11*(1), 19–28. https://doi.org/10.1177 /1362361307070992

Centers for Disease Control. (2019). *Spotlight on: Delay between first concern to accessing services.* https://www.cdc.gov/ncbddd/autism/addm -community-report/delay-to-accessing-services.html

Centers for Disease Control. (2020). *What is Autism spectrum disorder?* https://www.cdc.gov/ncbddd/autism/facts.html

Children's Hospital of Philadelphia. (2016). *Stimming; What is it and does it matter?* https://www.carautismroadmap.org/stimming-what-is-it -and-does-it-matter/

Clarke, T.-K., Lupton, M. K., Fernandez-Pujals, A. M., Starr, J., Davies, G., Cox, S., Pattie, A., Liewald, D. C., Hall, L. S., Macintyre, D. J., Smith, B. H., Hocking, L. J., Padmanabhan, S., Thomson, P. A., Hayward, C., Hansell, N. K., Montgomery, G. W., Medland, S. E., Martin, N. G., Wright, M. J., Porteous, D. J., Dreary, I. J., & McIntosh, A. M. (2016). Common polygenic risk for autism spectrum disorder (ASD) is associated with cognitive ability in the general population. *Molecular Psychiatry*, *21*(3), 419–425. https://doi.org/10.1038/mp.2015.12

Crespi, B. J. (2016, June). Autism as a disorder of high intelligence. *Frontiers in Neuroscience*, *10*, 300. https://doi.org/10.3389/fnins.2016.00300

Dabrowski, K. (1964). *Positive disintegration.* Little, Brown.

DeJean, V. (2008). *Vestibular re-integration of the autistic child.* iUniverse Inc.

den Houting, J. (2019). Neurodiversity: An insider's perspective. *Autism*, *23*(2), 271–273. https://doi.org/10.1177/1362361318820762

El Zein, F., Solis, M., Vaughn, S., & McCulley L. (2014). Reading comprehension intervention for students with autism spectrum disorders: A synthesis of research. *Journal of Autism and Developmental Disorders*, *44*, 1303–1322.

Faridi, F., & Khosrowabadi, R. (2017). Behavioral, cognitive and neural markers of Asperger Syndrome. *Basic and Clinical Neuroscience*, *8*(5), 349–359.

Ferri, S. L., Abel, T., & Brodkin, E. S. (2018). Sex difference in autism spectrum disorder: A review. *Current Psychiatry Reports*, *20*(2), 9. https://doi.org /10.1007/s11920-018-0874-2

Grandin, T. (2006). *Thinking in pictures: My life with autism* (25th anniversary ed.). Vintage Books.

Kang, D.-W., Adams, J. B., Coleman, D. M., Pollard, E. L., Maldonado, J., McDonough-Means, S., Caporaso, J. G., & Krajmaknik-Brown, R. (2019). Long-term benefits of Microbiota Transfer Therapy on autism symptoms and gut microbiota. *Scientific Reports, 9,* 5821. https://doi .org/10.1038/s41598-019-42183-0

Kanner, L. (1943). Autistic disturbances of affective contact. *Nervous Child, 2,* 217–250.

Kern, J. K., Garver, C. R., Grannemann, B. D., Trivedy, M. H., Carmody, T., Andrews, A. A., & Mehta, J. A. (2007). Response to vestibular sensory events in autism. *Research in Autism Spectrum Disorders, 1*(1), 67–74. https://doi.org/10.1016/j.rasd.2006.07.006

Markham, B. (1942/ 2021). *West with the night.* Warbler Classics.

Marom, M. (2018). Musical features and interactional function of echolalia in children with autism within the music therapy dyad. *Nordic Journal of Music Therapy, 27*(3), 175–196.

Masterson, B. A., & Biederman, G. B. (1983). Proprioceptive versus visual control in autistic children. *Journal of Autism and Developmental Disorders, 13*(2), 141–152. https://doi.org/10.1007/bf01531815

Meltzer, A., & Van de Water, J. (2017). The role of the immune system in autism spectrum disorder. *Neuropsychopharmacology, 42*(1), 284–298. https://doi.org/10.1038/npp.2016.158

Mize, L., & Hensler, K. (2008). *Echolalia: What it is and what it means.* https:// teachmetotalk.com/2008/06/01/echolaliawhat-it-is-and-what-it -means

Moyer, M. W. (2014, September 1). Gut bacteria may play a role in autism. *Scientific American.* https://www.scientificamerican.com/article/gut -bacteria-may-play-a-role-in-autism/

Mukhopadhyay, T. R. (2000). *The mind tree: A miraculous child breaks the silence of autism.* Riverhead Books.

National Autism Society. (2020). *Pathological demand avoidance: A guide for parents and carers.* https://www.autism.org.uk/advice-and -guidance/topics/diagnosis/pda/parents-and-carers

National Institute of Mental Health. (2017). *Any anxiety disorder.* https:// www.nimh.nih.gov/health/statistics/any-anxiety-disorder

Ostrolenk, A., d'Arc, B.F., Jelenic, P., Samson, F. & Mottron, L. (2017). Hyperlexia: Systematic review, neurocognitive modelling and outcome. *Neuroscience & Biobehavior Reviews*, *79*, 134–149. https://doi.org/10.1016/j.neubiorev.2017.04.029

Pathological Avoidance Demand Society. (2021). *Helpful approaches with PDA- Children*. https://www.pdasociety.org.uk/life-with-pda-menu/family-life-intro/helpful-approaches-children/

Ruthsatz, J., & Urbach, J. B. (2012). Child prodigy: A novel cognitive profile places elevated general intelligence, exceptional working memory and attention to detail at the root of prodigiousness. *Intelligence*, *40*(5), 419–426. https://doi.org/10.1016/j.intell.2012.06.002

Schulman, L., D'Agostino, E., Lee, S., Valicenti-McDermott, M., Seijo, R., Tulloch, E., Meringolo, D. & Tarshis, N. (2019). When an early diagnosis of autism spectrum disorder resolves, what remains? *Journal of Child Neurology*, *34*(7), 382–386. https://doi.org/10.1177/0883073819834428

Sensory Processing Disorder Foundation. (2021). *About SPD*. https://www.spdfoundation.net/about-sensory-processing-disorder.html

Seroussi, K. (2002). *Unraveling the mystery of autism and pervasive developmental disorder: A mother's story of research and recovery*. Broadway Books.

Smith, O., & Jones, S.C. (2020) "Coming out" with autism: Identity in people with an Asperger's diagnosis after DSM-5. *Journal of Autism and Developmental Disorders*, *50*(2), 592–602. https://doi.org/10.1007/s10803-019-04294-5

Stewart, R. (2000). Should we insist on eye contact with people who have autism spectrum disorders? *The Reporter*, *5*(3), 7–12.

Taira, M., Takase, M., & Sasaki, H. (1998). Sleep disorder in children with autism. *Psychiatry and Clinical Neurosciences*, *52*, 182–3.

Tammet, D. (2006). *Born on a blue day: Inside the extraordinary mind of an autistic savant*. Free Press.

Tidy, C. (2021, January 25). *Childhood disintegrative disorder: Heller's syndrome*. https://patient.info/doctor/childhood-disintegrative-disorder-hellers-syndrome

Venkat, A. (2016). *The complex relationship between autism spectrum disorders and epilepsy*. Epilepsy Foundation. https://www.epilepsy.com/living-epilepsy/epilepsy-and/professional-health-care-providers/joint-content-partnership-aes/complex-relationship-between-autism-spectrum-disorders-and-epilepsy

Webb, J. T., Amend, E. R., Beljan, P., Webb, N. E., Kuzujanakis, M., Olenchak, F. R., & Goerss, J. (2016). *Misdiagnosis and dual diagnosis of gifted children: ADHD, bipolar, OCD, Asperger's, depression, and other disorders* (2nd ed.). Great Potential Press.

Willingham, E., (2017, November 3). Mercury and autism: Enough already! *Scientific American.* https://blogs.scientificamerican.com/observations/mercury-and-autism-enough-already

World Health Organization. (2017). *Mercury and health.* https://www.who.int/news-room/fact-sheets/detail/mercury-and-health

Wright, J. (2012, February 12). Genetics: Autism, Tourette syndrome genes overlap. *Spectrum News.* https://www.spectrumnews.org/news/genetics-autism-tourette-syndrome-genes-overlap

3

I Don't Think We're in Kansas Anymore, Toto

Diagnosis

D-Day is how many parents refer to it. Diagnosis Day. The day there is a name put to what has been bothering you or you hoped was just bad parenting or you wondered if it was all in your imagination. Getting a diagnosis of giftedness generally lets you breathe and confirms your feeling that your child really is learning quickly and you aren't just bragging. Getting a diagnosis of autism can be a whole different set of emotions. As Ted Lieu, a US Representative from California (2017) has said, "There is little you can do to stop a tornado, a hurricane or a…diagnosis from changing your life in an instant" (para. 3).

Getting a diagnosis is absolutely critical to getting help. The Centers for Disease Control (CDC, 2019) estimated that 40% of children with autism are not formally identified until after age four, which means that they may miss critical early language development and interventions. But some help is better than no help. In today's world, no label means no services. Insurance companies (for those of you with insurance companies that do anything), Early Intervention programs, schools, therapists—*all* require a diagnosis. You cannot get treatment or help without a diagnosis. It is truly the ticket to help.

DOI: 10.4324/9781003237006-3

But oh, what a ticket it is. We spent Elizabeth's second birthday at a speech therapist's office. I had called a friend of mine in Colorado who knew someone in Florida, so we trekked the six hours to Jacksonville to meet with Judy, who was truly doing us a favor. No one would even take my calls until Elizabeth was two, and I was told at every corner that they would not even put us on the waiting list for evaluation until she was two. The waiting lists were two to three months long—just for diagnosis! I was also told that treatment waiting lists were even longer, but I couldn't even get on those lists until we got a diagnosis. I called Early Intervention and private speech therapists. After being told it was $150–$250 an hour just for diagnosis purposes, but *free* if I went through our state's Early Intervention program, I knew that Early Intervention was the way to go. Judy was charging us only $100 for our visit, and I figured that it was worth it: I could get a diagnosis, get on lists, and start the ball rolling. What I really wanted was to be told was that it was all in my head: I was a paranoid mommy, and my daughter really was fine. Nothing a little change in parenting couldn't fix. I wanted to be told I could fix it.

Judy was very nice, and I was amused, not for the first time, at how much fun speech therapy looks. She had toys all over her office and a very kid-friendly waiting room. I sat with Elizabeth as Judy played sound games with her—"What does the cow say?" "Moo! Can you say Moo?"—in a very cheery, friendly voice. However, I knew she was doomed.

To begin with, we did not live on a farm. We didn't even live near a farm. My husband grew up in Greece and is totally amused at how much farming is part of the American culture. As a cultural value, Americans teach our children to say farm animal sounds although they will probably only visit a farm a few times. It's much more useful to teach them what a phone sounds like, or the sound of an airplane, or what to say when ordering pizza. Really, when was the last time you, as an adult, were asked what a cow says? Therefore, we had not taught our daughter farm animal sounds.

Plus, she never copied sounds. She would watch my mouth, respond to directions, and put together 50-piece puzzles, but she would not copy sounds. She could say "mama" clearly, but that's it. No, she was not going to be copying Judy's farm sounds.

Judy came back with a diagnosis of dyspraxia or "lazy tongue." My first reaction was, "Huh? And here I was worried about autism!" Judy told us that she really didn't think that Elizabeth had autism: she made eye contact, she followed directions and understood what was said to her, and she responded to laughter and her name. We left feeling rather foolish and paranoid. Such a lack of diagnosis by a variety of professionals is common for smart kids with autism. But I still wasn't going to give up my place on those waiting lists. Regardless of *what* the problem was, we knew we still needed help. I called up Early Intervention services and was put on the waiting list for diagnosis. They were happy to look at Judy's data, but they had to do their own process. More waiting.

Early Intervention

Despite asking for someone to look at our daughter since she was 18 months, we were finally seen by Early Intervention (EI) when she was two years and three months old. EI is an amazing program funded through the federal government and required by law. All communities will have access to free diagnosis and therapy for kids with disabilities. The quality of the programs will vary, of course, but I have never been so thrilled as I was with our Early Intervention program.

To begin with, the EI folks came to our house *and* even made sure it was at a time when no one was going down for naps. These were people well used to working with the schedules of toddlers! I cleaned like a mad woman, of course. I was still wiping down the counters as they came in. I was *not* going to have them see the mess our house was in normally with two active and challenging toddlers. In other words, they saw a fake version of us. I knew that Ray would insist on being part of the process, so I sent him out with our babysitter for an afternoon at the park. There was a team of three people, and they got down on the floor and got out backpacks of yet more toys. They engaged Elizabeth in play and cheered for her when she dragged out her puzzle to show them she could put together a map of the United States (I'm telling you—the kid did and still does have an amazing sense of geography). She was showing off and loving it. No words, though. They tried gentle pressure—"Do you want Florida or Texas? Tell me." She solved the problem by grabbing Texas and putting it into place. I was pretty well convinced we had passed, which meant "failed," meaning we might get services.

I was *very* aware of time ticking. Elizabeth was now two years, three months old, and Early Intervention ended at age three by federal law. (That law was changed—it now ends at age six. Too late for us, but I was so happy at the change in the law.) We had already been on the waiting list for diagnosis for three months, but no help yet. More paperwork was needed. We then had to set up a meeting to make a plan. Luckily for my patience, that meeting was held only a few weeks later—but tick, tick, tick— Elizabeth was now two years, 3.5 months old.

At the meeting, the EI program folks told me she definitely qualified for "developmentally delayed," and I had another moment of "huh?" They explained to me that *all* children with delays were identified this way; they didn't use labels so that the services would match the child's needs and not the child's label. Even children with severe issues were diagnosed with this catch-all label. They didn't use the terms *autism, dyspraxia,* or *speech delay.* All services were to be free to me and to be as natural as possible. Wonderful! That meant that they would work with all of us: the family, her school, and her therapy. Fantastic! She qualified for speech therapy and occupational therapy. Great! Then they handed me a list of "qualified providers" (five pages worth) and left my house. Once again, I was in waiting list hell…

I called every name on the list. How on earth was I supposed to know which providers were "good" and which ones were just taking money from the government? The great irony was that I have a background in special education. I'm *supposed* to know this stuff. But I worked with public schools. I worked with teachers who are working with kids with disabilities. I knew nothing about how to pick a therapist. I went with the group that had the shortest waiting list—only two more months of waiting.

PICKING A THERAPIST

Choosing a therapist is one of the most difficult things to do—and one of the most important. However, you cannot let the knowledge of the importance of this task freeze your decision-making abilities. Time *is* of the essence, and you can always change therapists if it isn't working out. Of course, the best ones probably have waiting lists that are lengthy, so you will have to balance your sense of urgency with the availability of who you *really* want. Remember, just because a particular therapist worked wonders for a child of a friend of yours, doesn't mean that they are the only therapist for your child. According to Howard Erman (2006), you want to look for:

♦ **Connection:** Someone who will work with you and who you feel has your child's best interest at heart. It doesn't necessarily have to be someone you would be friends with, just someone who is willing to work with you.

♦ **Recommendations:** In today's electronic world, almost all reputable therapists will have a review listing somewhere. Read the comments and do a Google search to find the comments that might not be officially sanctioned. Do recognize that one person with a grievance can raise a lot of fuss. Look for patterns in the comments.

♦ **Training:** Check the therapist's professional lineage. Is her graduate school well-known and is it accredited? There are an awful lot of "pseudo" higher education institutions; make sure that your therapist comes with national or state accreditation or affiliation with an organization.

♦ **Insight:** Look for someone who sees your child with an eye for growth and can help you perceive things in new ways as well. Therapists are there to listen to you—but you want someone you can learn from as well.

♦ **Experience:** Ideally, the therapist should have a decade or more of working with children like your child. That being said, our speech therapist was brand new, and she was marvelous because she knew brand-new techniques. But she was in a partnership where there were other, more experienced therapists who all collaborated together and mentored her. Generally, the more experienced therapists get better results.

◆ **Cost:** You do yourself and your child no good if you go into significant debt in order to pay for the therapy. Go with the best you can afford, but make sure you can afford it. Most insurance companies will have some form of coverage, and many states are now requiring insurance companies within that state to cover services for children with autism. If you are not in one of those states, or, as in our case, your insurance explicitly denies speech or occupational therapy, ask the therapist if they know of any other (legal) approaches. And remember, there is always the list of free therapists through Early Intervention.

◆ **Location:** You will probably be visiting a speech, behavioral, or occupational therapist a lot—two or three or even five times a week. You will want to pick someone who is close to the rest of your life—your work, your home, and the child's school or day care. If you are in a rural area, consider the inconvenience of traveling an extensive distance for each visit.

Tick, tick, tick…Elizabeth was almost 2.5 years old when she finally saw a therapist's office. We spent six months of the one year that the system would allot us waiting for that help. And no one would let us start the process until the pediatrician gave the OK for there to *be* a problem. And the pediatrician wouldn't acknowledge any sort of problem until Elizabeth's language appeared as an item on the magic developmental checklist. Because she exhibited so many strengths, the areas of challenge were not seen as areas to be addressed until they appeared on the appropriate checklist.

Getting to Early Intervention

The biggest piece of advice I give parents who come to talk to me is "Push early, push often, push hard!" If I had realized that there would be six months of waiting for help, I would have started screaming earlier. The window of language development is very tight—the earlier you start language therapy, the more effective it is. The later you wait, the longer therapy takes to work well. Neurons have to be activated early in order to work later. If damage occurs at the wrong time and therapy does not start soon enough, there are sometimes irreversible problems.

However, the brain has a wonderful ability to be "plastic." In some cases, such as terrible car accidents where we know of specific damage to the brain, other parts of the brain can take over those functions after some time learning those functions. The brain has a remarkable ability to heal itself. It's why I'm in special education: I love the challenge of teaching a child to learn different ways "around" their problems.

It Is Never Too Late to Get Started, but the Earlier the Better

There are so many gatekeepers and so many layers of paperwork and bureaucracy to go through. "Early" Intervention—pfft! It should be called "Until we have time to get to you" Intervention. However, the waiting part was the *only* bad thing about the process: I have never worked with a kinder, more helpful group than the professionals who showed up at my door to help me help my child.

Every state is required to have Early Intervention—it's part of federal law and is funded through a combination of state funds and federal monies. However, each state has a different process by which it's activated. They also all have different names. Some states call it "Early Intervention," and others "First Steps." Whatever it's called in your state, it's there and pediatricians are the gatekeepers.

All pediatricians are required to keep in contact with the state's "Child Find" program, or some variation of that name. They report everything they do, from immunizations, to checking the weight of children, to medical issues they're seeing. When your child's doctor suggests that you contact Early Intervention, it is not a gentle suggestion like your neighbor might make—it means the doctor is making a report to the state that you have been referred. It sounds intimidating, but it's to help make sure that parents who don't know what they're doing get appropriate help for their children as quickly as possible. Pediatricians truly are looking out for the interest of the child.

However, because doctors are the gatekeepers, they also are the ones who allow or disallow you entry. I made the mistake of not pushing enough, and so we were locked out of help for several months. Another mother of a child who has since been diagnosed shared that:

> when he was little and kept crying about everything, we spent a lot of time struggling to get him to calm down. Why was he so irritable and frustrated? I took him to his pediatrician, and was told that he was fine and that I "needed to be more firm." Thanks. When he was 3 and about to start preschool, we took him for a check-up, and I mentioned the behavior issues. I was told that since he interacted with his younger brother so well, it couldn't be autism... Really?!

In many of the books written by mothers of children with autism, particularly those with smart autistic children, they each share how they changed pediatricians because they kept being told that their child was "fine" or that it was their fault. All of them were doing research on their own, and no one would listen. Unfortunately, this is all too often a common story among families. Not only are you struggling to help your child, but you're also trying to find others to believe you.

In their defense, pediatricians have to make a judgment call, based off limited experience with a child and only the strength of the parents' concerns. I am convinced that the standard "Oh, I'm sure it's fine" is not a diagnosis, but a test of the parents to determine the level of their concern. It's a trick I used with my own children. When they fell, I did not fuss over them because that would only make them think that every fall is a big deal. I told them they were fine. "Oh, Elizabeth, I'm sorry you fell. You're fine. Brush it off, and you can get right back up and play." If they were truly fine, they believed me and bounced right back up. If they weren't, they continued to howl, and I knew that it really was something serious. This approach is not, however, a good listening strategy. And when symptoms are vague and different mostly in severity from other kids, you leave your pediatrician's office convinced that you're being a worrywart. And the worst of all—you worry that you're a whiner of a parent, or worse, a bad parent.

There are tools available for pediatricians and you as well. The Modified Checklist for Autism in Toddlers (M-CHAT) (Robins et al., 2009) is available to use as early as 16 months. Although language is not a strong indicator at 16 months, there are numerous questions related to eye contact, use of pointing, communication efforts, and types of play. The ASD Video Glossary (Autism Navigator, 2018), developed by researchers out of Florida State University, shows videotaped differences between a typical baby or toddler and a baby with autism asked to perform the same tasks. Both resources are available free online.

Labels Are for Food, Not People

The Early Intervention folks told me that they didn't label. That sounds great in theory, but in reality, I was obsessed with finding out *what* was happening to my little girl, what I could expect, and what I could do. I often use the "University of Google." Go ahead and Google "developmental delay." In 2010, I got more than 2.5 million sites when I did that; in 2021, I got 143 million hits. Needless to say, Google didn't help me very much. I wanted words for what was happening. I wanted to *know*!

I spent hours that added up to days online. I read everything I could about dyspraxia, apraxia, echolalia, sensory integration disorder…and every site took me deeper and deeper into despair. I knew that I had a daughter who wasn't talking. I knew that she had signs of sensory integration disorder. I kept finding that these terms related to autism. But I also knew that she exhibited characteristics of giftedness. Did she have autism? The yes/no answer became an obsession with me. I read blogs; I read bulletin boards. I did *not* post anything—probably out of fear that someone would ask me, "Why are you here? She doesn't have autism!" Worse yet, someone might say, "Welcome to the mommy club of children with autism." I wasn't ready to commit either way. Part of me was still convinced that this was bad parenting—something I could fix with the right game, the right discipline strategy, the right...something, whatever that might be.

And oh, I cried. With every blog, with every posting on a bulletin board, I saw my daughter's future. I read of mothers who were celebrating their eight-year-old child's first three-word sentence. I read of children who drooled. I read of classmates teasing children. I read of children being forgotten on field trips. I read of emergency room visits from children banging their heads on walls. I read of parents who learned to let go of typical expectations and celebrate the small gains of their child. And in every blog, I tested the reality as my own: is *this* what's going to happen to *my* child? Is this her future?

During one of her speech therapy sessions, I brought up the issue of a label to the therapist. "What label do you think she'd qualify under if Early Intervention had labels?" I asked hesitantly. With great sympathy, the therapist said, "Autism." I finally had it—someone who knew about it told me my daughter had autism. And no one, anywhere, mentioned that she might be gifted, too. They were so focused on their concern with her disability that they didn't know that some of her behavior might be indicative of gifted behavior as well.

We finally got an official label the week she turned three. In the meeting where Elizabeth transitioned from Early Intervention to Special Education, the professionals informed me that she would qualify for services based on her label of autism. Now it was "real."

Too Much Information

I received so many pieces of paper about disabilities. At the pediatrician's office when we got the initial referral, I got information about Early Intervention and some of the developmental delays the office served. At Early Intervention and at every therapist's office, I received more information. I found unimaginable amounts of information electronically. There are literally hundreds of millions of sites that come up when you search for "autism" in Google. There are days I feel as if I've read every one of them, and yet, I'll find a new one, and a whole new community lives there. The amount of information on autism is beyond comprehension, and yet there is still so much to be known. I found myself in the bogs of information overload—too much to make sense of and yet I needed to make decisions now.

One of the traits that I share with my children is that I shut down when I'm overwhelmed. I did not seek out the very support groups that I was needing because I felt myself in too much of a panic. None of my immediate friends had a child with autism, and I didn't have anyone to hold my hand and lead me to a group. I also knew that my child did not have severe autism, and I felt guilty at crying about my child's issues when other mothers were dealing with much more significant issues. I now know how helpful a friendly voice would have been during this time and the toll it took on me, my marriage, and my friendships because I did not have a support network. But how can you take more time when you're drowning in information, decisions, and moment-to-moment experiences? And how do you find support when your child "fits" the classification but not the label of the support group?

D-Day: Getting a Diagnosis

One parent described D-Day (Diagnosis Day) as equally as earth-shattering as Birth Day—but not in a good way. Getting the diagnosis of autism for us was anticlimactic, but getting the diagnosis of developmentally delayed was…altering. I remember watching Elizabeth that afternoon, trying to see if she *really* was developmentally delayed, or if they had made a terrible mistake. Maybe we would all wake up from this, she would be fine, and I could relax, just an overly excited first-time parent. Maybe I really was overdramatizing this whole thing. Maybe the professionals just felt my panic. Maybe she just had some form of giftedness, and I was exaggerating something good to be bad. Maybe…I would not have been surprised if she had grown two heads or turned into a dripping, frothing monster that afternoon. I was so afraid that the label had changed her—or changed my perception of her. Elizabeth was, and still is, perfect to me in my eyes, but my perfect dream of parenthood was gone.

Sharing the New Map

Telling other people was tricky. Understanding it *myself* was hard. I couldn't use the term *developmentally delayed* because no one knew what that term meant. Trying on the word *autism* was like picking at a scab—it hurt an awful lot if I kept at it. My husband didn't have the preconceptions that I did; he wasn't in the field of education, nor did he grow up in the United States, and to him, autism was a word he related to "self" because of his associating it with the Greek language. He asked me to lead the way and to keep him informed—a pattern we established where I did the research and then processed aloud with him and sought his advice. We were both deeply involved but in different ways. He also was positive that we were headed in the right direction. Any action was better than no action. His practical and loving support helped us focus on what we could all do, rather than what she couldn't. He didn't understand autism, but he wasn't afraid of it.

I noticed that when I told people that my daughter had autism, there was either a reaction of, "Oh, Claire, you're making a much bigger deal of this than it is," or "Oh, wow…autism, huh?" and a drawing away. A common response was, "You must be such a saint." There is such a common perception among the general public that parents of children with disabilities are themselves somehow very special people—touched with "sainthood." The reality is, as anyone who knows me can tell you, I ain't no saint. I get frustrated, I cry, I swear on occasion, and I sulk. I'm afraid of what might happen, and I'm a tiger for my child. And don't *most* mothers feel that way? I roll my eyes at the "saint" thing because it's a way for parents of a typical child to (a) feel glad that *they* don't have to deal with challenging behaviors; and (b) keep any "taint" of autism away from them. In Greek culture, there is the concept of an "evil eye" or the idea that bad things will happen to you if you are too good or too successful. When people say that parents of children with disabilities are saints, I believe that what they are really saying is: "This could never happen to me. God only gives you what you can handle and I couldn't handle that. You, clearly, are such a good person that God gave this hard thing for you to handle. Good thing I'm not that strong!" It's a way of keeping the "evil eye" off of them—and it totally dehumanizes us. If we dare to complain, we must not be saintly, and are therefore not worthy of this burden we have been given. It's why I found solace in being with other mothers of autistic children. We can share all of our conflicted emotions, and there's no one judging us on how bad a parent we are.

I was amused to learn of a group of women who call themselves "Mothers from Hell." They have realized that they have to be their child's advocate, and they are prepared to take on the world. There are organizations whose entire mission is to be advocates and to help fight for children's rights. They are having tremendous impact on laws and insurance policies. I will discuss these organizations in a later section. But far from being "saintly," these parents and advocates focus on stirring things up, changing the status quo, and making sure that other parents do not have to go through what they went through.

Telling Others

Susan Senator (2005) described how she *acts* to let others know that her child has a difference. She acts very "in charge" and speaks loudly and clearly to her son, using short words, so that everyone around her can hear that she is treating him differently because he *is* different. She indicates by her voice that her son needs more coaching than other children, but that she is well in control. She noted how she would get appreciative glances using this approach, rather than the sighs and eyerolling she had gotten previously.

I've had a similar experience. There was a mother at the park whose son wanted to swing and we were on the only swing. Elizabeth was pitching a fit to stay in the swing, and Ray was starting to scream as well. The mother asked me, "Can't you just hurry her up?" I lost my temper and said, "No, I can't! She has autism!" The mother gave me a look of total shock and quickly moved her son to the other side of the playground. I wanted to yell at her, "He won't catch it!" but I didn't. The reality was that Elizabeth was just having the fairly typical fit of a toddler who didn't want to get off the swings. One good glare from me and a firm "When I count to three, you will get off of that swing" was all it took to stop that behavior. But I was tired and out of sorts and had been brooding and feeling sorry for myself. *Was* I using autism as an excuse? At that particular point, probably yes. But I was so tired of constantly having to monitor our movements: was this a good time to go to the grocery store? Do I have time to run into the pharmacy before tiredness/stress/anxiety made everything difficult? Could I take her to the speech therapist, drop her off to my husband at home, and still have time to make it to my class I had to teach?

The word *autism* comes laden with preconceptions. When I told teachers that Elizabeth had autism, they looked at her as though they expected her to start rocking violently and banging her head against the wall. I still remember being shocked when my daughter had a typical fourth-grade fight with Shelby, a neighbor friend of hers, but it was made more difficult because Elizabeth shut down and had no understanding of what her friend said to her or what to say. I went over to Shelby's family's house and was told "Why don't we let the girls just work it out?" I stated to the parents, "Well, that is a good idea, but since Elizabeth has autism, she has a harder time finding her words. I'm hoping I can help the girls learn to communicate to solve their problem." You would think that I had announced that my daughter had leprosy. The father immediately stood up and said, "We will have none of that here," and I found myself on the other side of the door. I never again went over to their house, despite living in the neighborhood for ten more years. I was shocked to my core, not for the first time or the last, at the outright prejudice. I then learned to introduce Elizabeth to schools by telling them that she has "language processing difficulties and some sensory challenges." I told her friends, "She has a hard time finding her words. You might give her some words to pick from when you're trying to talk to her."

Telling our friends was a bit anticlimactic. Many of them said, "Well, hadn't you suspected?" I found myself initially hurt that they didn't understand the trauma that came from having someone confirm my suspicions. None of them had had a child with a disability, and so my experience was new for them as well. But then, as now, I found myself struck at how they never placed expectations on me or my daughter. I soon learned which friends were real "rocks" with whom I could have catch-up conversations after months of being in research hell and who drifted away over time. I read where it was important to educate your old support network about autism in addition to finding a new support network. I didn't really have time to keep my friends in the loop (it was hard enough keeping my husband and family), but the ones who truly knew me just seemed to accept Elizabeth's differences as they accepted my quirks, and we moved on together.

Telling our family was another challenge. My mother immediately started seeking out brain treatments and sending me information to read. She listened to me, cried with me, and encouraged me to stop feeling sorry for myself and go do something. She also reminded me that Elizabeth was still Elizabeth. Getting a label did not change my child, and my job was that of any mother: helping my child be the very best she could be. A label simply gave me access to more help. My mother has never seen Elizabeth or Ray in anything other than a positive light.

My husband's family was a bit different. His aunts went to Jerusalem for a special silver icon and traveled to Cyprus to have it blessed by the bishop there. They told us that they were so sad and that they prayed constantly for Elizabeth to get better. In my anger and frustration one day, I yelled at my husband, "It's not like she has *cancer*, for God's sake! She's only autistic! It's not like she's going to *die*! We just have to deal with it, not *fix* her!" Other friends of mine have had their mothers blame them—"It's not really autism, you're just spoiling that child"—or blame their husbands—"You should never have married him." Reactions can vary widely, needless to say. Autism is so misunderstood and so confusing that parents and our families often don't know how to react.

I told Elizabeth and Ray, of course. My mother was deeply concerned that telling them would imply that I see them as anything less than perfect, and that children need to know that their parents love them unconditionally. Shuli Sandler and Michael Rosenthal (2015) stressed that it is important to tell your children early, in age-appropriate words, and with visual supports. Knowledge is power, and I will not have them blaming themselves. When I told Elizabeth about her autism, Ray, in unending sibling rivalry, immediately wanted to know what he had, too. In Ray's case, he has Tourette syndrome and anxiety disorder. He appeared pleased by the fact that his sister wasn't the only one who had a label, but he didn't appear overly curious.

However, Elizabeth is now a young adult and has not received direct services for autism since she was six. I got her permission to write the first edition of this book, but she was very hesitant to share additional stories for the second edition. In getting her permission for the first edition, I told her that she had a medical condition called autism that makes it harder for her to find words or talk with people, and that sometimes she feels things more than other people. As she got older and into her teen years, she became very aware of the prejudice surrounding disability, and does not see herself in "that" group. Because of the successes of Early Intervention and the language supports we were able to give her while growing up, she is less "different" now, and she sees autism as something she "used to have." I no longer see myself as an "autism mom," and I'm very comfortable in my role now as an "autism educator." I even begin to understand some of the aspects of being on the spectrum that I share with Elizabeth and Ray. Although I have not been formally diagnosed and don't know if I would meet the clinical diagnosis, I certainly have characteristics of autism.

I purposefully took the route of "medical difference" to let Elizabeth know that *she* did not cause this. I tried to explain autism like asthma: asthma doesn't have to stop you from being a professional athlete; you just have to manage it. Autism hasn't stopped her from doing anything she wants to—she just had to learn to manage it and even to use its characteristics to her advantage. Autism is *different*, but it does not have to be a *deficit*. Autism can be a gift, but it takes a lot of unwrapping.

I have learned since that there are several things you can do when the shock of diagnosis hits you. These include:

- ◆ **Taking time to process:** Grieve the way you need to, but do not isolate yourself.
- ◆ **Finding books and blogs written by other families of children with autism:** In the Resources Section, I list a number of these resources; they each had a different voice and something I could learn from. I felt like I was reading my story, and their strength gave me strength. They understood my hurt at the imperfect world that we have to deal with.
- ◆ **Talking to a therapist who has experience with families with disabilities:** The Early Intervention folks will probably know someone to recommend. Men often handle the shock of diagnosis differently than mothers do. They can find support at the Washington State Fathers Network at https://www.fathersnetwork.org.
- ◆ **Knowing that you have the power to share when and what you want:** Not everyone around you needs to know everything.
- ◆ **Realizing that autism is so common that it does not have the stigma that it used to:** The more you share with people, the more likely you'll find others with a story also.
- ◆ **Keeping your appointments:** Get your hair cut, go to lunch, get the car washed. Make sure your life rhythms stay as close to how they were before the diagnosis as possible.

"Traveling With" or "Traveler"?

In her powerful video essay "In My Language," Amanda Baggs (2007) noted that it is only when she interacts with the right things in the right way that she is considered to have thought. When she interacts, feels, tastes, or smells the wrong things in the wrong way, she is considered to be in a world of her own, rather than people understanding that she is experiencing the world in a different way. In a computer-aided voiceover, she noted that there was no meaning to her flickering her hand through the water in her video, no ulterior purpose—she was just engaged with the water, watching its flickering patterns, not searching for its relationship to anything else. She was merely interacting with the water as it interacted with her. She observed that she is considered to be limited when really it is others who are limited in their understanding of her. The piece is even more impactful when you know that the voiceover is provided by the computer voice "reading" the words she is typing. Amanda does not directly talk to the audience but allows us insight into her mind through modern technology. She is, indeed, human—but a human who perceives things that many of us do not.

However, autism can also separate us from others—and from ourselves. There is a strong temptation to interact with objects, words, and things that disconnect you from powerful emotions. In her book, Patricia Stacey (2003) noted that her son, rather than not feeling, would feel *too* strongly, and that autism allowed him to escape the pain of those powerful emotions. He would retreat into his "safe place" where he would not be scared, anxious, or distraught. Even powerful positive emotions would send him retreating by the very force of their impact. Temple Grandin (2006; Grandin & Johnson, 2005), in her amazing autobiographical explanations of autism, stated that she craved a feeling of safety that her "squeeze machine" could provide. This need for safety and trying to avoid feeling overwhelmed means that our family each have "our area" of the house, and we can easily get absorbed in screens rather than dealing with each other or issues in more productive manners. Conflict is something we all avoid.

In a powerful statement by Jim Sinclair in his 1993 essay "Don't Mourn for Us," he said, "This is what we know, when you tell us of your fondest hopes and dreams for us: that your greatest wish is that one day we will cease to be, and strangers you can love will move in behind our faces" (para. 9). Similarly, there is a very sad story of Karen McCarron, a mother from Illinois, who smothered Katie, her three-year-old daughter. When asked why she did this, Karen responded, "Maybe I could fix her this way, and in heaven she would be complete" (Mercer, 2008, para. 3). Of course, such stories are horrific beyond belief, but I can understand that desire to fix things for my daughter, while knowing that I have to teach her to handle things herself. Like any parent, I struggle to know and support who she is, not who I want her to be. We happily claim her gifts as part of who she is. Why not her challenges? I can't tell you the absolute answer, but I do believe that it is both to some degree—autism shaped her personality, and I struggled with keeping her "in the world" where she felt safe enough to deal with new situations and new stimuli. I worked on teaching her coping strategies and words for things she was afraid of and did not know how to explain, and I worked on helping her to observe herself and others. I worked on keeping her engaged with this world and away from the seductive world of "languagelessness" where she felt no pain or fear.

The Trip You Were "Supposed" to Have: Oughtism

My daughter had 75 baby dolls all named Lily. Actually, they weren't truly named Lily. Elizabeth was carrying one once when I was taking my children through the lobby of the hotel at a conference I was attending. Someone I knew stopped me to say hello and kindly leaned down to ask Elizabeth, "What's the name of your baby doll?" Elizabeth learned long ago to mumble a noncommittal "Lalable" when she can't think of what to say. "Lily? Oh, that's a nice name!" replied my acquaintance. Elizabeth nodded enthusiastically and said "Lily" the next time someone asked her what her baby's name was. Of course, it was a different baby doll...

Elizabeth loved baby dolls. Not necessarily because they *were* babies, but because other little girls had them. She didn't dress them, change them, or wrap them up—just carried them, and that made her happy. She also loved pushing them in a stroller. Not pretending, just pushing. Sometimes, she carried two of them. None of them appeared to be a particular favorite. But when asked five years in a row, "What do you want for Christmas?" she would always answer, "baby dolls!"

Presents

Finding presents for a child on the spectrum can be difficult. You're in a quandary of "Do I get them a toy that they want, or a toy that they need?" Choosing age-appropriate toys is not always right; your child may have no interest in dolls, games, or bikes. Yet, you're afraid that getting your child what they really want will either (a) highlight the differences between them and other children; or (b) add to the growing collection of obsessive items. Did Elizabeth *really* need one more baby doll to add to the 75 she already has? But she didn't want baby doll clothes, Barbies, or doll houses. She only wanted to carry around the baby doll. As a friend of mine said about her son, "We're trying to get him to play imaginatively. Do I *want* him to have blocks that he will just line up obsessively?" However, a very wise mother of an 18-year-old daughter who still loves Clifford the Big Red Dog shared with me that the purpose of a present is to give joy—and if the children feel joy, who are we to take that away from them?

Yet, on the other hand, buying them age-appropriate toys can have a two-fold purpose. First, toys provide the raw materials for teaching the child age-appropriate play strategies. My daughter had no idea what to do with baby dolls. However, she carefully watched other girls and decided that dolls were for carrying. Parents tell stories about playing with trucks and playdough, and modeling play activities for their children. Secondly, great toys can be an inducement for other children to come over to your house to play. We bought Elizabeth beautiful "dress-up" clothes, not because she necessarily enjoyed them, but because our house would be a treasure trove for the neighborhood children. Nicole was a little girl two years younger than Elizabeth who would come over every day to play in Elizabeth's treasure trunk. Elizabeth would dress up, too, and Nicole would take the lead in creating wonderful dramatic play. Elizabeth never initiated such play, but was more than happy to go along with Nicole's theater. Great toys can buy great friends. And it only takes one or two good friends to make a significant difference in a child's life.

Questions from well-meaning friends and family like "So, what does your child want for Christmas/his birthday?" can be quite a dilemma. Want or need? For them or for attracting friends? Presents become yet another issue in navigating your smart autistic child's interactions with the broader world.

Potty Training

Perhaps "oughtism" is most significant when it comes to toileting issues. So often we hurry the child because of our own timetable or our own sense of pressure. Tina, a friend of mine, was told by her behavioral specialist when her son was four that toileting issues are one of the most important things that you need to focus on; this is one of the first things that children will notice about each other in terms of differences. A child who is potty trained immediately looks down on other children who have not yet achieved this milestone. Children with high-functioning autism seem to fall into two groups: those who are potty trained early and those who are very late.

My family was in both groups because of Elizabeth's and Ray's sensitivities. At 18 months, Elizabeth had a bad diaper rash, so we were letting her play outside on the back lanai, or covered porch, stark naked. She peed, and I will never forget the look of absolute horror on her face as the urine ran down her leg. I cleaned her up and took her to the bathroom, where I showed her the insert toilet seat we had been given. I had read the manuals that suggested that the toilet seat be presented to the child but not pressured. She immediately sat on it and released some more urine. She and the potty were bonded. I hadn't planned it, but I was pleased.

Ray was almost completely the opposite. I tried rewards, regular visits to the bathroom, floating targets, "big boy" underwear, reading books…nothing seemed to help. Ray was finally potty-trained one day when I resorted to character Pull-Ups because of an upcoming trip. The Pull-Ups alternated Spiderman, his favorite, and the Incredible Hulk. The first day, I realized that we had made a terrible mistake because he was *thrilled* to pee in the Spiderman Pull-Ups; he was excited to have them and asked to have them. The next day, I pulled out the Hulk Pull Ups and he pulled away in fear. "*No*, Mommy! *No!*" I quickly threw the package behind me that had the next Spiderman Pull-Up and told him that the Hulk was the only kind of diaper we had, and he was going to have to pee in the Hulk ones. "*No,* Mommy! *No!*" He was really crying now in terror and fear. I was so sympathetic and even loved on him, but kept insisting that the Hulk Pull-Ups were the only ones we had left. If he wanted diapers, he would have to use them. However, if he wanted to pee in the potty, he could wear his Spiderman "big boy" underwear. I'll never forget his little teary voice as he said, "I pee in the potty, Mommy. I pee in the potty." And literally, from that moment on, Ray never had an accident. We laughed that we potty trained him through fear and intimidation, but it wasn't fear of us, it was the fear of the Hulk. Sometimes you use what you have to in order to get kids past a developmental milestone.

Other children with autism have had much greater issues with toileting. Because some children with autism have problems identifying cues from their own body, they may not recognize when they have to go to the bathroom. Similarly, teaching them to feel "proud of themselves" may not be something they understand. Finally, they are so resistant to change in their routines that moving from a diaper to the bathroom is a major hurdle for them. Some suggestions include:

◆ **Know that it will take a long time:** Most toileting manuals suggest a period of a few weeks to a few months. Be patient and know that it will happen—just slower, and with greater consistency.

◆ **Introduce the bathroom and potty in stages:** Let them learn the word *bathroom,* reward them for coming in the bathroom, sit on the potty dressed for a while, and then present how to take down clothes in stages. It helps during this time to have clothes that are easy to get in and out of.

◆ **Go to the bathroom often:** Some programs recommend every 15 minutes, and one program I read about had the instructor play with the child in the bathroom during the regular times when bowel movements were more likely to occur. There are several potty-shaped watches available from Amazon that little children can wear that beeps as often as you want it to—every 15 minutes for example—and reminds children to go.

- ◆ **Make going to the bathroom a visual reminder:** The key is to be firm and consistent—make going to the bathroom a part of the daily routine and remind the child visually with a cue. Friends of mine do the sign language "T" for "toilet" to remind their son. That way, it's a reminder without drawing attention to him.

- ◆ **Reduce distractions so that they can focus on the feelings they are having:** Because bright kids with autism are so easily distracted by sensory information, it will help to talk to them about what muscles they feel. One little boy I knew talked about his belly button being his "on" switch because he became aware of the groin muscles helping him release.

- ◆ **Reduce your own stress about this—if you can:** Toilet training is one of those things that schools and mothers-in-law have very strong opinions about, but the reality is that this is one of the first opportunities that your child has to learn about themselves. They have to listen to their own responses, determine their own needs, and then take action to help themselves. Nudging, but supporting, is key.

Finding a New Normal

We often are given the belief in our world that "If you do the right things, things are going to be great!" In our educational, generational, and cultural spaces, we are led to believe that we can have it all: the great career, the great house, the perfect child. We read that if we avoid drugs at childbirth, eat organic, watch educational shows, breastfeed, wear seatbelts, and put our children on their backs, that we will be OK—we can avoid so many of the mistakes that our parents made. Somehow disability has been perpetuated as a "mistake" because if you do everything right, then you should be protected. When misfortune does strike, there is a tendency to whisper and to look away. In fact, a 2009 study by Dr. Yamamoto and colleagues from the Harvard-affiliated McLean Hospital found that women in particular do not like to look at babies with deformities—they glance away and reject the pictures. We feel pain and discomfort for things that disturb our image of perfection.

As human beings, we are born with an innate desire for a "normal," and our children are especially dependent on the illusion of stability. Any change to that normal, and our children react. What I have learned is that the times during change are incredibly hard. We hold on until we can sense a "new normal" coming. My husband and I will sometimes ask each other, "So, is that new normal here yet?" We have tried not to grieve the old normal, but to hold on—normal's comin'. It's a wonderful way to sustain each other and our family as we strive toward a routine. But normal takes time, and sometimes it takes help. There are a variety of ways to achieve it and lots of information to take in.

References

Autism Navigator. (2018). *ASD Video Glossary.* https://autismnavigator.com/asd-video-glossary/

Baggs, A. (2007). *In my language.* https://www.youtube.com/watch?v=JnylM1hI2jc

Centers for Disease Control. (2019). *Spotlight on: Delay between first concern to accessing services.* https://www.cdc.gov/ncbddd/autism/addm-community-report/delay-to-accessing-services.html

Erman, H. (2006). *Thoughts on how to choose a therapist.* https://howarderman.com/how-to-choose/

Grandin, T. (2006). *Thinking in pictures: My life with autism* (25th anniversary ed.). Vintage Books.

Grandin, T., & Johnson, C. (2005). *Animals in translation: Using the mysteries of autism to decode animal behavior.* Harvest Books.

Lieu, T. (2017). Why I boycotted Congress "moment of silence" after the Texas shooting. *NBC News: Think.* https://www.nbcnews.com/think/opinion/why-i-boycotted-congress-moment-silence-after-texas-shooting-ncna819161

Mercer, D. (2008). Mom convicted in autistic girl's death. *The Associated Press.* http://www.usatoday.com/news/nation/2008-01-17-3456189394_x.htm

Robins, D. L., Fein, D., & Barton, M. (2009). *Modified checklist for Autism in toddlers, revised.* https://mchatscreen.com/

Sandler, S., & Rosenthal, M. (2015, April 15). Should parents tell their children they have Aspergers? *Autism Spectrum News.* https://autismspectrumnews.org/should-parents-tell-their-children-they-have-aspergers/

Senator, S. (2005). *Making peace with autism: One family's story of struggle, discovery, and unexpected gifts.* Trumpeter.

Sinclair, J. (1993). Don't mourn for us. *Our Voice: The Newsletter of Autism Network International, 1*(3), 2–3.

Yamamoto, R., Ariely, D., Chi, W., Langleben, D. D., & Elman, I. (2009). Gender differences in the motivational processing of babies are determined by their facial attractiveness. *PLoS One, 4*(6), e6042. https://doi.org/10.1371/journal.pone.0006042

4

Down the Rabbit Hole

Treatments and Therapies

Research, Research, and More Research

Let me just start by telling you that Elizabeth is "cured" of autism. I use "cured" in quotes, not because she got over a dread disease, but because after the age of seven, she no longer qualified for services because her speech was age-appropriate, her practical living skills were strong, and her social skills were only slightly delayed—and her academic abilities were far above grade level. She falls into that group of children whom mothers, doctors, and others claim are "cured" of or "recovered from" autism. Of course, she received a tremendous amount of formal therapy, we provided an intensive amount of coaching in a structured home environment, and she works *very* hard to master tasks that are set before her. Is the autism gone? No, but we can live with it now. And now there are new labels of ADHD and anxiety…

There are many, many strategies and therapies currently available out there—most cost money, and only a few are well-researched. A 2009 study by Dr. Deborah Fein and colleagues found that up to 20% of children with high-functioning autism who receive intense interventions are "recovered" by age nine.

DOI: 10.4324/9781003237006-4

More recent studies have found that although 7% of all children with autism might "lose" the label later in life, only 3% do not replace the ASD label with something else (Schulman et al., 2019). Being one of those statistics, I certainly advocate intensive treatment. Some people have told us that Elizabeth never *really* had autism; she just grew out of odd behaviors. Others have stated that she had *temporary autism*. Dr. Shulman and colleagues (2019) noted that those children who were able to move off of the spectrum label were those children with fewer support needs who were provided intensive, effective treatments.

I believe that my family headed off significant issues by doing lots of things, and I also know that we're still dealing with issues—Elizabeth now takes medication for ADHD and anxiety. I call them the "A labels." Although her needs at age two were in the areas of speech and regulation, her needs are now related to attention and anxiety. I still review her papers for random uses of indistinct "this" and "that." And she still has difficulty processing information on audio-only calls. Facetime and Zoom have been very helpful to her!

When Elizabeth was five, we moved and changed states. In the new state, the IEP team determined that she didn't need occupational therapy. After about six months, the speech therapist told us that because she was then "within age-appropriate limits of speech," she no longer qualified for services for autism. That meant that my daughter had "beaten" autism after three years of intense therapies. I didn't know whether to cheer or cry. I was thrilled that Elizabeth had made progress. But I knew that there was still so much more to go.

I asked the speech therapist if she felt that Elizabeth was speaking at her *ability* level and was told, "No. She's very bright. But because she's speaking at the level of a five-year-old, she doesn't need services anymore." I was, and still am, so angry at a system that would give up on a child simply because she met a certain level. Never mind that she was able to solve problems and analyze and could read already but did not have the language level equivalent to all of that. Never mind the fact that social skills were still a foreign language to her. I was now on my own with her interventions.

Since then, I have had Elizabeth tested so that I could have numbers to back up my intuition. Schools often just pat parents on the head when a parent says, "My child is very bright but has some challenges." Elizabeth's IQ test, which overall was not high enough to qualify her for a gifted program, showed her visual processing abilities to be in the 99th percentile—higher than 99% of other children her age! Her language processing speed was in the 16th percentile—below 84% of other children her age. And her achievement levels? All above grade level. She did not qualify for gifted services at the time, although the psychologist told us that she "is gifted—clearly." She did not qualify for special education either. We were on our own after this point. Did she still have autism? Officially no. Did autism impact her growth and development? Oh yes...The place where a child is now will be different tomorrow, the next day, and next year.

As a parent, I needed to know that there were lots of things that could help my child. The question is of course, what? What do I buy, use, try, and believe? When I was searching the "University of Google," the problem wasn't finding information; the problem was too much information for me to process. I was already trying to process why this happened, my guilt over what I could have/ should have/might have done, and what was going to happen, that I was completely overwhelmed by the number of strategies for what I could do. The amount of information is staggering, and when researching I often shut down in frustration, feeling completely overwhelmed, only to log back on the next day. I can completely relate to Elizabeth's need to shut herself in her closet and rock herself until she feels less overwhelmed.

It is important to do your own research. But do talk with other parents! As Karyn Seroussi (2002) said:

> I...learned that an open-minded parent with an autistic child and Internet access could learn more about the biology of autism than a closed-minded clinician with twenty years of experience in developmental disabilities, and that other parents were a better resource for practical advice than professionals.
>
> (p. 124)

Keep a balance between science and story, parents and professionals, and go with your instinct as long as it doesn't hurt you, your family, or your child.

I'm not here to tell you what you can/could/should/might do. I encourage you to do what I have done: research, talk to your family, and find a professional who listens to you and gives you advice that you can live with. Most importantly, find a professional who believes in the abilities of your child as much as you do or who is open to learning more. Bright children with autism break a lot of stereotypes, and professionals have to be willing to believe that some behaviors are not problems but are symptomatic of ability as well.

Know that you might have to change professionals and change yet again when your family has learned all that you can from one professional. Every child on the spectrum is unique, and every family situation is unique. What works for one child may not work well for another. There is no one "best" strategy. Trust your instincts, trust your child, and trust that the professionals really are doing their best.

However, although professionals may know their strategy or the latest research in their particular area, and other parents may have had their own successes or insights, they do not know your child as well as you. You are the only one who sees your child in the holistic context and sees them progress from birth to adulthood. *No one* knows the track your child has followed, the progress they have made, or the implications on their whole life experience like you. *You are an expert on your child.*

There is a wonderful phrase, "Go with your gut." Some fascinating research by the Harvard Medical School (2009) has suggested that the 30 feet of intestines in your body actually have their own system of nerves that are independent of the other nerves and that communicate directly with the brain. Called the enteric nervous system, it's a hotline connecting emotions, digestion, and brain functioning. You really do "know it in your gut" and experience "gut-wrenching" hurt, while poor decisions can "make you nauseous." Your gut may, indeed, know the right choice before your brain.

The goal is to find a match between your child and a strategy. And when your child changes, the strategy may have to change as well.

As for me, I just wanted my daughter to develop, to find her path, and to be loved and appreciated at the same time with all of her differences. The dual nature of autism is just like the dual nature of light—both a wave and a particle, both a difference and a disability. But the road map you choose will depend on your understanding of autism, the research you undertake, what you feel you can do, and the professionals you work with.

Finding the Mapmakers (aka Professionals)

It is very important for you to find a professional who will listen to you—just as it is important for you to have a list of things to tell and ask the professionals. My family interviewed several speech therapists who all immediately jumped into "textbook" mode and told me what I was supposed to be doing without listening to me first. I got so tired of the "Oh, and you need to..." or "You might try..." statements from more polite therapists. We already *were* putting subtle pressure on our child to encourage talking. We already *were* being consistent with discipline and not giving in to tantrums. We already *were* putting pictures around for her to point to in order to communicate. I was raised a good Southern girl who never talks back, and I'll never forget the speech therapist I finally told off when she said, "You need to be encouraging her to talk, but not pressuring her too much that it shuts her down." I finally snapped and said, "We *do*, damnit! I want to know what *else* I can be doing!" Zeppelin, the therapist we went with, was the first one who asked, "So, tell me what you've been doing with your daughter." Here was a partner in the process, not an "expert."

The other element I learned to look for was the therapist who truly wanted to learn about my child *before* starting to work with her. I was so irritated the day a speech therapist said, "Wow, you know, she really responds when you tell her *why* you're doing something." I had previously told the therapist that Elizabeth really wanted to understand why she was supposed to be doing an activity, not just to do it. I knew that explanations helped her ability to stay engaged. I had told the therapist that as well. It was not the first time I felt shuffled aside as "that mom."

Professionals often perceive parents as emotional and unable to separate their love for their child from their decision-making process. I was guilty of this as a teacher myself, listening to parents say that their child was completely misunderstood—that the problem was the teacher/school/system/other students...anything other than their own child or their own parenting. It wasn't until I became a parent of a child with a difference that I fully understood the pain of being told that there's something wrong with your baby and you might be the cause. Now, when I talk with parents, I don't use the disability label or focus on what's "wrong" with their child. I talk about how the school, society, and other children are very different than their child, and what's not working is the "fit" between all of these components.

It also is important to teach society, teachers, and other people about accepting people with autism. I recently heard a story of a mother who, when she explained that her son was yelling because he had autism, was told, "Well, he should wear a sign or something." Clearly, our society has a long way to go to understanding differences. But we also can work on helping our children understand their impact on others. And you play a key role in that process.

You have the right to be listened to as an equal partner in the process. You should feel comfortable sharing with and educating the professional about your child. You should feel confident that the professional really listened to you and made a fair decision based on their expertise and what you share. You should be able to trust that they are listening and not ridiculing. And you need to change professionals if you don't. Your responsibility is to be clear and informative, to follow their suggestions for working with your child, and to listen—and to change professionals if it's not a good fit. Your responsibility is to do the best for your child that you can.

For example, when Elizabeth was being evaluated for her aptitude by the occupational therapist, she was in a hyperanxious state, and I asked if I could be present. The therapist first gave Elizabeth four small colored blocks and then gave herself four blocks, and she asked Elizabeth to make the same shape she did. She made an L shape with the blocks and said, "Now, you make that." Elizabeth just sat there, looking hard at the blocks and idly fingering them—appearing to be unresponsive. Knowing my daughter, I waited and finally said to the therapist, just as she was going to mark a 0 on that question, "She's looking for the white one. You gave her different colored blocks than you have. She's trying to make the exact same as you and can't with different colors." "Oh!" said the therapist, and gave Elizabeth the same colors, who immediately made the same shape *and* color combination. Details are highly important to Elizabeth, and she notices small things—someone with expertise in autism should have known that. It made me really wonder how many kids are misdiagnosed or underestimated simply because the therapist didn't know how a kid's mind worked. Or because the mom isn't pushy enough.

By Air and by Sea, on Foot and on Wheels: Finding Therapies

No matter what vehicle you use for treatment, it is important to keep in mind that everyone has the same goal: helping your child improve. Now, some will aim for curing, and others will aim for improvement; some are doing studies to make advances to the field, and others are trying to make money. There are passionate advocates for many of these various treatments who believe deeply in one approach, and there are others who are trying to debunk myths and use data in their decisions.

It is important to note that there are research-based interventions that can be used for smart kids with autism. The National Standards Project from the National Autism Center (2015) and the National Clearinghouse on Autism Evidence and Practice (Wong et al., 2014) have databases of 27 effective practices for children with autism. These can be grouped into three different areas (Hughes & Henderson, 2017), including: (a) applied behavior analysis-based interventions; (b) cognitive and physical supports; (c) social and relational interventions. However, although most of these involve professionals with differing approaches, you have control of the single most important impact: supportive and loving parenting.

Intensive and Intentional Parenting

It cannot be overstated that the first line of therapy or help is what *you* provide. Parenting a child with high-functioning autism is intense—their responses are dramatic, their anger more intense and more frequent, and you are left wondering if what you're doing is making any difference.

The answer is yes! In fact, intensive parenting is the best form of therapy for these children and they, perhaps even more than typical children, *need* the parent to read to them, share their quiet spaces, help them find their abilities, focus on what they can do, connect with them, help guide them through the tough times, and love them really, really hard, particularly when loving them is difficult. In other words, be a parent—really be a parent!

In his book *The Mind Tree*, Tito Mukhopadhyay (2000) discussed how much work his mother did—she read to him, tried diets, taught him to ride a bike, and never gave up on him. In a battle about whether they were going to go to his uncle's wedding, Tito communicated with her that she had to choose between her brother and her son. "For you, I give my life. For him, I give three days," she responded (p. 64). She went to the wedding but reassured her son that he was important to her.

Perhaps the hardest part of parenting intensely is the lack of overt response that you may get from your child. You know that they love you in the way that they may cling to you at times but feeling intense love when there is no eye contact can be difficult. Talking to a child and engaging in communication with a child who doesn't talk back can be very difficult. Continuing on in the face of silence and pain can be overwhelming.

However, I cannot emphasize how key you are—you often provide the first translation to the rest of the world for your child.

Tina, a friend of mine, shared how she would spend her afternoons at the grocery store, engaging in conversations with her son: pointing out colors of food, listening to sounds of carts, and watching the toy train move around the top of the store. Her son would jump at the thunder sound that happened when the sprinklers watered the vegetables, and she would laugh, showing him that it was alright. She talked about rain, textures, and shapes with him, helping him to unite his perceptions with language. He was functioning so well at the age of 13 that he no longer qualified for autism services, and some professionals she worked with questioned if he "really" had autism. She and I fully believe that "parent therapy" is the most effective form of intervention that you can provide.

Although I had a child who hugged and kissed, and looked me in the eye, I did face the inherent difficulty of teaching someone to talk and helping her to acclimate to her environment. We read, and we read, and we read. Elizabeth soon learned that I would stop anything I was doing if she appeared with a book in her hand. I would sit down on the nearest chair or even the floor, take her in my lap, and I would read it to her. Through reading, she listened to my voice and looked intensely at the pictures. There are many "baby" books I cannot now throw away because I have such sweet memories of reading them to my children over and over again.

Similarly, once we realized that we were going to have to teach Elizabeth how to talk, we started trying to work around the verbal part and focus on the communication aspect. I found pictures of common foods, laminated them, and taped them on the refrigerator so that Elizabeth could ask for what she wanted by pointing, rather than just screaming ineffectually. We asked her question after question and gave her choice after choice to give her opportunities to talk. "Do you want the cheese or the grapes? Do you want the pink dress or the blue one? Do you want to go fast or slow?" Each forced choice, question, and visual cue was an effort to reach her, to get her involved in our world.

Sometimes I just stopped and enjoyed her and tried to see things the way she saw them. If her attention was caught by a passing train, I watched it, trying to see it through her eyes—the blur of the cars, the rhythmic clack of the rails—and I would find myself nodding and bobbing as well, in total sympathy with her feeling that this was a moment in which the world was ordered and safe and in rhythm. I let her swing and swing and swing, feeling the swaying of the world as it rushed past her, the brush of the wind, and the head rush on the way back. I too felt the lure of thoughtlessness and only experienced sensation along with her. But I always knew that it was my job to bring her back to the world that, in the words of Tito Mukhopadhyay (2000), is "a suitable place for the social beings and not beings like us" (p. 124).

It also is the task of intensive parenting to track changes in your child. Tina still has her notebook of charts and graphs that she maintained on her refrigerator. For three years on a daily basis, she tracked bowel movements, behaviors, and medication intake. I kept lists of words spoken and activities to try at home. And I researched and researched, thinking there was something else I could try to help me at home and, ultimately, to help Elizabeth.

The following sections list treatments I either sought out or researched. I have divided these into the different means that are used: the different approaches therapies can take, the various specific therapies available, and the environments in which therapies can take place. Please do not use this as an exhaustive list! There is so much autism research out there that my list is going to be outdated within weeks. Also, many of the treatments are controversial to some degree. I'm a great believer in throwing the whole shebang at a problem. The hard part was deciding what to try and what to spend my time, money, and energy focusing on. My mother offered to do Reiki—energy healing work that reeks of "woowoo" New Age stuff and that she seems to have a strange knack for. Go right ahead! My husband's aunts went to Cyprus to get a silver icon that has been blessed by the Greek Orthodox Patriarch. Wonderful! My girlfriend included my daughter's name in her prayer circle. Fantastic! We opted for speech and occupational therapy as well as Montessori education. We did *not* do the gluten-free/casein-free (GFCF) diet or Alternative/Augmentative Communication (AAC). The approaches that did not take up too much of my time or money, I was more than happy to accept. I learned early in my life never to laugh at other people's "magic" because sometimes magic does happen. My daughter improved and that was magic to me.

Philosophical Approaches: Behavior, Mind, or Body

Applied Behavior Analysis

Applied behavior analysis (ABA) is the gold standard of autism treatment. ABA is the system through which children are taught to stop doing inappropriate behaviors and to use appropriate behaviors using rewards. It is a very clearly established process by which a target behavior is determined, the steps to reach that behavior are identified, and the child is rewarded when they begin to come close to that desired behavior. It's a process of breaking down a goal into very specific steps to master first. It's very similar to the system used by grandmothers: "When you eat all of your dinner, you can have dessert." Structured by Dr. Ivar Lovaas in the 1960s (see Lovaas, 1987, for more information) for treatment of children with special needs, ABA principles have been found over and over again to work for kids with autism. ABA is the most successful treatment and is even recommended by the U.S. Surgeon General (Hagopian et al., 2015).). It's often the *only* thing to help students with more severe forms of autism. The philosophy has many names—discrete trial teaching, behavior modification, stimulus-response—but any program that uses the words "behavior" or "skills" in it is probably rooted in this philosophy.

ABA assumes that kids will respond to reinforcers that they want. Schools typically will use ABA in their approach to teaching. Educators will offer rewards and consequences to encourage children to behave, learn, and engage socially. I have seen a kid stop making moaning sounds for five minutes in order to get a Skittle. I have seen kids learn to point in order to get a lollipop afterward. ABA is not concerned with *why* kids change their behavior, just that they do. There also are some amazing computer programs and even robots that have emerged out of this philosophy (collecting points and getting scores are used in these programs as forms of reinforcers). These cutting-edge programs teach kids with autism what to say in different social situations, to identify people's emotions on their faces, and to replace repetitive motions, such as hand flapping, with more socially acceptable ones, such as foot tapping.

There are many people who object to ABA for several reasons, one of which is that it is very similar to animal training. Whether you're teaching a child to say "hello" at appropriate times and rewarding them with hugs and praise or teaching a dog to "come" with treats, ABA uses the same foundational principles of rewarding appropriate behaviors and then fading the reward once the behavior has been learned. I used to laugh that I got a puppy at the same time I started my teacher education program, and the dog's obedience classes and my discipline classes were very similar. I was a better teacher because I was a dog owner. In her 2006 book, *Animals in Translation*, Temple Grandin noted that she often feels more at home with animals than she does people—she understands how they react to things. I happen to adore my dog and have no issues recognizing the underlying similar motivations in both of us because there is a basis of love and respect. But others do see problems in the use of ABA.

Perhaps the most impactful criticism of ABA is that it "reinforces ableism" rather than valuing the idiosyncrasies of autism (Shyman, 2016). Numerous autistic adults have stated that they felt like they were treated as defective and that their desires and needs were ignored in favor of ableism. The practice of ABA has changed significantly over the years, but the essential differences still exist in the goals. Humanistic interventions strive to help people become the best person that they can be. ABA can be interpreted as is trying to shape individual behavior to fit expectations of an environment, coupled with a value judgment about the behavior being exhibited. It follows the "medical model" of intervention that focuses on the individual, rather than the adaption of the environment.

Another concern that some people note is that ABA works on the symptoms, but not the underlying causes or issues. You can teach specific skills, but because generalization is so difficult for children on the spectrum, they often don't move those new skills forward on their own. I personally use ABA as a tool, but I much prefer cognitive interventions because they allow a smart autistic child to use their own cognition to help themselves.

Cognitive Interventions

Still focusing on the individual but encouraging the child to take the lead, cognitive interventions focus on metacognition, or teaching children to plan and to think outside themselves about their own thinking. Such strategies have been found to be highly effective for children with emotional and learning disorders and obsessive-compulsive disorder (OCD), and there is growing research on metacognition in children with autism, especially for some of the core aspects of anxiety and social difficulties. In children with obsessive-compulsive disorders, for example, Dr. John Marsh (2007) found that when children were taught to "talk back" to themselves (and when they could realize that their compulsions were simply the manifestations of OCD, *not* a measure of their own capability of as a person), they were able to reduce obsessive actions and thoughts more effectively than with medication. An example of this dialogue might be: *I'm not really wanting to check the light switch/oven/wash my hands again. It's just the biology of the OCD that is making me think I need to. I can outwait the chemicals that are firing in my brain.* While it can be important to help your child reframe an experience, care should be taken that their experiences are validated. Joely Williams (2019) shared,

> As someone who has autism, I am exposed to unintentional gaslighting on a daily basis, from people, who often don't wish me any harm, and sometimes, they're even trying to help...They can make you feel like you are wrong, or guilty or responsible for not getting better. They tell you to "get over it," because "It's all in your head and you can control it."
>
> (paras 4, 7)

Cognitive behavioral interventions are listed as one of the 14 evidence-based interventions for kids with ASD in the National Standards Project (National Autism Center, 2015) and are particularly suited to bright children who can use language to help themselves.

Similarly, when children with learning differences are taught how to plan to learn—"What do I need to do first? What should I do after that?"—rather than just doing something, they become better at managing their own learning. Studies by Karen Harris and Stephen Graham (1999), for example, found that time after time, teaching children to plan out the process through which they're going to do something is incredibly effective at raising their performance. They found that children with multiple types of language processing problems often have huge growths in thinking when they are taught specific steps and questions at each step. It's hard to do without training because it can devolve into the frustrated screech of a mother who asks, "Why did you do that?"

Cognitive intervention does, however, assume that children have a certain degree of theory of mind: that they can plan ahead, separate themselves from their behavior, and recognize that other people behave and think differently than they do. Such abilities are not always present in children with autism. But can they be used and taught? Certainly, in bright children, cognitive interventions have a very strong possibility of success.

In our house, we used both strategies of ABA and cognitive intervention. Elizabeth and Ray were rewarded for completing their work, doing dishes, or sitting in their seats at restaurants. They got computer time taken away if they have a tantrum. But often, I asked them, "What can do you do? What might happen, and what can you do about it? What do you need to plan for? If you feel a tantrum coming on, what can you do instead?" We had lists of steps visually represented for tasks like "clean your room," "feed the dog," and so on to help them visualize what tasks they were responsible for and increase their positive behaviors.

Elizabeth really responded to this kind of instruction. For example, when she was a baby, she *hated* the sand on her toes; she would try to climb up me if I bent to put her on the sand. It was such a drag to live near the beach and not be able to go. One day, I got a rock and brought it to her in the backyard. She looked it over and I pointed out things about it—it was bumpy and hard. We pulled on it a bit and little pieces of it came off. In a very excited, happy voice, I told her, "Look Elizabeth! The rock crumbles! It gets smaller!" Then, I brought out some sand in a bucket and she pulled away, not about to put her hand in it. "It's OK, darling," I said. "You don't have to touch it. But look! Sand is little rocks. It's the rock all smooshed up into little pieces. Can you crumble the rock? You're making sand! What a great, strong girl you are!" Very tentatively, Elizabeth reached back to the rock, put her hand on it, and looked carefully at the sand. I exclaimed in a really excited tone, "That's right! Sand is just little teeny rocks. Smooshed rocks!" The next time we went to the beach, I reminded her ahead of time. "We're going to see sand. Remember what sand is?...(long pause for gentle pressure for possible speech interaction—didn't happen)...It's rocks all broken up and smooshed into sand! I know it feels yucky, but you have to remember it's just rocks."

The first day back at the beach was quieter. She wouldn't let me put her down, but she leaned waaaay over in my arms to watch the sand. It didn't do anything scary, and within two days, she was down on it. I started this intervention when she was about ten months old, and it took her until she was more than two years old to really lose her fear of sand, after many reminders that the sand was just rocks. Now she will go for walks on the beach and even "lay out" with her friends. But she won't bury herself it in nor dig her toes in it at the edge of the surf. But that's OK—we all have a great time at the beach!

Included in the cognitive group are also physical interventions that help trigger certain ways of thinking. Visual schedules and visual reminders are probably the most common ways to help smart autistic kids keep track of a complex world with minimal language stress. We had pictures of chores, maps, and calendars all over the house to help my children remember what they were supposed to do. We started using pictures of food for Elizabeth to choose. Today, she is in college, and her notes are works of art, color-coded with charts and graphs to help her keep information straight. She takes notes from the book first and then checks her notes against what the professor says, knowing that she will be more apt to miss information if it's told to her auditorily. Although "learning styles" have been debunked as an absolute means of learning, Elizabeth still has auditory processing challenges and overcomes them with careful visual notes.

Relatedly, there are a number of physical interventions that help with symptoms of stress and anxiety. Regular exercise that stretches "big" muscles reduces negative responses and meltdowns. I had a student, Jason, whom I regularly sent to carry a big load of books over to Mr. Smith's classroom on the other side of the school. He would haul them over there, and Mr. Smith would thank him profusely and then give him another big pile of books to bring back to me. Somehow, he never noticed that we were just simply exchanging the same piles of books! The use of "heavy" work that is repetitive can calm kids down. And the cost of exercise is relatively cheap, compared to the other forms of therapy—plus, it's very socially acceptable. My son uses weightlifting as a means of reducing his anxiety and has formed several friendships around the gym. Elizabeth did competitive cheerleading; the repetition, the intensity of the lifting and tumbling, and the development of friendships within the stunt teams were all strategies that helped her deal with anxiety.

Relational Approaches

Developed by Dr. Stanley Greenspan (Greenspan & Weider, 2006), Floortime is a time of active engagement with a child with autism. I first learned about Floortime from the book *The Boy Who Loved Windows* by Patricia Stacey (2003), who worked extensively with Dr. Greenspan. We did not have the treatment available to us, but I read up on it considerably, bought the book, and talked about it with our babysitter Irene.

Floortime involves watching the child play and then following their lead with anything that attracts their attention—creating moments of engagement or "circles of communication" (Greenspan & Weider, 2006) through novelty and positive reinforcement. The emphasis isn't on skills, but on social engagement, with the attempt to increase the number of times your child communicates. You are to playfully interrupt your child's stimming or withdrawal, and attract them back to the world through lively, novel, and happy communication. We exaggerated our actions and our happy, positive emotions when we were talking with Elizabeth to attract her attention. It is a highly stimulating form of playing with your child, and it is exhausting.

Never the most gregarious person, I would tire quickly after about half an hour of talking in a very excited manner and trying to play with Elizabeth's toys with her. Luckily, our long-term babysitter, Irene, all of 17 years old at the time, excelled at this form of therapy. She had an amazing knack for making Elizabeth laugh during her preschool years. I would watch her open her eyes wide at Elizabeth, roll on the floor in reaction to any reaction of Elizabeth's, talk with a wonderfully dramatic voice, and give lots of hugs and high fives when Elizabeth would respond. Irene was a natural at creating therapy moments, and although she wasn't formally trained, she could think of activities and ways to communicate and engage with Elizabeth that I could not. I am deeply grateful to Irene and include her in our list of professionals that I give credit to for helping Elizabeth learn to cope with her autism and engage with us.

My friend Tina credits this relational approach for her son's improvements. She joined him in his perceptions, and he would share his joy of colors and movement with her. He lost his label of ASD at age 13. He is now 25 and still very close to his mom, although he is still dealing with high levels of anxiety and social challenges.

Biological Diet Approaches

There is a growing body of evidence that autism is caused by a complex set of genetic and environmental interactions, resulting in a whole host of protein and intestinal issues that lead to psychological challenges. For many years, there has been a deep division between psychological issues, which autism is classified under, and physical issues, which include the study of disease and bodily functions. However, as anyone who gets cranky when they're hungry or fights with their partner when they're tired knows, there is a significant relationship between the mind and the body. Although ABA and cognitive interventions focus on the management of the symptoms of autism, biological interventions focus on the management of the cause of autism. Gluten-free/casein-free (GFCF) diets that seek to remove the gluten and milk casein that can cause gut issues have had some successes with some kids.

As a layperson, I have to admit that I didn't know what to make of all of the fierce arguments over the various diets and physical interventions. I didn't know enough to make an informed decision, and the amount of work it would take to become up to speed on these issues appeared daunting. Certainly, there are powerful arguments for the presence of biological factors. There is so much research going on that I was unwilling to take a stand either way. I went with what appeared to work for *my* children. I have respect for all parents trying their very best to help their child, and I resent close-mindedness of any type. There appears to be a combination of biological and environmental causes and responses that can be taken. Twenty, ten, or two years from now, I hope that we have a much clearer picture and that this argument is considered anachronistic.

Combining all of these theories we know about in real life? It's called parenting.

Therapies: Main Roads and Byroads

My family was open to most things that we came upon. We tried some and didn't try others. We balanced family needs, time, money, and our goals. We listened to a variety of people and read and read. I was determined that we were not going to try one thing for a week or two, just to try something else new again. I was committed to letting the strategies we chose work. Did we pick the best strategies? I have no idea. But given our time pressure, our financial situation, our level of knowledge, and our needs, we did the best we could. Resource information for many of the therapies listed here is provided at the end of this book.

Speech Therapy
This is the first place almost all autism interventions start. I had heard stories upon stories about how three-year-olds pester you with questions, and I was so sad when we didn't have that experience. I asked the speech therapist why that was so important,

and she told me that without questions children can't learn and make connections. They ask questions for two reasons: (1) to get an answer; (2) to figure out what they want to know. Three-year-olds do not plan ahead, and so they do not plan their questions until they ask them. It is through the very asking that they are learning how to learn. The answers are not nearly as important as the process of asking. I knew that it was key to engage Elizabeth in conversation, so I turned to a running monologue. "Da?" she would ask, pointing to the sky. "Oh honey, those are clouds. The big puffy ones are cumulus clouds. Isn't that a great word—cuuumuuuulous? They build up to make rain. Rain comes from clouds, and the grayer the cloud, the more rain. If the clouds are flat on top, those are called thunderheads, and that's when we hear the big booms..." I would exhaust my entire knowledge of clouds and rain and try to provide as much information and language support as I could. To her credit, she would listen patiently (at least I always thought she was listening) and then turn and point to something else. "Da?" And I was off and running talking about kinds of cars. I truly had no idea what she wanted to know, and I hoped that somewhere in the enormous verbiage that I was giving her, she would get what she needed.

I've worked in schools most of my professional life and only occasionally worked directly with speech therapists. If I had to do it over again, I might go into speech therapy. The therapists we worked with were truly outstanding. They would work one-on-one with Elizabeth, bring out toys and games, and engage her in back-and-forth conversation. They would exert gentle pressure on her to talk:

"Do you want the blue bear or the green bear?"

"Boo."

"Good girl! Here's the bllllue bear!"

I learned that I had to tell them to explain to Elizabeth what they were wanting her to do, and she would be much more cooperative. From the beginning of her life, it seems, Elizabeth wanted to know "Why?" (This is something she probably inherited from her inquisitive parents! "Why" can sometimes be interpreted as questioning authority, when in reality, we truly want to know the meaning behind the question. I totally understood where she was coming from.) When we would explain to Elizabeth that she was sorting bears by color because we wanted to see how well she knew her colors, she would happily commence sorting. When asked, "Can you sort these bears by color, Elizabeth?" she would sit and look at you, because that was a question and the answer to it is a yes/no answer and she was pondering the response, not understanding that it was NOT a question but was actually a direction for action.

When she turned three, speech therapy took place at her school. The speech therapists were focusing on her use of language at that point and working with the teacher on using active strategies to involve other students in her activities. I would get a daily notebook that gave details. When we moved to another state, speech therapy was covered by our insurance company. Glory, glory! I was quite angry that the thousands of dollars that we had paid in one state were covered by another! Now, insurance companies are being pressured to help families with autism, and it can't happen fast enough in my opinion. Without speech therapy, I shudder to think of where we might be.

Many bright children on the spectrum do not receive speech therapy until they are in elementary school. The speech therapy focuses not on the production of words, but on the use of words. Many bright children with ASD have a monotone, pedantic manner of speaking. Speech therapy then moves into a communication aspect in which children are taught listening skills and how to respond to what others say. Communication becomes a very cognitive task in which children are taught to listen for key words to which they respond.

For bright children on the spectrum, communication is not the easy, automatic skill that it is with typical children and adults. For this reason, speech therapists are central figures in any form of intervention. They can teach the child to use their intellectual and analytical skills to break down the steps of communication, and great progress can be made.

Occupational Therapy

This is really where Elizabeth's therapy got strange. She needed occupational therapy to help her learn to deal with the sensory input that was causing her to get anxious or afraid. She sat in pools of plastic balls, spun in swings, rolled on big therapy balls, listened to modulated music on headphones, and had to be "brushed" with a hard plastic bristle brush. The therapist listened to my questions patiently and explained how all of these are various calming and alerting techniques that can "wake up" or "calm down" neurological impulses that are being misinterpreted by the body. I was fascinated and more than a little skeptical. Swinging was something we did at the park; how could this be an activity by professionals? However, I did notice an improvement within months. Elizabeth could go to the beach. She wasn't wandering around aimlessly as much.

Related to occupational therapy, sensory rooms attempt to either stimulate a depressed sensory system or calm down an overanxious one. The first time I went into one, I was convinced that the person who first came up with this idea had done serious LSD in their time. The sensory room at the Home of the Innocents in Louisville, KY, has water bubbling in large floor-to-ceiling tubes, lit from within with lights that change color. Music that is very instrumental and vaguely Indian in its tonal quality is played. The floor has sections of different textures. Elizabeth loved her experiences in her therapist's sensory room. We didn't visit it often, but she enjoyed the room and appeared to be calmer when we left. Did it make a tremendous change in her? No, but it was worth trying. For many children, taking them to a place where their senses become overloaded in a rhythmic manner can be intensely calming. However, it is important to note that many of these therapies have little research data behind them and are often expensive to implement. Elizabeth also calmed down after an intense afternoon at the trampoline park—and exercise is a well-researched intervention.

Medication

A whole range of medications are used to treat the symptoms of autism. There is no medication specifically for autism, but medications for depression, seizures, sleeplessness, anxiety, hyperactivity, and irritability all can help to control the problems associated with it. I would recommend that you work closely with a psychopharmacologist who can advise you about various side effects, dosages, and other issues you may face. It is critical that you keep track of the dosages and the effects on your child. A friend of mine, Tina, kept a behavior chart that noted timing and size of dose as well as timing of behavioral issues. She knew exactly when a medication kicked in and when a medication did not appear effective. During any time when you are trying a new medication, be sure not to introduce any other new things into your child's system. Introduce new medications when you can follow your usual routine so that you can determine if any changes are indeed due to the medication and not other factors in your child's life.

I was that mom who never wanted to medicate my child. I hated how some parents would rather medicate their children into compliance rather than doing the hard work of teaching appropriate behavior. I hated how as a culture we tend to turn to medication to solve many problems rather than learning internal skills. However, my viewpoint was changed by three comments at three different times.

The first was in a session about a brain imaging study of ADHD (Castellanos, 2000), when the scientist shared that behavioral therapy helped approximately 50% of children, and medication also helped around 50% of children. But when behavioral therapy and medication were used together, the number of children who were helped was in the neighborhood of 85%–90%. The scientist discussed how the medication allowed the child to be more receptive to the instruction of the behavioral therapy. I realized that it is hard to learn something when the message can't get through; medication can sometimes provide that cognitive calm that allows therapy and other strategies to work.

The other realization I had was during a conversation after overhearing the comment, "If you don't think that chemical imbalance can affect your mood, try thinking clearly when you're hungry." "Hangry" is a thing! When we are hungry, our brains need certain chemicals. If our bodies cannot produce a particular chemical, we have to find it from outside. That outside source might be sunshine for Vitamin D, an orange for Vitamin C, or a pill for an appropriate level of dopamine. Some people cannot tolerate a certain level of sugar and have to take insulin to function. Some people cannot tolerate a certain level of sensory stimuli and have to take Adderall to function. Much as I dislike medicating away problems, I do see the value of providing the body the fuel that it needs to function.

Lastly, a teacher friend of mine, while watching a couple of young men downing Red Bulls, stated, "You know they're just self-medicating. It's too bad they aren't doing it under a doctor's guidance." So often, people who are not treated pharmacologically will seek to find the same "balance" with other substances—legal and illegal. Studies have found that kids with untreated mental health issues will more frequently abuse drugs that mimic the feeling they might get from prescriptions (Bhandari, 2019), but in inappropriate quantities with severe side effects. So, an anxious kid might take opioids, while a kid with ADHD might take cocaine. Not all kids who abuse drugs are self-medicating, but it did make me think about the effect that kids are seeking to feel better about their mental states.

Augmentative and Alternative Communication (AAC)

AAC is one of the recommended practices from the National Standards Project through the National Autism Center (2015). The range of technological innovations available today to children who are unable to talk fluently is mindboggling. From simulated voice technology to iPhone apps, such as Proloquo2Go, that allow children to click on icons to make sentences, technology is making leaps and bounds to bridging communication barriers.

Text-to-speech technology allows the computer to do the talking for the child. When the child types, the computer then reads the material aloud to someone else. There is a wonderful YouTube video by a woman named Mel (Amanda) Baggs (2007), who had severe autism and was completely nonverbal in oral speech. In this video, she stims, makes no eye contact, and provides a running computerized monologue. She shares how autism is "her language" and then notes that she is treated differently because she does not communicate well in our language, yet no one tries to learn her language. Her thoughts are coherent, very logical, and fascinating to listen to. The computer is doing the "talking" for her, and you truly feel as though it is translating for you. Without the use of her computer and its voice, Mel would appear to be noncommunicative. The computer provides a fascinating insight into the world of a person with autism.

However, technology is not the only means of allowing children with difficulty conversing to communicate. AAC can include visual schedules, the Picture Exchange Communication System (PECS), and requesting puzzles. All of these strategies tend to use a visual picture that the child selects to represent a word. The child can communicate with others using pictures rather than words. The key element of AAC is that the child *initiates* communication and does not just respond to directions or situations; the beginning of the communication cycle is maintained by the child.

Sensory Diets

The term "sensory diet" was created by Patricia Willbarger in 1984 to explain how sensory experiences could be designed so that the person can better function within their environment. These activities can be planned to calm senses down or to stimulate other senses in order to find and maintain emotional and behavioral balance. The activities can be planned around a child in the area of tactile, vestibular, proprioceptive, visual, and auditory needs. See Table 4.1 for some ideas and strategies adapted from Carol Kranowitz (2006) and Colleen Beck (2018).

Chiropractic Therapy

I was at a "mommies group" one morning when my family was just starting the process of identification. Elizabeth wasn't talking and hadn't said a word. My anxiety levels were off the charts. One of the other moms said that she had taken her daughter, who was just identified with autism, to Dr. Suzanne, a chiropractor who specialized in sacro-occipital therapy, related to craniosacral therapy. The other mom's daughter was running around with the other children, laughing and screaming as they jumped in the pool together. I was frustrated because my family's appointment with Early Intervention wasn't for another six weeks, so I got Dr. Suzanne's name and number.

TABLE 4.1 Sensory Strategies

Sensory	Stimulating Strategies	Calming Strategies
Tactile	• Drawing • Working with clay or Playdoh • Eating snacks with diverse textures • Light scratching • Velcro • Cold water play	• Soft pillows • Tying the arms of sweaters around the body • Massage • Hugs • Fidget toys • Warm water play
Vestibular	• Swinging • Rock climbing • Jumping on a trampoline • Wiggle cushions	• Swimming • Walking on a balance beam • Crawling through tunnels • Sitting cross-legged
Proprioceptive	• Pushing lawnmowers, wagons, etc. • Ripping paper • Popping bubble wrap • Playing catch/ throwing the ball • Chewing gum • Chair pushups	• Walking with books or bags of rice on the head • Stretching up to the sky • Pushing palms together • Weighted blanket • Sipping water through straws
Visual	• Blowing bubbles • Dancing with scarves • Lava lamps • Coloring	• Taking photographs • Darkened room with a flashlight • Flashlight shining through a hand or different colored papers • Study carrells or trifold privacy screens
Auditory	• Playing an instrument • Listening to music • Dancing to music • Snapping fingers	• Singing • Instrumental music • White noise • Beating a drum

Dr. Suzanne manipulated Elizabeth's back and head and seemed just to apply pressure in strange spots. Elizabeth was very squirmy on the bench and then went still. On the way home, she spoke her first word beyond the names of our family— "Seepy"—and she went to sleep right there in the car, something she *never* did. I sat at a red light and cried that I had heard my daughter's voice for the first time. Before this, she had used a garbled "Diddle-la" which meant both "Cody-dog" and "home," and nonverbal gestures, but she had never spoken a word out of the blue like that.

In one really stunning visit, Elizabeth got manipulated when she had had a particularly trying day. She was sing-songy, stimming, and didn't seem to hear us. Any attempts to touch her made her pull away and giggle uncontrollably. She went up on the table, and the doctor pressed on the top of her head and inside her mouth. Elizabeth squirmed away, shrieked loudly, and then collapsed. She slept all the way home and woke up clearheaded and coherent. Coincidence? Possibly. Was she a completely changed child after that? No. But she was improving in her behaviors.

I didn't really care if hard science showed that this works or not. It did for our family.

Prayer/Reiki

I put these two approaches together because they both involve working with higher powers. Elizabeth's name was written on a card and prayed over by my husband's aunts. They lit candles and sent us icons blessed by the Greek Orthodox Metropolitan, similar to an archbishop. My best friends included Elizabeth's name in their various prayer groups. And my mother did Reiki.

Reiki is a Japanese healing energy that focuses positive growth on a particular illness or hurt. Mother, who is a scientist by training and holds a degree in geology, is a certified Reiki Master and has a very odd ability to diagnose and heal, called "intuitive healing." She sensed a "dark spot" in Elizabeth's brain near the Broca's area, related to language. She worked on lighting up those synapses, getting them to respond and connect. The momentous day that Elizabeth called me "Mommy" for the first time, my mother called me to see if there had been a change, even before I could call her to celebrate.

Again, coincidence? Possibly, but it didn't matter to me at all. If higher powers, head adjustments, speech therapy, Floortime, and occupational therapies were working, we would stay with them.

As a professor, I would recommend to parents to start with the strategies with significant documentation and evidence of effectiveness, such as ABA and speech therapy. **Do not delay** these approaches so that you can first try alternative therapies! As a parent, as long as you have the time, the energy, and the money, you should try what works best for your family and the techniques in which you see improvement. But you absolutely should include strategies that are well-established and productive. Form a foundation of the well-established strategies and, with the leftover time, energy, and money you have, try others as well.

Other Kitchens, Other Sinks

There are a whole host of other things that my family did not try. We did not try them because I didn't know about them then, the negatives of trying them outweighed the positives, or I was too busy trying other things that I simply didn't have time. I list them only as a reference; you will need to do your own research to see if these strategies are things to try, believe, or reject. Parents need to be informed because professionals have such contradictory information.

Son-Rise Program
A positively focused intensive therapy, the Son-Rise Program, offered through Autism Treatment Center training programs conducted through video workshops provided around the world, is based on the premise that autism is at heart a relational issue. As a result, this program focuses on active, dynamic play therapy over the course of several five-day workshops. Rather than stamping out stimming and repetitive behaviors, the parent or therapist joins the child in their activities, sharing the experience with the child. Through a focus on increasing the motivation of a child, skills such as eye contact, vocabulary, and interactive attention span are developed and nurtured.

Biological Approaches
Brain Balance
Brain Balance appears to be a "non-medical and drug-free" program that focuses on physical exercises, nutritional guidelines,

and academic training (Benderev, 2018). Although there is tremendous positive family feedback about this approach, there are few studies, and none were scientific with randomized or double-blind controls. It is a little unclear exactly what the program does, other than that it's "personalized" and that there are various forms of training available.

Biofeedback

Sometimes referred to as electroencephalographic (EEG) biofeedback, neurotherapy, or brain wave therapy, biofeedback is a noninvasive computerized process that works to retrain brainwaves to function in a normal state, providing long-term results with minimal side effects. During biofeedback therapy, children wear electrodes on their head and learn to control video games by exercising the parts of the brain related to emotional regulation and attention. Considered alternative therapy, biofeedback seems to hold some significant promise as children literally learn to control their own brain functions. It is the biological feedback to teaching a child to pay attention to their own thinking processes. It is expensive and not covered under most medical plans.

Gluten-Free/Casein-Free Diet

In the gluten-free/casein-free (GFCF) diet, gluten, which is found in wheat and most binding agents, and casein, which is found in dairy products, are taken out of the diet. A sugar-free diet is just that—a removal of sugars and other carbohydrates—while yeast treatments remove unhealthy bacteria buildup and candida. Other diets restrict oranges, apples, tomatoes, red grapes, and bananas because of their high levels of phenols and sugars. The yeast treatment often means the taking of Nystatin, a medication that does not go into the bloodstream but removes the yeast in a person's digestive tract. Some parents have reported that once the yeast was out of their child's system, their child showed remarkable improvement and a reduction in the "drunken walk" or the tippy toes gait that many children with autism exhibit.

There is a great deal of debate about this type of intervention. In a randomized, well-controlled study, the GFCF diet was found to have little impact on the functioning levels of children with autism (Hyman et al., 2016). The use of diet has even been used as "abuse" evidence in divorce cases. It certainly is confusing—following a sugar-free, gluten-free, casein-free, and phenol-free diet would leave a child with very few food options to eat. Parents have to research what works for their individual child if they decide to go down this route.

Supplements

Some autism advocates propose that children be given large doses of magnesium and vitamin B6, while others are finding that Vitamin D plays a role in reducing the impacts of autism. Magnesium is needed for the proper functioning of every cell, particularly muscle and brain cells, while B6 is needed for more than 60 biological processes. Magnesium is found especially in green vegetables, seeds, nuts, and whole grains. Vitamin B6 can be found in avocados, liver, nuts, chicken, fish, wheat germ, and bananas. The National Institutes of Health found that high doses of Vitamin D can also alleviate some symptoms of severe autism in 75% of children (Cannell, 2017).

Magnesium is toxic at high levels, and too much B6 can cause nerve damage in adults, so care should be taken for proper dosing. In the last 15 years, however, there have been only three cases of chemical toxicity of Vitamin D, and no one has died. Vitamin D therapy appears relatively harmless. I would highly recommend that you consult with your child's pediatrician before undertaking vitamin or supplement therapy.

Chelation

Chelation is a treatment for acute heavy metal poisoning, such as mercury, iron, arsenic, lead, uranium, and plutonium. Parents who believe that mercury in immunizations are the cause of their child's autism are the ones most likely to seek this out. However, chelation is considered to be quite dangerous and has been largely abandoned since 2005 when Abubakar Tariq Nadama, a five-year-old boy with autism, died during chelation because of a resultant elevated heart rate. *I would strongly discourage this therapy.*

However, there are a number of websites that describe "natural chelators," such as cilantro, garlic, and methylsulfonylmethane

(MSM; also known as dimethyl sulfone), a naturally occurring sulfur compound found in fresh vegetables, seafood, and meat. Suggestions for starting this therapy include "juicing" and eating lots of protein in order to flush out the heavy radicals in the body.

Hyperbaric Oxygen Treatment (HBOT).

In HBOT, children breathe pure oxygen in a pressurized environment. According to Rossignol et al. (2012), the therapy can help fight bacteria, reduce inflammation, and promote growth factors and stem cells that can reduce the impacts of autism. However, the FDA has issued a warning to beware of false or misleading claims for using HBOT for treating autism (Sakulchit et al., 2017).

Transcranial Magnet Therapy

Children who receive magnet therapy sit in a chair while a magnetic coil is placed near the scalp. This process creates an electric current that researchers say enhances the ability of specific cells to protect the brain from sensory overload in one region. Researchers at the University of Louisville Medical School (2009) have mapped how tiny strands of brain tissue, called cortical cell minicolumns, develop and connect. That research suggested defects in the minicolumns that interfere with information processing, and has created interest in the possible improvement with children with autism. Very new, this therapy only seems to result in mild headaches for the participants.

Withholding Immunizations

This strategy isn't as much of a way of "treating" autism as it is "preventing" it. *However, it is extremely dangerous.* As my grandmother has said, "People just don't remember the iron lung for polio." I'm also very concerned by the message that it gives that parents are willing to risk the possibility of their child's death over the possibility of their child getting autism.

A study in the journal *Pediatrics*, by Jason Glanz and colleagues (2009) of the Institute for Health Research, found that 1 in 20 children who did get not get immunized came down with whooping cough, compared to 1 in 500 children who were immunized. Although no parents would want their child to get these terrible diseases, some people feel safe not immunizing their children simply because so many other people *do* immunize. Counting on others to keep your child healthy places an unfair burden on others.

There are, of course, risks to immunizing. The Vaccine Injury Compensation Program tracks court cases and compensates families for issues caused by vaccines. Over 12 years, from 2006–2018, the vast majority of cases came from the flu vaccine; more than 3,820 people had significantly adverse reactions to the flu vaccine. The MMR vaccine, the bogeyman of autism conspiracy theorists, had only 130 cases. From 1988–2021, a period of 35 years, there have been noted 62 deaths from the MMR shot, or approximately 1.7 a year. Although having anyone die of a vaccine is still highly unacceptable, in unvaccinated countries approximately 3–6 per 1,000 die of measles, 3–5 per 1,000 die from mumps, and 3–5 per 1,000 die of rubella (World Health Organization, 2012).

This is an issue on which so many people have staked out their viewpoints, but what truly is needed is dialogue. Distrusting results means distrusting science, and if you distrust science, then all that is left is faith and bias. Let's just keep everyone as healthy as possible.

References

Baggs, A. (2007). *In my language.* https://www.youtube.com/watch?v=JnylM1hl2jc

Beck, C. (2018). How to create a sensory diet. *The OT Toolbox.* https://www.theottoolbox.com/how-to-create-sensory-diet/

Benderev, C. (2018). "Cutting edge" program for children with autism and ADHD rests on razor-thin evidence. *NPR.* https://www.npr.org/sections/health-shots/2018/06/18/616805015/cutting-edge-program-for-children-with-autism-and-adhd-rests-on-razor-thin-evide

Bhandari, S. (2019). Risks of untreated ADHD. *WebMD.* https://www.webmd.com/add-adhd/childhood-adhd/risks-of-untreated-adhd

Cannell, J. J. (2017). Vitamin D and autism: What's new? *Review of Endocrine Metabolic Disorders, 18*(2), 183–193. https://doi.org/10.1007/s11154-017-9409-0

Castellanos, F. X. (2000). *ADHD in gifted children* [Paper presentation]. The National Association for Gifted Children annual conference, Little Rock, AR.

Fein, D., Barton, M., Eigsti, I. M., Naigles, L., Rosenthal, M., Tyson, K., Troyb, E., & Helt, M. (2009, May). *Cognitive and behavioral profiles of children who recover from autism* [Paper presentation]. International Meeting for Autism Research, Chicago, IL, United States.

Glanz, J., McClure, D. L., Magid, D. J., Daley, M. F., France, E. K., Salmon, D. A., & Hambridge, S. J. (2009). Parental refusal of pertussis vaccination is associated with an increased risk of pertussis infection in children. *Pediatrics, 123*(6), 1446–1451. https://doi.org/10.1542/peds.2008-2150

Grandin, T. (2006). *Thinking in pictures: My life with autism* (25th anniversary ed.). Vintage Books.

Greenspan, S. I., & Weider, S. (2006). *Engaging autism: Using the floortime approach to help children relate, communicate, and think.* Da Capo Lifelong Books.

Hagopian, L. P., Hardesty, S. L., & Gregory, M. (2015). Overview and summary of scientific support for Applied Behavior Analysis. *Kennedy Krieger Center.* https://www.kennedykrieger.org/sites/default/files/library/documents/patient-care/centers-and-programs/down-syndrome-clinic-and-research-center/aba-scientific-support-9-2015.pdf

Harris, K. R., & Graham, S. (1999). Programmatic intervention research: Illustrations from the evolution of self-regulated strategy development. *Learning Disabilities Quarterly, 22*(4), 251–262. https://doi.org/10.2307/1511259

Harvard Medical School. (2009). *The sensitive gut: A Harvard Medical School special report.* Harvard Medical School Press.

Hughes, C. E., & Henderson, L. M. (2017). Addressing the autism spectrum disorder "epidemic" in special education. In W. W. Murawski & K. Lynn Scott (Eds.), *What really works with exceptional learners* (pp. 225–243). Corwin.

Hyman, S. L., Stewart, P. A., Foley, J., Cain, U., Peck, R., Morris, D. D., Wang, H. & Smith, T. (2016). The gluten free/ casein free diet: A double blind challenge trial in children with autism. *Journal of Autism and Developmental Disorders, 46*(1), 205–220.

Kranowitz, C. (2006). *The out-of-sync child has fun: Activities for kids with sensory processing disorder.* TarcherPerigree.

Lovaas, O. I. (1987). Behavioral treatment and normal educational and intellectual functioning in young autistic children. *Journal of Consulting and Clinical Psychology, 55*(1), 3–9. https://doi.org/10.1037//0022-006x.55.1.3

Marsh, J. (with Benton, C. M.). (2007). *Talking back to OCD: The program that helps kids and teens say "No way"—and parents say "Way to go."* Guilford Press.

Mukhopadhyay, T. R. (2000). *The mind tree: A miraculous child breaks the silence of autism.* Riverhead Books.

National Autism Center. (2015). *National standards project, phase 2.* https://www.nationalautismcenter.org/national-standards-project/phase-2

Rossignol, D. A., Bradstreet, J. J., VanDyke, K., Schneider, C., Freedenfeld, S. H., O'Hara, N., Cave, S., Buckley, J. A., Mumper, E. A., & Frye, R. E. (2012). Hyperbaric oxygen treatment in autism spectrum disorders. *Medical Gas Research, 2,* 16. doi: 10.1186/2045-9912-2-16

Sakulchit, T., Ladish, C., & Goldman, R. D. (2017). Hyperbaric oxygen treatment for children with autism spectrum disorder. *Canadian Family Physician, 63*(6), 446–448.

Schulman, L., D'Agostino, E., Lee, S., Valicenti-McDermott, M., Seijo, R., Tulloch, E., Meringolo, D., & Tarshis, N. (2019). When an early diagnosis of autism spectrum disorder resolves, what remains? *Journal of Child Neurology, 34*(7), 382–386. https://doi.org/10.1177/0883073819834428

Seroussi, K. (2002). *Unraveling the mystery of autism and pervasive developmental disorder: A mother's story of research and recovery.* Broadway Books.

Shyman, E. (2016). The reinforcement of ableism: Normality, the medical model of disability and humanism in Applied Behavior Analysis and ASD. *Intellectual and Developmental Disabilities, 54*(5), 366–376. https://doi.org/10.1352/1934-9556-54.5.366

University of Louisville Medical School. (2009, September). New autism treatment earns EUREKA award from National Institutes of Health. *University of Louisville Medicine Magazine, 4.*

Williams, J. (2019). Autism and gaslighting. *All Thing Autism.* https://www.psychreg.org/autism-gaslighting/

Wong, C., Odom, S. L., Hume, K. Cox, A. W., Fettig, A., Kucharczyk, S., Brock, M. E., Plavnick, J. B., Fleury, V. P., & Schultz, T. R. (2014). *Evidence-based* practices for children, youth, and young adults with Autism Spectrum Disorder. University of North Carolina, Frank Porter Graham Child Development Institute, Autism Evidence-Based Practice Review Group. https://cidd.unc.edu/Registry/Research/Docs/31.pdf

World Health Organization. (2012). Surveillance guidelines for measles, rubella and congenital rubella syndrome in the WHO European region. https://www.ncbi.nlm.nih.gov/books/NBK143264

5

Everyday Strategies

"Life hacks" for smart kids with autism can be invaluable and can save your sanity. Because smart kids with autism have strong cognitive abilities, there are a variety of everyday, household strategies that show promise of effectiveness because of their ability to use a child's mind effectively. As a family, we have learned a whole host of ways to cope and ease some of the challenges faced by autism. None of them work all of the time, but I try to think of them as a toolbox with different strategies I can use at different times. These are strategies that we have collected from various professionals and have implemented in our house over the years.

Scripts

One of the first things I realized when Elizabeth started being able to talk was that although she could *make* the word, she couldn't always *find* the words. She didn't know what to say in certain situations. So, we practiced scripts.

> **Me:** Elizabeth, when the lady at the store says "hello,"
>   you should say "hello" back to her.
> **Elizabeth:** (nod)
> **Me:** Let's practice. "Hello there, little girl!"
> **Elizabeth:** Hello. (whispered)

DOI: 10.4324/9781003237006-5

> **Me:** Good! Now, when the man at the restaurant says "Hello, big girl," what do you say?
> **Elizabeth:** Hello?
> **Me:** Yes—same answer! Good! Now, this one is trickier, but I know that you can do it. The lady says, "Hello, little girl. How are you?" You don't say "Hello," you say "Fine." Listen for her voice to go up at the end. That means that she's asking a question and wants an answer. Let's practice, "Hello, pretty thing! How are you today?"
> **Elizabeth:** Fine?
> **Me:** Excellent!

We practiced scripts for introductions, making friends, presentations in school, restaurants, ordering pizza…Every chance I got, I asked Elizabeth to speak, making sure that we practiced ahead of time. She became quite good at combining scripts, and most of her conversation looked typical. She has shown amazing determination and creativity in how she analyzes how scripts go together. My husband even taught her conversational scripts in Greek so that she could converse with her aunts in Greece! Those scripts are much shorter, but I understand that she has an excellent accent—amazing for a kiddo who couldn't talk for so long.

Circular Conversations

One of the interesting strategies that my family has adopted because of our shared emotional sensitivities is a communication style we call "circular talk." When it is necessary to talk about a subject that is going to cause tension, anger, or distress, we allude to it—set the stage first. Then, we talk about something else. Then, we discuss it in general, and then go off on yet another subject or perhaps back to the first distracter. It pays to keep up with current events in my family—we use them as conversational fillers. Then, we work on more of the "real" conversation, only to dance away when emotion threatens. We chatter on about something else, give the other person time to recover, and then go back to the topic, but in a problem-solving frame of mind. It's a well-timed dance of conversational skill that requires that you pay attention to when the other person can handle talking about the topic again. No screaming for us. No yelling, no overt shows of emotion. So many people in my family are fragile emotionally and feel things intensely, including Elizabeth. When Elizabeth feels anger, she is *angry*. When she's sad, she is intensely distraught. Is it autism? Is she just a member of our family? Perhaps our family has undiagnosed autism running through it? Is it our Southern heritage? Who knows? But circular conversations are our coping strategy and have been very effective with Elizabeth.

Crisis Books

I know of other parents who have used this strategy extensively. If you know of a situation that is coming up that is going to stress your child out—going to the doctor, Christmas, visiting Disney theme parks, or anything that can be a novel and potentially frightening situation to your child—you can prepare them by creating personal books that they can look at about the new experience. Modeled after Michelle Garcia Winner's "Social Thinking" (2020), the books can use pictures of the family or the child and should tell the child what is going to happen. My family used this once for a move. Each sentence had a picture, and the words were very simple:

> All of our stuff is going into boxes.
> Nothing will be left behind.
> There will lots of boxes all over our house!
> Elizabeth and Ray will put their toys and books into boxes.
> Bunny and Bear will stay with Elizabeth—they do not ride in boxes!
> …
> Elizabeth will find her clothes in the boxes and hang them in her new closet.
> She will find her book *Princess, Princess* in a box and put it on the bookshelf.

Elizabeth, Ray, Mommy, and Daddy will sit down to eat at the
old dining table in the new dining room.
They will be tired and happy.
The end.

Providing children a visual sequence of what they can expect to
happen, using their own names and pictures, figuring out what
anxieties they might have, and ending on a good note with something familiar are good strategies that help reduce anxiety and
fear. Plus, with a book or a stapled set of papers to hold and refer
to, the child feels a bit more in control.

Social Stories

Scripts and crisis books are very related to social stories in
which children are taught ways to appropriately respond. A
social story, as originated by Carol Gray (2000), is a structured
approach to a social situation that prepares the child for an
uncertain event, shares important information, and gives the
child a strategy to deal with it. In *The New Social Story Book*,
Gray defined a social story in this way: "A social story is a short
story that describes a situation in terms of relevant social cues
and common responses, providing a student with accurate and
specific information regarding what occurs in a situation, and
why" (p. 1). She often pairs a visual cue with the appropriate
response. I personally broke up the process into two steps—
providing an action together with a script for memory purposes, and then removing the physical action but adding lots
of verbal repetition because I knew that I couldn't always be
there to provide Elizabeth with the visual cue. For example, we
would dramatize how to answer a telephone or how to talk to
her grandmother. Then, I would verbally remind her of what
she could say if the telephone rang and it was her grandmother.
We practiced scripts using the context of her real life, and I used
the crisis books for events that were outside of a typical day,
such as a move or a trip.

Social Thinking

Made popular by Michelle Garcia Winner, social thinking breaks down "complex social concepts…into understandable and doable parts" (Social Thinking, n.d., para. 1). It ties the concept of making meaning in social situations to identifying and adapting our social behaviors to impact how others feel about us and how we feel about others. This "social emotional chain reaction" helps individuals with autism connect emotional responses with appropriate social interactions.

- ◆ How will what I do make the other person feel?
- ◆ How will they treat me based on how they feel?
- ◆ How will I feel about them based on how they treat me?

There is fairly strong research evidence that by intellectualizing the social and emotional processes, children with autism can become better at navigating the social waters. By breaking down the process into intellectual exercises, bright autistic kids can begin to understand more about how relationships are formed.

Visualizing

I learned to make everything visual for Elizabeth. Luckily for us, this included language-based things such as lists, but if a list wasn't in front of her so that she could see it, it didn't get done or understood. She had lists for how to make her own lunch, household chores, morning routines to get out the door, work plans for school, and how to do long division. She would ask, "What's for dinner?" a hundred times until I show her the menu. Baskets in her room were labeled, first with pictures and then with words, to help her keep things in place. When we moved, I had to write out a list for her about our itinerary and the schedule we would follow. All of these helped with her understanding and helped her keep anxiety at bay. I learned, often the hard way, that when she was struggling, I need to give her room to cool down and then work up a list or a series of pictures to help her deal with the situation.

There are many other uses for visualizing. There is a strategy of linking colors and shapes with certain actions. For example, overly honest opinions are a fairly common action that can often lead to hurt feelings and social rejection. I worked with a teacher who taught her students to classify their thoughts as Red, Yellow, or Green Light Thoughts, adapted from Joel Shaul's "Green Zone Conversations" (2014) and Social Thinking (Winner & Crooke, 2020):

◆ Red Light Thoughts are those thoughts that will most likely be negatively received, or are negative in meaning. They are thoughts that aren't very complimentary, even if you are asked your opinion. Red thoughts are ones that you can think but probably shouldn't say, such as, "Your hair is a really ugly color."

◆ Yellow Light Thoughts are those thoughts that you should only share if you trust the person, or should be directed only to specific people. "I would like more water, please" should only be said to someone whose job it is to get water. "I feel sad" in response to "How are you?" should only be said to someone who is a close friend, not an acquaintance.

◆ Green Light Thoughts are positive or neutral in nature or are complimentary and can be shared with anyone. "It's a beautiful day," "Birds are so interesting," or "Do you think it's going to rain?" are all comments that engage the other person.

Replacement Behaviors

Particularly for the issue of stimming, I quickly learned from research and advocacy sites (Kapp et al., 2020; Children's Hospital of Philadelphia, 2016), that the repetitive motions were done to reduce stress or to rebalance for focus. Children can stim during moments of high stress or high joy. The tic or the repetition can ease cortisol levels of anxiety. Some stims are expressions of joy and should not be focused on because they are not creating a problem for the person. However, some stims are harmful— banging heads, pulling hair, etc. Thus, the solution is not to get rid of the stim but to replace it with something that also can help reduce the anxiety. Also known as *habit response therapy*, the goal is not to get rid of the need for the harmful tic or the stim, but to find a replacement. "And since the brain can't do two things in the exact same instant" (Coffey, 2011, para. 4), the brain is tricked into accepting the new movement. My family particularly encountered this with fingernail chewing. Elizabeth's fingernails were bitten down to the quick and would bleed. We tried using nail polish as a reward for not chewing her nails—no success. We tried gentle reminders to stop—no success. Finally, I read about replacement behaviors and tried to get her to press her fingers hard against a surface. That would provide the sensory input that she was wanting and get rid of the "itches" she said she had in her fingers.

Similar to replacing behaviors for tics or stims, we learned to intentionally distract for replacement behaviors during moments of stress. When a meltdown or a confrontation appeared imminent, I would ask the children, "What are three things you can see?...What are three things you can hear?...What are three things you can move right now?" At the conclusion of our "Three Things" game, they had been distracted and their anxiety was often lessened. They were the ones making the observations and they could gain self-control over their responses.

Counting

To handle things, I have learned to count them. This was brought home to me by my son's incredibly wise teacher when he was 18 months old. The school had indoor activities and outdoor activities, and because we were in Florida, the door between the indoors and outdoors often was open to allow the children to go back and forth. I picked Ray up from preschool one day, and his teacher had "that" look on her face.

"How was Ray today?" I trepidatiously asked.

"Oh, it was a little tough," she said with a tired smile.

"Oh...?" I asked.

"He really wanted to bring the outdoor trucks and toys inside, and we had to keep reminding him that outdoor toys stay outside."

"Oh...?" I asked, feeling there was more to the story than this.

"78 times," she said.

I am truly not exaggerating. The teacher had to "remind" my son 78 times to keep the trucks outside. I was struck by several thoughts:

◆ What a patient teacher—there is no way that I would last 78 times before I lost my temper.
◆ The teacher truly believed that her job was not to "correct" Ray; instead, she "reminded" him.
◆ Often, the secret to kids is just outlasting them. Knowing this taught me a coping strategy to being more stubborn than they are: counting!

The next day when I picked Ray up, I asked how it went that day. The teacher was all smiles and said, "Only 25 times today." This *was* progress!

I have used this counting strategy innumerable times since. We counted all kinds of things as a family. For example, Ray did *not* want to sit down in the bathtub. I placed him in a sitting position 27 times the first day I tried this strategy. The second day was 18, the third nine, and by the fourth day, he had learned that bath time meant sitting down.

We counted successes. Elizabeth's words grew from five at age two to 50 by age 2.5 to beyond counting at age three. We counted how many they got right in the daily multiplication timed test. We counted how fast they can get dressed.

I timed Raymond's tantrums. The first one, when we were visiting family and he was two, lasted an hour. The next, when he was three at Thanksgiving dinner, lasted an hour and a half. The next, after a move when he was four, lasted two hours and 45 minutes. These were full-on, screaming, ranting, and hurling-himself-against-walls tantrums. I sobbed through every one of them, and just counted, knowing that they would have to end sometime, and I would get my son back from the dark place his issues took him to.

I counted to let my kids know how close they were to getting in trouble: "I will count to three, and if you have not gotten quiet/closed the door/gotten off the computer/stopped annoying your sibling by the time I hit three, you will go to time out/lose privileges/go to bed early." I tried my best to make the consequence fit the issue, but I followed one critical rule—I always followed through and never did things like counting "one, two, two-and-a-half, two-and-three-fourths," because I have learned the hard way that children try to see how far past two they can push the situation. My children knew that two means two, and that a consequence is coming soon.

Sometimes, just the threat of counting works. My mother was babysitting one night and was getting fed up with the kids. She gave them her best stern face, and said "One...TWO," at which they promptly stopped teasing each other. When my husband and I came home from a rare date together, she laughed that it was a good thing that they stopped because she would have had no idea what to do if she had gotten to three!

Counting helps us all. It lets kids know the extent of their behavior. My children asked me to count things for them, and they knew that Mommy was getting fed up and controlling her own frustration when she started counting. Counting also provides us all a way of coping. I have learned that counting provides a structure for the children to feel secure within. It is during unsupervised time or lack of rules that both Elizabeth and Ray would get into mischief, whine, or provoke each other until a fight ensued. They liked knowing how much time was left in an activity, how far they had pushed my level of tolerance, and how much they had improved.

Writing

Although Ray has fine motor issues, we have encouraged him to use writing as a means of communicating. It is a strategy that is highly effective in my family, both immediate and extended. When we are uncomfortable or have to deal with challenging issues, rather than retreating (always a preferred option), we write. Email and texting have been saving graces for us, as we have become much more communicative with each other. Any form of confrontation—personal, business, friendly, or unfriendly—is difficult for us.

However, the power of writing goes beyond the emotional aspect of confrontation. There are times that I don't know what I feel until I write it down. Emotions can be such a cascading tidal wave that to process them requires time. Making ideas visual and seeing them on paper allows us to better identify our emotions and communicate them clearly. It's a characteristic of the spectrum that I recognize in myself and other members of my family. I well remember a "fight" my husband James and I had over the course of several hours as we sent first furious, then huffy, then problem-focused, and finally conciliatory texts to each other. The texts gave us space to deal with things and an opportunity to identify and work toward communication, rather than completely shutting down. James and I flirted and courted over email, and it's a medium we still go back to. I encouraged my children to sit down at the computer and write to whoever upset them. Through writing we can deal with our emotions.

Writing it out also is a strategy strongly supported by research. According to Joshua Smyth and Danielle Arigo in the March 2009 edition of the journal *Current Opinion in Psychiatry*, expressive writing and other school-based therapies showed significant ability to help children learn to regulate their emotional outbursts. Therapeutic writing is a strategy for helping one identify, define, and explore emotions (Sargunaraj et al., 2020). Such use of writing allows tension to be released without directly impacting others.

Intellectualizing

One of the original defense mechanisms suggested by Sigmund Freud, intellectualization is the avoidance of stressful emotions by focusing on fact and logic. Many of the strategies I've described encompass this idea, but with intellectualizing there is an added effort to make things intellectual rather than emotional. Because my children were such passionate, tender little souls with strong cognitive abilities, they would scream out their frustrations, anger, or even enjoyment of things. They shut down when there was any suggestion of change or emotional judgment. To help with all of these issues, we asked them to examine the impact of their behavior before we told them how to change their behavior: "Elizabeth, how are people reacting to your screaming? I know that you're having a good time, but is there something else you can do that won't scare other people? Ray, how do you think Max felt when you screamed at him? What do you think you could have done differently?"

Such intellectualizing as a coping mechanism is rooted in research dating back to Freud's original psychological studies. Alison Dandoy and Alvin Goldstein (1990) found that when children are taught intellectualizing skills, the biological reactions of stress decreased; people were better able to handle their emotional outburst to a stressful situation. In the book *The Regulation of Emotion*, Pierre Philippot and Robert Stephen Feldman (2004) discussed the process of living an authentically emotionally healthy life, being able to function within society's guidelines for emotional outbursts, and not allowing stress and anxiety to rob a person of their ability to function. The use of intellectualizing questions is not designed to stifle children's emotional development, but to give them space in which to work out their emotions. It also is a process of teaching and reinforcing theory of mind—to help children understand that there are different ways of perceiving things. Because children with high-functioning autism have cognitive abilities that may be impacted by autism, they have the potential to learn the sequential steps of taking another's perspective. I also want to give them a feeling of internal control over the situation, rather than fighting me or someone else for that control. It's hard to not react and tell children what to do, and it's hard for them to think about other people's perspectives, but progress is progress, even when it's slow.

Whatever you do, do it thoroughly. None of these various therapies work with half-hearted attempts. Give the strategies time to work. On the other hand, if a treatment is going to be effective, you will see changes within a few weeks. Just because something worked for your neighbor's child doesn't necessarily mean that it will work for yours. Be willing to let go of something if it's not working. Other parents who tell you that you're doing your child harm aren't in your shoes. In his book *Not Even Wrong*, Paul Collins (2004) wrote, "Autistics are the ultimate square pegs, and the problem with pounding a square peg in a round hole is not that the hammering is hard work. It's that you are destroying the peg" (p. 225). Remember that your child is ultimately becoming who they are.

Getting Good Mileage—for Them and for You

Things have calmed down considerably from the chaos that was my family's experience for so many years. We learned that tantrums would end eventually; we learned that some days were worse than others. We learned that there are successes and there are failures. We learned that our daughter is becoming an amazing young woman. We learned that our son had his own unique set of challenges without the support of a label. Autistic meltdowns lurked around our house, and most of the time they were kept at bay, only triggered by tiredness, anxiety, hunger, lack of structure, transitions…in other words, life.

I have, however, learned some global coping strategies for me and for our family.

Exercise
For my children, deep, stretching exercise was absolutely critical to their ability to focus and their ability to regulate their own emotional states. We called it "getting the evil jujus out." I often

challenge them to a good run around the park in front of our house. They were enrolled in formal sports activities since they were tiny because of their need for focused, large muscle, physical activity.

For me personally, yoga has been a tremendous source of strength. I find that the calm breathing activities as well as the stretches help me center myself and, indeed, get rid of my "evil jujus." I introduced it to the children, but it was slow going. They would rather be very active, and yoga requires concentration. However, they enjoyed the stretching, so we did that in small bursts. Dion and Stacey Betts (2006) wrote a very useful book called *Yoga for Children With Autism Spectrum Disorders: A Step-By-Step Guide for Parents and Caretakers* that we found to be helpful.

Structure

Counting worked so well as a coping strategy that we used it pretty extensively. But we also had strong routines that we established for consistency. At times, I even asked the children how they would prefer we do things. One day when he was around six, I was fussing at Ray for not brushing his teeth—a sensory experience he did not enjoy. "What do we need to do to help you remember to brush your teeth? Would a reward work? A schedule? You can't get out of brushing your teeth—what would help you finish it?" I asked. He opted for a visual reminder and a toothbrush that lit up that he could watch while he brushed. My children crave structure, and as much as possible, I tried to get them involved in the process of creating it.

I generally think through what is going to happen so that I'm very clear about consequences for my children's behaviors: "If you don't get in bed by the time I count to three, you will not be allowed to play quietly for ten minutes, and I will turn the light off right now" or "If you don't stop arguing over the computer game by the time I count to three, I will turn off the computer."

We've even used time as a measure to self-manage behavior: "You may have it for ten minutes, and then it's Ray's turn," "I have three things to do, and then I will leave to come get you," or "You have two minutes to put as many things away as you can. How many things do you think you can pick up?" My kids love numbers, and so I used that love to help them control their lives. Of course, when they were little, I could announce how long things lasted, "Oops! Ten minutes is up!" Once they could read clocks, they set their own time frames. But it was a nice trick while it lasted…

Targeted Rewards and Consequences

It's important to know your child and set up rewards that they desire and consequences that they don't want to occur. Know what you're going to teach your children when you're planning rewards and consequences. I learned this very clearly when my son was three. He had colored on the walls in dramatic strokes—really expressed himself. I informed him that when we make messes, we clean them up and that he was going to have to clean up that mess *right now*! He was thrilled! Scrubbing the walls was great fun for him. He turned a delighted smile up to me, and I realized that I was in trouble. Kids on the spectrum often love gross motor movements—actions that involve the whole arm or the whole body, things that build strength. Scrubbing the walls… what a great activity! I knew that we were in for many more days of colored walls if I went down this route. I informed him with great sternness that he was not going to be allowed to clean this up because we do not write on the walls, and he was going to have to *sit there and watch*! I commanded him to sit on the step and watch me commence scrubbing. He cried, and I realized that I was totally doing a Tom Sawyer. Ray never colored on the walls again, and I used to offer for him to scrub walls as a reward for cleaning his room. We still "invite" him to wash the cars, which is a continuation of when he was "allowed" to do dishes and "allowed" to mow the lawn.

Brainwashing? You betcha! I purposefully "allowed" the children to do things that I wanted them to do. They were not "allowed" to do dishes unless we had a quiet dinner. They were "allowed" to help me clean the garage if they did not fight in the morning.

Consistency

Structure only works if you're consistent with it. It is so tempting when you're tired to let little things slide. I have found that if I have the thought "Well, just this once," I'm in for it. "Just this once" is interpreted by kids as "If I push/scream/yell/stim enough, I'll eventually get my way. It worked once—it might work again." Gambling addicts are hooked because of the rush that they get when they win *finally*, after so much frustration. It is the winning every now and then that makes the brain get hooked. I'm telling you: you're in for trouble if you go the "just this once" route.

That being said, there are lots of things that my husband and I were inconsistent on, like popcorn before bed ("OK, just today because we're watching the finale") and cleaning their room ("I'll do it for you this one time, and then you're responsible"). But for important things—homework, politeness, not hurting things—we remain consistent.

There are lots of things that we were been pretty successful with because of consistency. My children never ran into traffic because of my absolute insistence on holding hands *every time* we crossed the street. Elizabeth and I would find a way to touch when crossing the street until she was a teenager. The few times my kids tried to run ahead of me when they were toddlers, I would grab them, go back to the beginning, and try it again. There was one day we had to practice crossing the street 11 times before they realized that I was going to win that battle. It also helps that my children were slightly fearful of streets, a fear that I encouraged. I noticed every dead squirrel and expressed sorrow: "His poor squirrel mommy is so sad because he didn't hold her hand." (However, although they don't need therapy as young adults about traffic, it may have backfired on me because my children hate driving and are more than happy to have me drive most places.)

Clarifying

My son and I had a major altercation when he was ten when we were working on his homework. I had picked him up from his afterschool program and had asked, "Do you have everything?" He confidently replied, "Yup!" When we got home, he was missing his homework calendar. I fussed at him and said, "You said you had everything!"

In tears, he replied, "Mommy, I don't know what you mean by 'everything'!"

I had to constantly rephrase things and break them down into component parts. Typical parental orders like "Clean your room," "Get dressed," "Are you ready for school?," or "Do your homework" get lost in the muddle of language that surrounds Elizabeth and Ray. I tried to keep my patience as I broke global ideas into specific tasks.

I sometimes had to take a very analytic path as well. My two are very sensitive, and any sort of reprimand could lead to a waterfall of tears or completely shutting down. Ray has what we call his "scowl," where he will go into a black, dark place where he cannot hear you nor respond to you. I learned to ask my kids to tell me what worked and what did not. When they got in trouble, didn't do well, or made a mistake, I learned to keep them in the world by asking them, "What did you do right, and what happened to make it go badly? What else could you have done?" This strategy depersonalized the emotions that they couldn't handle and used their skills of analysis for rules.

This has huge social implications, of course. Other mothers and teachers use global commands all the time. "Be nice" is a rather global idea to get along. "Be polite" and "Treat others as you would like to be treated" are rules for living that have to be explained, broken down, and shown how they connect to other things.

Crisis Mode

There are many smart autistic children who, during moments of anxiety, will appear to purposefully stir things up. A friend of mine's son, who is diagnosed with Level 1 ASD, has been known to urinate on her curlers, smear feces, go into his brother's room to break toys, and generally cause severe mayhem. In her memoir, Helen Keller (Keller et al., 1903) shared how she became a "wild thing," scratching and screaming at her family. Other children will thrash around, pound their head until it bleeds, or bite.

Such actions typically are done because the child needs some form of interaction, some form of stimulation, or some reassurance of ritual. It is easier to get attention and emotional responses doing negative things than it is to get positive attention. A child can almost be guaranteed a response with violent behavior—a predictable reaction that can therefore be counted on. Screams and yelling are more intense than hugs and smiles. When a child is particularly anxious or feeling disconnected, any attention can ground him. Tito Mukhopadhyay (2000) noted that he felt disconnected from his body and couldn't understand what he felt unless it was a very strong feeling. Some descriptions have included things like "flying apart" or "disconnected," and such feelings can bring out a fight-or-flight sensation. Susan Senator (2005) related how her son would have dilated eyes and rapid breathing. Strong sensations, such as deep pressure or strong emotional reactions, can be the only things that autistic children feel keep them together—emotionally and physically. They are, in a sense, fighting for their lives.

This understanding, of course, doesn't help when you or someone close to you is the one being bitten, screamed at, or otherwise abused. Although ignoring some behavior can reduce its impact, often the child will just try harder for a reaction, and when someone is being hurt, you cannot ignore such behavior.

There are, however, a variety of other choices for you. You can:

◆ **Remain passive, even in the face of great volume:** If the child is trying to provoke a response, then removing that response can eventually decrease the behavior. Consistency is key, as is depersonalizing the situation. The child does not truly have this level of anger at you—just at the situation in which they cannot count on a reaction.

◆ **Remove the child from the situation, calmly and efficiently, with little to no reaction:** A school I worked at had "removal rooms" where children were placed if they were behaving violently. There was no yelling back at them, no matching of emotion, just removal to a room where they could not hurt themselves or others. In our house, we used a small room that was darkened when my children were out of control. I was usually crying on the other side of the door, holding the knob, but crying quietly, and I would only repeat the expected behavior in a monotone voice. It should be noted that these are NOT restraint rooms, but places of safety where the child is held until they can find their calm.

◆ **Focus on helping them find their own control, rather than controlling them:** Many "old school" adults will encourage physical discipline at times like this. I've been told (and so many friends of mine relate that they've been told this also) that "What that child needs is a good spanking." As a parent of a child who's different, you know that a "good spanking" often will simply make the situation worse. Spankings moderately work as a temporary means of discouraging a child who is using a tantrum or misbehavior to get what they want. When a child is truly out of control, an adult who also is out of control will terrify them, and it will take even longer for the child to return to a state where they can hear the adult or even respond. I have bittersweet memories of Ray, five years old and tear-stained, desperately trying to catch his breath after a tantrum, repeating, "I be good now. I be good now," as he fought for control. He needed me to model for him and encourage him to find his own control. He did not need me to be shrieking at him, spanking him, or doing anything other than providing a haven from his own swirling emotions.

◆ **Interrupt the crisis early on, before it escalates, with a strong, positive reaction:** I watched a child once who had let out a good scream and was building rapidly toward a tantrum. His teacher sat down hard next to him with a dramatic movement and threw back her head and laughed—not at him, but a shout of laughter. He looked startled, and then let out a laugh along with her. She gave him a big hug and held him firmly. You could see him physically begin to calm down as the tension eased out of him. The need for stimulation is there and is great, but you can provide a dramatic response that is positive. Temple Grandin (2006) shared in her autobiography that she would squeeze herself in small spaces when she was stressed out. She was seeking grounding feedback, and the pressure all over helped her regain her control. I have found that tickling helps my children when they are needing strong responses from me.

◆ **Breathe, just breathe:** Many parents report that talking to their child during a meltdown can exacerbate the issues. Deep breathing can (a) help you calm down; and (b) model for your child breathing techniques that they can use to center themselves. When a child is heading into crisis mode, learning to deep breathe through it can reduce the stress cortisol levels, and according to Stephen Porges (2007), increase the blood flow to the parts of the brain that are shutting down, reducing the fight-or-flight reaction that is a crisis attack. I have found that yoga helped me tremendously to find that core of quiet within myself through breathing. I have a very sweet memory of when I was six years old, being on my bed with my own mother, coloring in a coloring book with her. I was aware of her breathing, and I changed my breathing to match hers. The peace I felt as we breathed together in synchronization was so powerful that I felt part of her and part of a bigger universe at the same time. Breathe with your children and encourage them to breathe with you.

◆ **Consider medication:** You cannot cure autism with medication. What medication can do is moderate some of the effects at particular times. You may find that what works at 8 does not work at 12 and needs changing again at 16. In very severe cases, risperidone, an antipsychotic medication, has been found to reduce irritability in children with autism. Approved for use for children with autism, although used off-label for some time, it has been found to reduce rapid changes of mood and self-injurious behaviors. Guanfacine is another medication that often reduces anxiety and irritability. We had a psychiatrist that we called "Dr. Pill" because her first reaction was to change medication rather than to look at the whole picture. It is important to try behavioral therapy both before and during the use of medication because they can truly help each other. Stay in communication with your doctor about possible side effects, such as drowsiness and weight gain and don't be afraid to change doctors if you don't like the way yours is treating you or your child.

It is important sometimes to "Declare victory and get out," as Susan Senator (2005) said in her memoir (p. 217). Every year, month, week, and day will bring new challenges. The need for consistency, clarity, and structure does not change, but the way in which you make those happen will change based upon the needs of your child. Be flexible, enjoy the ride, and know the incredible difference that you can make in the life of your child.

References

Betts, D. E., & Betts, S. W. (2006). *Yoga for children with autism spectrum disorders: A step-by-step guide for parents and caretakers*. Kingsley.

Children's Hospital of Philadelphia. (2016). *Stimming; What is it and does it matter?* https://www.carautismroadmap.org/stimming-what-is-it-and-does-it-matter/

Coffey, B. (2011). *How habit reversal therapy works for tics and Tourette's.* https://www.youtube.com/watch?v=gbrUzRtRGTk

Collins, P. (2004). *Not even wrong: A father's journey into the lost history of autism*. Bloomsbury.

Dandoy, A. C., & Goldstein, A. G. (1990). The use of cognitive appraisal to reduce stress reactions: A replication. In J. W. Neuliep (Ed.), *Handbook of replication research in the behavioral and social sciences* (pp. 275–285). Select Press.

Grandin, T. (2006). *Thinking in pictures: My life with autism* (25th anniversary ed.). Vintage Books.

Gray, C. (2000). *The new social story book*. Future Horizons.

Kapp, S. K., Steward, R., Crane, L., Elliott, D., Elphick, C., Pellicano, E., & Russell, G. (2020). "People should be allowed to do what they like": Autistic adult's views and experiences of stimming. *Autism, 23*(7), 1782–1792.

Keller, H., Sullivan, A. M., & Macy, J. A. (Eds). (1903). *The story of my life*. Doubleday, Page & Company.

Mukhopadhyay, T. R. (2000). *The mind tree: A miraculous child breaks the silence of autism*. Riverhead Books.

Philippot, P., & Feldman, R. S. (Eds.). (2004). *The regulation of emotion*. Erlbaum.

Porges, S. (2007). The polyvagal perspective. *Biological Psychology, 74*(2), 116–143. https://doi.org/10.1016/j.biopsycho.2006.06.009

Sargunaraj, M., Kashyap, H., & Cjandra, P. S. (2020). Writing your way through feelings: Therapeutic writing for emotion regulation. *Journal of Psychosocial Rehabilitation and Mental Health, 8*, 73–79. https://doi.org/10.1007/s40737-020-00198-1

Senator, S. (2005). *Making peace with autism: One family's story of struggle, discovery, and unexpected gifts*. Trumpeter.

Shaul, J. (2014). *The green zone conversation book: Finding common ground in conversation for children on the autism spectrum*. Jessica Kingsley Publishers.

Smyth, J., & Arigo, D. (2009). Recent evidence supports emotion-regulation interventions for improving health in at-risk and clinical populations. *Current Opinion in Psychiatry, 22*(2), 205–210. https://doi.org/10.1097/yco.0b013e3283252d6d

6

Education

Joining the Highway

You probably have some critical memories of high school and oh boy, middle school. Elementary memories tend to be sweet, but they often set your perspectives on things for years. Your school life was an intense time of your life, and you are naturally very concerned about what it is going to be like for your child who marches to the beat of their own drummer. Schooling is one of the most problematic areas for smart kids with autism. There is one absolute guideline you need to follow: find teachers and schools that are focused first and foremost on what your child *can* do, and who then try to reduce the negative impact of disability on the development of your child's abilities and talents.

The identification and development of your child's abilities has to be the driving focus of their schooling. As human beings, we define ourselves by our strengths—we pick our professions, our friends, our areas of interests, and our purpose around those things that we can do. If our failures are the focus of our lives, then self-esteem, drive, motivation—all of it suffers.

Although the rates of autism have skyrocketed, schools have been unable to keep up. A 2017 study by Elizabeth Keefe found that 77% of special education teachers felt underprepared at the end of their teacher preparation program to teach students with autism. Christina Samuels (2019) reported that special educators

DOI: 10.4324/9781003237006-6

felt that less than 15% of their general education colleagues were prepared to work with children with disabilities at all, much less children with autism. And yet, we turn our children over to other people that we trust to love our children, implement the best therapies, listen to us, make accommodations for our children, develop their abilities, and tell us how things are going. Trusting educators is a process, and the more that you know, the better able you will be to facilitate the communication.

Our First Choice: Montessori Education

Let me be *very* clear: Montessori education is *not* set up for kids with severe disabilities. Montessorians do not ever claim that their method of education is an effective intervention, and often do not have special services for children with autism, low support or not. However, originally created for the "lost children" of poverty and neglect, Montessori education follows the child in their own developmental growth. This means that it allows children to progress at their own rate, with a system based on the concept that children will watch first, then try, and then master. For my children who were bright, not talking, and watched people before interacting with them, I decided that Montessori education was the perfect thing for them. And it was. I credit our Montessori school with much of their progress.

To begin with, Montessorians do not lock a child into a particular academic or social expectation, and the needs of each child are looked at from an individual perspective. Knowing that Elizabeth had language problems when she turned two, I immediately enrolled her in our local Montessori toddler program, designed for children aged 18 months to three years old. I wanted her around typical children because she watched other children so intensely. I also wanted her in an environment that would not pressure her to join the group but allow her to watch and try new tasks at her own rate. Lastly, this program was so tactile and hands-on in nature that I knew it would be a great way to gently acclimate her to sensory things. By learning to polish shoes, for example, she would be learning how to handle slippery things.

When she was 2.5 years old, the teacher of the toddler program suggested to me that she be moved up into the early childhood classroom for children who were ages three to five. Elizabeth was not doing the tasks of that age, but as the staff said to me (and I am eternally grateful to them for this), "She needs to be surrounded by language, and the kids in that age group have higher language levels than the toddlers." I did *not* suggest this change and was amazed that her teachers would suggest something that was outside the "rules" to meet the needs of my child. This truly was an outstanding school that looked at each child as an individual and focused on meeting those needs. It's an ideal you rarely see.

It was one we paid for, though. There are some public Montessori programs, but they are few and far between. Private Montessori schools tend to be expensive, but although the cost was far beyond what we could comfortably afford, it was money very well spent. My daughter entered public school in third grade (when we moved) two grade levels ahead in reading and three in math, and I credit this gain to the individual approach her teachers took in her educational process.

Our Montessori experience with our son was much less positive. We had both children in an early childhood Montessori school in Kentucky, and Ray was starting to exhibit signs of dysgraphia, or fine motor difficulties when he was five. Upon my suggestion and after her own research, the teacher began to incorporate the program "Handwriting without Tears" for Ray—a wonderful program that teaches all students to write in such a way that those students with difficulties are less impacted. The Director of the school heard of this, saw that it was a "program that helped students with special needs," stated emphatically that "this was *not* a special education school," and refused to allow its usage. I sent her a very angry note at the end of the year right before I pulled Ray out that my son now had a writing disability that could so easily have been averted. My experience with Elizabeth's early language intervention had shown me the power of providing intervention right when a child needs it. Not every educator understands that sometimes those aspects of education that are essential for some kids can actually help all kids.

It is worthwhile to note that the word *Montessori* is in the public domain, which means that any school can call itself a "Montessori school" regardless of teacher training or beliefs. I would encourage parents, if Montessori education looks appealing, to make sure that the school is accredited by either one of the Montessori-accrediting agencies and that the teachers have received training from a Montessori-accredited teacher preparation program. Such training and accreditations are more likely to ensure that the school is committed to accepting individual differences and to developing the abilities of its students. Also, be sure to interview the directors and teachers to find the best fit for your child.

Our Next Choice: Private Education

There are a whole host of private schools that specialize in working with children with autism. There are a growing number of schools that focus on twice-exceptional children (who have both gifts and disabilities), and they have large populations of smart kids with autism, so there certainly are a large number of choices. Good ones, however, are more difficult to find.

Private schools, in general, are under no legal obligation to educate children with autism. If your child has a label, no matter how high-functioning they are, private schools have the right to deny you services, based on the premise that they cannot meet the diverse needs of your child. However, labels are confidential information—you can reveal information as you see it necessary. But you do need to think before you enroll your child in a program without disclosing his issues. A friend of mine works in a private school and shared how parents try to "sneak" their children in. It almost always backfires, particularly when the child is having a meltdown or a bad day. Difference looks different, and teachers are experts at knowing what level of difference their school can tolerate.

In our case, we found that Elizabeth needed a private school for gifted children in high school because she was so far ahead in her public middle school. We found a school that had a generous scholarship program because although we are professionals, we are not wealthy. We know that we were very fortunate to have this choice because she had done so well in public school and because I could navigate the system for her.

At this new school, I found that it was better to highlight Elizabeth's strengths, describe her learning challenges, but to steer away from the label she had had because it had so much baggage associated with it. I brought in IQ and achievement test scores to back up my claim that she was "very smart but learned differently," noted that she had sensory issues, and explained that although her language was strong, teachers had to give her time to respond. I relied on her testing data to communicate with teachers, not the label. She had some amazing teachers who were very understanding of her learning differences but were also well aware of and helped her develop her strengths. Others refused to bend in their methods of teaching, with an attitude of "If she can't learn this way, she shouldn't be here." Private schools are a mixed bag—they can be very, very good, or very, very bad.

There are other private schools that specialize in children with disabilities, but many of them do not accept children with autism and often are significantly confused about children with high-functioning autism. These schools tend to be designed for children with typical social skills but poor reading skills. Autism is perceived as such a high-needs area and so specialized that most private schools are not willing to take on the behavioral and learning needs of children whose needs are literally all over the spectrum. The perception among educators is that children with autism are harder to teach, and that generalization may or may not be applicable to an individual child.

There are, of course, numerous private schools that accept only children with autism, and here is one of the biggest dilemmas parents face. Because these schools only take children with autism, there will be only children with autism for your child to be around. Similarly, these schools are used to a population that often is severely cognitively impaired. There will be few role models, but there should be a staff who is caring and understands the complexities of autism and who are more likely to communicate and work with you. Such skilled expertise can be expensive.

Schools can commonly be $50,000 a year and more. And public schools generally are unwilling to pay the cost of private school placement because these are the most restrictive placements possible. Children who do best in these placements tend to either have such severe autism that the impact of peers is negligible or have faced such extreme teasing and abuse in a more inclusive setting that they're deeply unhappy. In a school for children with autism, everyone understands autism, and the child is better able to be their own person, free from the expectations of the label.

Perhaps one of your options, if your child is strong enough to compete academically, is a private school for children with gifts and talents. These schools are used to children having diverse academic abilities, and many of their students have social challenges as well, so they are well-prepared to work with children with diverse needs. However, instruction and interaction in a school for gifted children tend to be highly auditory and language-based. Most children who attend a school for gifted children are very fluent in language and make jokes and puns that may be beyond your child's abilities. In addition, your child's visual needs or language challenges may not be appropriately met here.

One of the most promising possibilities, of course, is a school for twice-exceptional children. There are a growing number of them, and because of the overrepresentation of autism among gifted populations, these schools tend to be aware of, and responsive to, smart kids with autism. Like many other options, they tend to be very expensive and in major population centers. However, if you are lucky enough to live in Los Angeles, New York, or Colorado, you can take the opportunity to see if these schools are right for your child. Most twice-exceptional schools focus on developing areas of interest and passion, encourage creativity, and offer considerable counseling for students and their families. Teachers are highly trained and understanding of the tension between the talents/strengths and areas of challenge for kids and families.

An issue in private school settings is that there tends to be a tremendous turnover rate among staff. Most private schools do not pay teachers what public schools can or offer the same benefits. Teachers at private schools might be there to get their first years of teaching down and then move to a public system, or they may have retired from the public system and are supplementing their income until they "really" retire. Often, teachers at private schools are financially secure and are there for the purpose, not the paycheck—but they can be less sympathetic to families who are struggling. Because stability and routine are so important to children with autism, losing a favorite teacher can be truly traumatic. Also, the effectiveness of the interventions may be based on the training of the individual teacher.

You will need to balance many factors when considering schooling. If you are checking out private school options, be sure to ask the director some of the following questions:

- ◆ Are you licensed? (Licensing means that they have to meet certain health code and operating requirements.)
- ◆ Are you accredited? (Accreditation means that an outside agency is holding them accountable for meeting their goals and for operating in a certain manner. No accreditation means that anyone with any agenda can open up a school.)
- ◆ Are your teachers licensed and by whom? What percentage are credentialed?
- ◆ What is your retention rate among teachers and staff… among students and families?
- ◆ What is your approach to discipline? Do you use restraint, time out, or behavior modification?
- ◆ What is your approach to education? What philosophy or treatment style do you use? What is your emphasis—academic skills…social skills…functional skills?
- ◆ What role do you see the parents playing in your school? How do you want us to be involved?
- ◆ How and how often do you evaluate student progress?
- ◆ How do you communicate with parents, and how often? What kinds of formal and informal communication strategies do you use? What can I expect to hear from my child's teacher on a regular basis? What kinds of communication do you expect from parents?

- ◆ Is there a learning or behavioral specialist on the team?
- ◆ What other supports do you offer, such as occupational therapy, speech therapy, or art therapy?
- ◆ Do you offer any special classes, such as art, music, PE, or sports?
- ◆ When students leave your program, where do they generally go? What forms of support do you provide for this transitional period?

You should have an idea of what answers you want to hear from them. You will rarely, if ever, get all of the right answers from the same place. The goal is optimization—the highest number of the best answers from one place. There may be a place that does one thing exactly the way you like it. Weigh that in consideration with the other issues and make the best determination you can.

Be prepared to change. Schools can say one thing and do something completely different. One school my family visited had the greatest person selling the school. She verbalized exactly what we were looking for and seemed to be in alignment with my philosophy. I sent my children off, content that they were being taken care of and cared for. In reality, the principal had little follow-through and poor communication with her staff. My children had a great teacher, but when she left, we left.

Homeschooling

For parents who cannot find a system that works for them, or who perceive that no one else has the specific knowledge of what works for their child, homeschooling is an option that is growing rapidly in popularity, especially since the COVID-19 pandemic. There is a significant financial element to consider because homeschooling generally requires the full-time involvement of at least one parent, as well as training costs for the parent who is providing the educational interventions. Hidden costs come in as well as you provide social engagement opportunities for your child. Camps and sports activities where children can meet and engage with other children cost money because they aren't provided through the school. Homeschooling also can put stress on a marriage when one parent is providing direct treatment and the other is not.

However, the education is absolutely tailor-made to your child. If your child is obsessed with cars, then math, reading, and history instruction all can focus on cars. If your child has an attentional issue one day, you can back off. If they're interested in one thing all day, you can adapt to that as well. The parent understands what can motivate and move a child forward. Also, because homeschooling is such a growing movement, there are thousands of websites dedicated to curriculum and activities for children that parents can access. Most larger communities will offer social activities and connections to other homeschooling parents. Our local sports facility offers homeschool swim classes during the day for families to interact with each other, and local museums will offer field trip opportunities for homeschooling families.

Each state will have different requirements for the homeschooling process. Some of them will require extensive daily logs, testing, and portfolios. Others will require that you check in every now and then. Research the laws, and join your state's homeschool organization to advocate for needed changes. When homeschooling is done poorly, children can suffer significant neglect. However, when done well, homeschooling can be a fantastic experience for the child and the parent.

Virtual Schooling and Hybrid Home/School

One option to consider is online schooling. Similar to home schooling, the curriculum can be adaptable to your child's needs. Our children were taught through virtual school through the public school system when we lived abroad for a year. They disliked it because of the lack of authentic social interactions, but they were well-prepared when the world went online during the pandemic in 2020! Their achievement grade-wise was high, although the depth of their learning was more limited. However, online learning allowed us to explore some of their interests and offered incredible flexibility. Virtual schooling as a hybrid between going it alone in home schooling or through a school system is a distinct possibility for some families and can be a solution—temporary or long-term—to many issues.

Acceleration and Dual Enrollment

A child should *never* be held back in what they can do because of what they can't do. If a child is capable of reading chapter books in kindergarten, then they should be provided chapter books, even if their reading comprehension isn't yet strong. If a child can do math three grade levels ahead, then they should be provided opportunities to do so.

Two national reports, *A Nation Deceived* (Colangelo et al., 2004) and *A Nation Empowered* (Assouline et al., 2015), found that acceleration is one of the powerful and impactful interventions that can be done to develop the talents and strengths of strong students. The removal of barriers from learning and the progression of topics that allows a child to learn something new and to move forward are powerful motivators, and acceleration is one of the most effective interventions for helping smart children succeed.

Depending on your location and your state policies, dual enrollment should be considered as a possibility. Dual enrollment is where a high school student can enroll in a local college or community college and take classes that count for both high school and college credit. English 1101 can count for both the senior year of high school's English as well as the first year of college's requirement. For children who are bright and autistic, dual enrollment is a means to accelerate the academic strengths of a student. It has additional advantages for students with disabilities because the social pressure to fit in is reduced. They are already different from their peers, so additional differences are often tolerated in ways that they are not by age peers.

I encourage teachers and parents to think of gifted education as the primary education focus for a smart child with autism. Most special educators tend to think about providing inclusive strategies for the general education classroom and curriculum. In the case of a twice-exceptional child, inclusive strategies should be used to provide access to gifted education.

Strengths Orientation

The most important thing you can fight for as a parent of a bright child with autism is to recognize and develop your child's strengths and talents (Hughes, 2017). The goal that I seek in IEP meetings, 504 development, and inclusion in gifted education is "Develop the abilities and mediate the impact of the disability."

There are two verbs in that sentence, and each one is very important. The first, "develop," means that you and schools must focus first and foremost on what your child *can* do. You need to define them by their abilities. Are they a jumper, swimmer, puzzle solver, or writer? Can they do math operations, read, identify dates, or see things others miss? My son has always had the ability to catastrophize—he was the anxious six-year-old who pointed out the different ways that someone could break into our house. After putting up a whole lot of locks, we introduced the concept of probability. It might have been *possible* for someone to drive a car through the front window to get in, but what was the *probability*? There is an entire career in risk management where a skill like my son's can be a very valuable asset. He just needed to make it to seven years old without an ulcer. Helping him intellectualize and cope with dread has been an ongoing process, but we introduced strategies early on. Although his ability to see what all could go wrong is part of his anxiety disorder, in a different context, it can be a strength. Guiding questions to ask are: Where might this skill of my child's be an asset? How could they use this to benefit themselves or others?

The second verb is "mediate." Mediate means to resolve differences and to find the space between where there is balance. I have intentionally not chosen the word "mitigate" because to mitigate something means to reduce its impact or downplay it. Smart kids with autism are not seeking to "cure" their autism or even to reduce its impact, but to find an environment or approach where the strengths and the challenges are balanced. There are numerous fields and areas where the characteristics of autism *are* the strength. We cannot "get rid" of autism, and we do not want to—it is so much a part of our children that we cannot reduce its impact without changing who our children are. But we can help them live with themselves, find others who can appreciate them, and become better versions of themselves—not different but strengthened.

One way to do this is to change the language from a negative perspective to a positive one. Autism educators frequently state that topics are "obsessions" or that autistic students "perseverate." No one has reached eminence without being passionate about something and persevering. Table 6.1 presents a different viewpoint of negative language that is focused on finding positive.

Programs of Note

There are some amazing schools for twice-exceptional children. Perhaps one of the most well-known ones is the Bridges Academy in Los Angeles, CA. In addition to an innovative curriculum approach in which student interest drives the development of individual learning contracts, the school offers age-appropriate exploration and creative development experiences. Bridges also provides significant professional learning opportunities and offers graduate degrees to their teachers in twice-exceptional curriculum and counseling. A documentary about being and teaching twice-exceptional children, *2e: Twice-Exceptional*, was filmed there.

Montgomery County, MD, offers one of the oldest and most established public twice-exceptional programs in the country.

TABLE 6.1 Different Views/Same Behavior

Deficit Perspective	Observed Behavior	Strengths Perspective
Perseverate	Intense focus on one thing	Persevere
Obsession; restricted interests	Intense interest	Passion
Refusal to follow social norms	Not being impacted by expectations of others	Authenticity
Sensitivity	Responding to stimuli	Awareness
Inappropriate responses to emotions	Difficulty responding in emotional situations	Coping
Rigid thinking	Preference for routine	Structured
Difficulty with speaking	Limited speaking	Reflective, thoughtful

Although Montgomery County tends to focus more on gifted children with learning disabilities, such as dyslexia, the schools are well-prepared for the wide range of needs that gifted children with various disabilities may exhibit. They provide numerous resources for educating twice-exceptional children that offer significant guidance to teachers.

Other systems are doing amazing things with smart kids with autism. Pleasant Grove Elementary, a public school in Indianapolis, IN, has a "wiggle room" in which kids with autism can retreat when they are feeling overwhelmed and need a break before they have an outburst. The CHIME Institute's charter school in Woodland Hills, CA, specializes in inclusive education for children, starting with preschool and going through middle school. There are a number of excellent private schools for children with autism that focus on one type of therapy or another. However, where my family lived, none of these were options.

Special Education

As I have mentioned before, I was thrilled with the intensive therapy provided by Early Intervention. I cannot say the same for the services from the public schools once Elizabeth turned three. At three, she moved from EI to special education within our local school district. I was so annoyed that the group who had gotten to know her so well would be cast off with no follow-up possible.

At her Individualized Education Program (IEP) meeting, we went over goals: yes, Elizabeth would be using age-level language skills. Yes, she would be interacting with other children to learn how to ask for things. All good. Then, the staff turned to me and said, "We have two options for services. The first is a full-day self-contained program for children with autism and the second is a part-time self-contained program for children with autism." I was livid!

Elizabeth, then and now, is a mimic of behavior. She tries so hard to figure out the code of social acceptance that she will watch everyone around her and act in that manner. If things were calm, Elizabeth was calm. If things were chaotic, Elizabeth was in the middle of it. The *last* thing my daughter needed was to be in a self-contained classroom of other children with autistic behaviors. She had been in a Montessori classroom with typical peers and had been doing very well. "Can't she get services that were deemed to be necessary and appropriate just a week before?" Well, no, the staff told me, sorry. The school system didn't offer that. Sometimes, they did have kids from neighboring preschools come and play with the kids in a structured environment. This— *this*—was inclusion?

"What about the therapy?" I asked.

"Well, that's in a group setting."

So, I thought, let me get this straight. She's moving from personalized, individualized, one-on-one services that come to her school to a self-contained program with group therapy, and I'm supposed to be OK with this?

Special education is caught in a bind of what is called "free appropriate public education," commonly known as FAPE. "Free" is what it sounds like: Services are to be provided at no cost to families so that money does not play a role in a family's decision. The sticky part of FAPE is "appropriate." The 1982 Supreme Court case *Board of Education of the Hendrick Hudson Central School District v. Rowley* clarified that "appropriate" does not mean "best" or "maximizing." It means "appropriate for growth to happen." A recent case of *Endrew F. v. Douglas County School District* (2016) found that children should be offered IEPs that "are ambitious" and that "every child should have the chance to meet challenging objectives." However, the court in *Endrew* did not require districts to provide opportunities to children with disabilities "to achieve academic success, attain self-sufficiency and contribute to society that are substantially equal to the opportunities afforded children without disabilities" (Alsante, 2017). As a result, very few practices have changed to require IEPs to maximize student potential.

What this means for children with high-functioning autism is that schools are required to serve the *disability* but are not required to serve the child's *strengths*. If a child is managing to function at grade level, even though their abilities may be higher or there is a significant struggle to do so, no services are federally mandated. In the states that provide gifted education services by state law, advanced services have to be provided for children who are outperforming their peers, but not necessarily for children who have the potential for high performance but aren't achieving to that potential because of a disabling condition.

In my family's case, I had not a legal leg to stand on if I were unhappy with what the schools had to offer. Now, in some egregious cases, parents have taken their school districts to court to provide better services for their child and won. That option was not available to us.

I was in a unique situation. The degrees I hold meant that I was treated very, very carefully. I was particularly irritated one day when the school district set up a meeting close to the time Elizabeth was to turn three. I assumed that it was a planning meeting to go over options for her treatment. I had to find a babysitter willing to work with my two active and sensitive little ones, plan around my teaching schedule, and go down to the school district's central offices. At this meeting, I was told that that purpose of the meeting was to let me know that a planning meeting would be necessary because Elizabeth was turning three, and we would no longer be served under Early Intervention, something I had already been told clearly by both the therapists and the EI people (I also had signed a paper stating that I was aware of these changes). I was so angry that they would waste my time and money scheduling a meeting whose only purpose was to schedule another meeting. But they had to make very sure that they covered themselves legally with me. Because I knew the law (heck, I taught the class!), they were very careful with me. I'm not saying that they weren't this careful with everyone, but I did not feel the gentle helpfulness I had felt with the Early Intervention folks. There was nothing I felt I could do with the school system. I opted out, and my family decided to go it alone for the next five years, which cost more money...

I know that other school districts are not so limited in their choices. There has been so much publicity since then and so many more advances made that many school districts now offer a wide range of services that are appropriate for the diversity found among kids with autism. With the expansion of Early Intervention to age six, those wonderful services we had can now last for much longer than we were limited to. Most preschool settings are now fully inclusive and offer numerous choices to many children. Many states are offering full-time preschool or kindergarten classes. Elizabeth was just a year too late.

The following is a synopsis of special education. For more information, please go the Center for Parent Information and Resources (https://www.parentcenterhub.org), Wrightslaw (http://www.wrightslaw.com), or the Office of Special Education and Rehabilitative Services through the U.S. Department of Education (http://www.ed.gov/about/offices/list/osers/osep/index.html) websites.

Funding Issues

Public education is free—all of it. If specialized programs, equipment, technology, and services, including people to individually assist your child, are deemed necessary to help your child, all of it is free to you. However, it is important to realize when you are working with the school system that the staff have to operate under significant financial constraints, and all of their dealings with you will take that into consideration, even though legally they're not supposed to. Susan Senator (2005) referred to it as the business model of education—not a bad metaphor.

Special education in the public schools is required by federal law, known as the Individuals With Disabilities Education Act (1990), commonly called IDEA. It is reauthorized by Congress, with significant changes made every seven years. The last update was conducted in 2004. (If you're doing the math, you will realize that IDEA should have been reauthorized in 2011. At this time in 2021, IDEA still had not been reauthorized because Congress has not been able to get it through.) About 33% of the federal education budget is taken up with special education. Because approximately 10%–20% of students in schools are in special education, there is an unequal distribution; it is clear that it is more expensive to educate children with disabilities.

However, all of this federal money only pays for approximately 10%–15% of the actual cost of special education borne by a school district—a far cry from the 40% the law was originally supposed to pay to schools (Griffith, 2018). The remaining 90% of the monies have to come from the state and the district—most often from the district. IDEA is very close to an unfunded mandate from the federal government: districts are required to follow very specific procedures and provide specific services, and yet they are given very little money to do so by the federal government. In cases where districts have claimed that they are unable to provide such services because of their economic woes, the Supreme Court has told them that they must—and they must simply take the costs from other operating expenses. Thus, it is in the interest of school systems to keep their special education costs under control but provide enough services that students benefit.

There is a legal definition of the word "benefit" as well: The education for any one child has to provide a setting in which it is expected that that child will make progress. It is *not* required that the educational experience be maximized for optimal growth of that child, nor purely for social reasons. This means that school districts are always trying to balance what is a "good enough" education for a child and the desires of the parents. When I teach the special education law class, I tell my students that special education has been shaped by court cases, and that although individuals may want to do the best for children, the system has to maximize its public tax dollars for all children. Thus, there is an inherent tension built in between the needs of the school district to provide adequate education for all of their children with the budget that they have and the needs of the parents to have excellent educational opportunities for their child.

This doesn't necessarily mean that the process has to be overtly adversarial, though. Districts and parents are not automatically on opposite sides; in fact, they do have the same goal—to educate the child in the best manner possible and to help them grow. It's just that the word "possible" means different things depending on which side of the table you're sitting on.

IEP Versus 504

All public schools are required to serve all of their students, so special education is designed to work with students who (a) have a disability *and* (b) have some form of school problem that *only* a change in instruction would address. If there is an adverse effect on educational achievement, but a change in the accessibility to the instruction would address it, students may have a disability but not qualify for special education.

If this is the case, but they still need some accommodations or modifications in order to perform well in school, parents have the right to ask for a 504 plan. Section 504 is part of the Rehabilitation Act of 1973 that requires employers to provide equal access to their employees in order to do their jobs; employers cannot discriminate based on the employee's disability and the employer's requirement to provide access. For example, if your office is on the second floor, you are not allowed to deny a person in a wheelchair a job if they are capable of doing the job once they have access to the office. The employer has to provide ramps, elevators, or some form of access. If you think of children with disabilities as employees, they have the right to access the traditional school curriculum and not have their disability get in the way of that access. Schools have to make accommodations. A 504 plan is where the school, the parents, and sometimes the child plan what kinds of accommodations are needed to access the regular curriculum. Students on a 504 plan do not need specialized instruction, but they may need more frequent breaks, the opportunity to move around more, or even special equipment. My son, because he was on grade level for his academic work but needed accommodations because of his anxiety and Tourette syndrome in order to remain there, was served under a 504 plan.

A 504 plan protects both the district and the child. An individual, fabulous teacher might make some classroom accommodations for a child—allowing them to get up out of their seat or giving them extended time for projects and tests. But if the child is moved to a classroom with a teacher who is more inflexible, a 504 plan will *require* that teacher to make specific changes to their classroom. That teacher does not have to change the curriculum, but they will be required to change how they instruct, based on the specific needs of the child. Additionally, the district is protected by a 504 plan because it documents that the school is not discriminating against a child with a disability while providing access to the curriculum. There are fewer parental rights under a 504 plan than there are under an IEP. However, parents do have the right to call a 504 plan meeting at any time to review its effectiveness, request additional assessments, and so forth.

If a child qualifies for a disability *and* it is determined that they need particular services in order to progress, an IEP will be written. An IEP spells out what the educational plan is for *that* child, based upon their strengths and areas of challenge. IEPs are not supposed to be "cookie cutter" plans in which every child in a classroom is working on the same goal. They are supposed to be specific to the child and followed by every teacher and professional within that school. The IEP is a document full of legal protections for the child and the parents that ensure specific steps will be followed, or there will be legal repercussions.

However, such repercussions are rare. Although the IEP process often is based upon an adversarial relationship rather than a collaborative one, the implementation of the plan requires collaboration efforts in which both schools and parents must engage. It is in the best interests of everyone to collaborate and work together to create a positive educational experience for a child.

Special Education Processes

Getting to an IEP is a process firmly established by federal law. However, there are small, but significant differences between states and districts in the way they translate the law. You will need to check out the specific processes for your individual state. Essentially, there are seven steps:

◆ **Initial problem:** The child is observed by the classroom teacher to have difficulties or problems in school. Problems can be academic, behavioral, or social. Alternatively, the parents can bring the plight of the child to the attention of the team, sometimes called a Student Support Team (SST) or prereferral team.

◆ **Prereferral team:** The teacher (or the parents) brings the name of the child to the team with a description of the problem. The team generally is a group of general educators with some limited participation by special education professionals. The parents are rarely directly involved at this point, but they do have the right to be there and are notified of the team's decisions. The team then makes recommendations that can be implemented relatively quickly as well as any screening assessments that might be done by teachers. In a school system that is following Response to Intervention (RtI), these recommendations have to be carefully documented and based on research. A waiting period of about six to nine weeks generally is recommended to give the strategies time to work and for documentation to be gathered to determine their effectiveness.

◆ **Referral team:** Once the data of the prereferral team have been gathered, the referral team will decide whether to move forward. If the strategies were effective in bringing about changes in the child, then it is decided that there probably wasn't a disability—it was just a gap in the learning process or a mismatch between the educational environment and the child's learning style. However, if little to no progress has occurred, the team can make an official recommendation for formal assessment. Parental permission is required, and generally the school's psychologists become involved. In more progressive school districts, special educators and school psychologists are involved early in the process. In some states, they are prohibited from doing so. It is important to note that when a parent insists on assessment or when a child comes to a district with a diagnosed disability that has already received services, such as autism, most school districts move directly to the assessment step.

◆ **Assessment:** The purpose of the assessment process is to determine the nature of an educational problem— whether it is academic, behavioral, or social. Assessments can be tests, observations, interviews, or checklists. Often schools use a multidisciplinary assessment that explores all of the needs of the child within a school environment. Your child may have a fully developed autism diagnosis, but the school will still need to do a thorough assessment for educational purposes. Once the assessment is completed, there has to be an eligibility meeting.

◆ **Eligibility:** Required by federal law to be held within 60 days of the parent's written consent to formal assessment recommendation (the definition of days as calendar days, school days, or business days is up to the state; if a parent never formally signs consent on paper, the timeline has not started), the IEP eligibility meeting determines if the child meets the educational definition of disability. Each state has a slightly different version of its eligibility requirements. You will need to check with your own state to see if it follows federal suggestions, the DSM-5 guidelines for autism as delineated by the American Psychiatric Association (2013), or its own. I laugh with my students, with no real sense of humor about it, that the best way to "cure" some disabilities is to move. It also is important to know that there is a difference between an "educational definition" and a "medical definition" of a disability. This distinction is most commonly seen in the issue of dyslexia, which is a more medical/psychological term for great reading difficulties. Dyslexia can fall under the educational term of *specific learning disability*, but it doesn't always. A child might meet the definition of dyslexia provided by a private psychologist but not meet the definition for learning disability. Although somewhat historically rare for children with autism, there are a growing number of cases where a school system has denied services because the child doesn't meet the educational definition of autism. If this is the case, the parent needs to get a written copy of what the state's educational definition of autism is, because the federal suggestions mirror medical guidelines. However, some states and districts have placed more restrictions on its autism label, excluding some of the higher functioning children. This was our issue: when we moved, Elizabeth qualified under medical guidelines but not under educational ones—and there wasn't a darn thing we could do about it unless we wanted a fight.

◆ **Need for services:** This decision usually is conducted at the eligibility meeting, but it is a federally defined separate decision process. The team decides if the child not only meets the definitional test but also needs specially designed instruction in order to benefit from schooling. If the child has a disability but does not need specialized services, they may be eligible for a 504 plan. But if they do need specially designed instruction (SDI), they are to receive an IEP.

◆ **IEP meeting:** Generally held immediately after the need for services decision, but not always, an IEP is written if the child was found eligible for special education. In the next section, I detail the parts of an IEP, but it should be emphasized that the IEP is written by the team; it should never be the sole creation of a single person—teacher, therapist, or parent. Although most teachers and schools may come in with a draft of goals written ahead of time, all goals are up for discussion and negotiation. The IEP spells out what it is that the schools are going to do for your child, and it is an agreement regarding the services and programs that will be provided. Some schools will have drop-down menu options for goals. Parents need to insist that goals be written for the specific needs of their child, not just what is convenient or what is typically offered. Schools must provide the services, programs, and accommodations that are listed on the child's IEP.

Rights Under IDEA

IDEA is an education act that guarantees that eligible children with disabilities will receive a public education that includes special education and related services as directed by the child's IEP, based on the child's individual needs (para. 3).

There are several basic assumptions that IDEA is founded on. These all translate into specific parental rights. These include:

◆ **Zero reject:** No child, no matter how profound their disability, can be denied educational services. This does not guarantee all children rights to the *same* educational experiences, but all children have the basic right to an education that is appropriate for them.

◆ **Free appropriate public education (FAPE):** This is the underlying assumption of the law. According to the Learning Disabilities Association of America (2004):

  ◆ Free requires that the education of each child with a disability be provided at public expense and at no cost to the child's parents. The only exception is that incidental fees normally charged to nondisabled students or their parents as part of the regular education program also may be charged to students with disabilities and their parents.

  ◆ Appropriate means that each child with a disability is entitled to an education that is appropriate for their needs. Appropriate education is determined on an individual basis and may not be the same for each child with a disability.

  ◆ Public refers to the public school system. Children with disabilities, regardless of the nature or severity of their disabilities, have the same right to attend public schools as their nondisabled peers. The public school system must educate students with disabilities, respond to their individual needs, and help them plan for their future. Private schools are not held to the same requirements to provide services as public schools.

◆ **Language accessibility:** Assessment shall be given in the child's strongest language if English is not their first language. This is to make sure that English language learners are not found to be poorly performing because they were tested in English, rather than their native language. However, if these students perform more strongly in English than their native language, they can be evaluated in English.

♦ **Due process:** Districts must follow due process, which means that they must follow the rules that they set for themselves. If they do not, the parents can hold them liable. If schools state that they operate within a time frame, they must follow that time frame. If they state that they have to communicate in writing, they have to communicate in writing. Parents and school districts might disagree, but if the school districts did not follow due process, they have no hope of winning if legal repercussions are brought against them. In the law, Congress states that one goal of IDEA (1900, reauthorized 2004) is "strengthening the role and responsibility of parents and ensuring that families of such children have meaningful opportunities to participate in the education of their children at home and at school" (20 U.S.C. 1400 (c)). In other words, the school district *must* try to include parents at every step along the way.

♦ **Least restrictive environment (LRE):** Children with disabilities have the right to be educated to the greatest extent possible with their nondisabled peers in the least restrictive environment. This means that separate classes, programs, schools, or other removal of children with disabilities from the regular education environment occur only when the nature or severity of the disability is such that education in regular classes with the use of supplementary aids and services cannot be achieved satisfactorily. If schools are to provide separate experiences, they must justify such placement.

♦ **Instruction and services:** After reviewing the educational data available, the IEP committee must design special educational instruction to meet the unique needs of the child with a disability, coupled with any additional related services that are required for the child to benefit from that instruction.

Other Parental and Family Rights

Before you go into any official meeting, it helps to know what you have the right to ask. For more complete lists of parent rights, please go to your state's special education regulations or Wrightslaw (https://www.wrightslaw.com). The Wrightslaw website has an excellent description of the various laws and application to parents. You have the right to:

♦ Be present at all school meetings about your child. The school can hold the initial set of meetings without you, but you must be invited to the eligibility, determination of need, and IEP meetings in writing.

♦ Bring anyone else you want to any of the meetings. I have been a parent advocate at numerous meetings because I speak "educationalese" and can facilitate the process for them. Know that if you do bring an advocate, you might put the district on the defensive, because the presence of an advocate can be the first step in a lawsuit, and the focus of the meeting can shift away from meeting the needs of your child to the district covering its legal bases. However, you also can play the roles of "good cop/bad cop" and let the advocate do all of the demanding while you do most of the accommodating.

♦ Give or refuse assessment of your child. If you want your child assessed by the school district, that permission must be granted in writing.

♦ Have an independent educational evaluation (IEE) that has to be considered in addition to the data provided by the school-based assessment team. Parents have the right to have this information, but they might have to pay for an IEE themselves. For example, the school might find that a student does not meet eligibility based on the evaluation results. However, an independent psychologist might very well find different results. Schools have to take both sets of data into consideration.

♦ Ask for mediation, an impartial due process hearing, if you are not pleased with the process or the outcomes of the meetings. Mediation is designed to avoid a court case if possible. Parents and the school both have the right to request mediation and then move to a court case if the decision in mediation is not acceptable. However, if you request a court case and lose, you may be required to pay the court costs.

- Inspect and review your child's educational records.
- Be given written prior notice on matters regarding the identification, evaluation, or educational placement of your child.
- Be given a full explanation of all of the procedural safeguards. You also can ask questions about what the jargon means.
- Appeal the initial hearing decision to the State Education Agency (SEA) if the SEA did not conduct the hearing (the school district has the right to do this as well).
- Have the child remain in their present educational placement, unless the parent and the school agree otherwise, while administrative or judicial proceedings are pending.
- Participate in, and appeal if necessary, discipline decisions regarding your child.
- Call an IEP meeting, even if it is not the scheduled time, to address concerns or changes that have occurred.
- Receive special education services until the child is 21 or until they graduate high school with a regular diploma, whichever comes first.

Writing a Good IEP

The IEP is made up of several interrelated and significant parts. These include:

- **Present Levels of Performance (PLOP):** Also called Present Levels of Educational Performance (PLEP) or Present Levels of Academic Achievement and Functional Performance (PLAAFP), these statements summarize any testing data that is present on the child and any documented progress or changes in the child. PLOP should include information on a child's behavior, academic levels, real-world functioning skills, and/or social-emotional states. PLOP also should include statements of student strengths and areas in which the child is making growth. These statements of performance must then directly lead to the child's goals. There cannot be a goal written unless there is documentation that such a need exists in the PLOP.

◆ **Annual goals:** These goals must be measurable and objective. They should be as specific as possible. This means that vague, fuzzy terms like "appreciate" or "understand" should not be used. Even fuzzier goals like "improve social interactions" should be made much more specific. IDEA (2004) took away the short-term objectives that may have guided schools in their determination of progress. I teach my students to follow a "formula" for goal writing—ABCD:

  ◆ **Antecedent:** Under what circumstances will the goal be reached? ("Given a third-grade level book, the student will be able to...")
  ◆ **Behavior:** What is the verb involved? ("Describe...")
  ◆ **Content:** What is the child working with? ("...the plot of the story")
  ◆ **Determinant:** What is the degree to which the student should master the skill or behavior, and how will it be measured? ("At a Proficient level, as determined by the fourth grade standards...").

  Some examples include:
  ◆ In the classroom, Elizabeth will be able to engage in social conversation at an appropriate sound level with her teacher and familiar peers 50% of the time, as based on observations by the school psychologist.
  ◆ On the playground, Ray will be able to play with one or two age peers for a period of 15 minutes with sustained attention, as determined by classroom teacher observation.
  ◆ Given a math test, Brandon will be able to multiply two-digit numbers with carrying at 90% mastery, as determined by classroom work.

◆ **Program provided or special education services provided:** The IEP team will have to describe how long the services should be provided and where they are to take place, keeping in mind the need for the least restrictive environment. Similarly, the amount of time that the child will interact in the general education program also must be specified. Some districts have a more inclusive approach than others. Inclusion, simply defined, is the concept that rather than having the student move to the special services, the services come to the child. The child tends to stay in the general education classroom, and special education teachers and other specialists come into the classroom to provide direct services to the child. Generally, teachers collaborate, coteach, and plan activities together that allow the child to participate as fully as possible in the general education curriculum. However, there may be many variations of this model in a school. Other districts may rely more on a continuum of services model in which students might go to a resource room for a smaller student-teacher ratio during specified periods of time. Students might be in a self-contained class or even a special school. You will have to decide which approach is more important to you.

◆ **Related services provided and length of time provided:** All of the services, such as occupational therapy, speech therapy, and adaptive physical education, and the length of time that service is to be provided have to be specified. Sometimes, this is provided in minutes over the course of a week or a month. The longer the time frame, the more likely it is that the school may not be providing exact amounts of service per week. You should ask for it in terms of the smallest increments you can get the team to agree on. How long each day does your child get to see the specialist? Once a day for 15 minutes might be more effective than twice a week for 30 minutes or 120 minutes each month. You will have to decide this as a team. But you can certainly always ask for as much service as you feel would be beneficial!

◆ **Modifications and accommodations:** These are the changes that are necessary within a classroom that will allow the child access to the general education curriculum. Modifications are changes in the standards, while accommodations do not require changes in the general education curriculum. Accommodations generally inform the teacher of the changes they will need to make, such as preferential seating, allowing frequent breaks, extended time on tests, or a scribe to write for a child. This section also can include various forms of technology that may need to be present to help the child communicate, such as a Picture Exchange Communication System (PECS) or a computer with vocal abilities.

◆ **Means and frequency of communicating to parents:** A report documenting a student's progress toward their goals has to be specified in the IEP. Often, this is on the same schedule as other students' report cards. However, you can request more frequent communication if there is a new therapy or strategy you're trying at home. Also, the assessments and methods of evaluation toward the accomplishment of the goals must be specified. Schools are required to collect, monitor, and analyze IEP progress data throughout the IEP timeline. Parents can ask to review samples of evidence to ensure that the regular reports are not simply a hunch or unspecified observation but rather a systematic process designed to ensure that the Specially Designed Instruction is working or not. This is particularly important for students with autism.

◆ **Testing accommodations (if any):** When students are given high-stakes tests that determine their progression to the next grade, or the school's overall performance on its goals, some students are allowed to receive alternative tests. However, such alternatives are limited by the state to around 2% of the population and generally are given to students with more profound disabilities. If you have concerns with the administration of inappropriate tests, you should talk to your school test administrator about this. However, administration of these tests can be modified, such as allowing the test to be given in a smaller environment or read aloud.

◆ **Time frame of the IEP:** Generally, IEPs are good for a year, but IDEA allowed states to choose to do three-year IEPs if parents agree in writing. Most states still require an annual IEP review and meeting to write new goals for the next year, but some are considering moving to a more flexible, long-term format.

◆ **Statement of transition:** By the time the child is at least 16 years old, although some states require it at the age of 14, the IEP team must start thinking about the goals of the family and child after high school. Adult services start getting involved at this time so that the movement from school placement to adult living is as smooth as possible.

Professional Boundaries

Notably missing are the specifications of educational approaches or therapies. Rarely do IEPs tell teachers and therapists how to do their jobs; they just specify what they are to have accomplished at the end of it. It assumes that teachers are professional enough to be able to select the most effective instructional approach and do not require additional teacher training. However, if you have a particular therapy program that you have been using that has been successful, you can request that it be put into the IEP. You may not get very far with that, and there is no legal right given to you to require it, but you certainly can ask. It can be very confusing to a child to switch from one therapy program one year to a different one the next year, so you should emphasize the educational, behavioral, and social impact of such changes.

Getting the Most Out of Your IEP Team

Realize that an IEP or 504 meeting is a negotiation. It is in everyone's best interest to collaborate and provide a plan for your child's educational experience that helps the child. There are a number of things that you can do to help facilitate this process.

Attitudes

Believe that the teachers and administrators involved ultimately have your child's best interests at heart also. They may have different rules and different expectations, but they are in the profession of helping children. Recognize different areas of expertise. You are the expert for your child, and you will have a better idea than anyone about what might and might not work for your child. However, the professionals involved have been trained in disabilities and may have expertise in a process of education that you do not. The IEP meeting is an excellent way to match your child's needs with the variety of strategies that the district can offer. You both can learn from each other.

Be prepared to be very firm on some things and to allow the education professionals some leeway as well. Be ready to give in and to insist. Also be prepared for "happy talk" that says very little. "Elizabeth is delightful" makes everyone feel good, but it is not useful in order to write a goal. "Elizabeth should be provided puzzles in order to strengthen her spatial abilities" is more specific and practical.

Relatedly, be ready to insist on the school addressing your child's strengths as well. An IEP meeting is designed to meet the needs of the whole child, which can include areas of strength. These strengths just have to be documented and stated in the PLOP. Most people tend to focus on the "can'ts," but the IEP also should focus on the "cans." Most importantly, effective IEPs seek to mediate the impacts of a disability to allow strengths to be developed.

Also be prepared for private matters to be discussed. Your child's potty training history, who lives with you, and the relationship you might have with your child's father or mother are all relevant information to your child's educational progress.

Before the Meeting

Be prepared. Come early, and have all of your child's documentation. Plan through what you would like to see happen at the IEP meeting. Familiarize yourself with the format of the IEP form so that you can more easily discuss it. Have some draft goals you might like to see happen.

You also should familiarize yourself with your child's testing and evaluation data before the meeting. You have the right to see it ahead of time, so consider requesting this well in advance of the meeting. It can be beneficial to ask if you can meet your child's teachers and therapists ahead of time, and you should visit the new school or classroom if possible.

During the Meeting

Take thorough notes. Ask those speaking to slow down if you need them to. Document any disagreements in writing. Make sure that the goals being set for your child are challenging yet realistic. If you get upset about the team's decision, you can ask for a moment to calm yourself down before discussing it further. Most members of the team will understand.

During the meeting you should feel comfortable speaking up even if you're not asked a direct question. Often, the school professionals will outnumber you, and they are very familiar with each other and the process, so there is a tendency to steamroll right over the parent. Insist on being heard. Don't allow yourself to be bullied, but also don't be a bully. Just maintain as calm an outlook as possible.

At the same time, you want to listen very carefully to what is being said. Teachers and administrators often are not able to say things that you are, but they can delicately suggest to the parent what is possible. For example, when I was a teacher, I could not suggest that children be evaluated with a nonverbal IQ test, because that would make the school district liable for the cost of the evaluation and it was something that was outside the normal evaluation process. But I *could* say, "Do you have any nonverbal IQ information for your child?" Most parents don't know about the existence or power of a nonverbal IQ test. Similarly, when I was a teacher, I used to carefully explain to parents their rights when I felt that the district was taking advantage of them. I couldn't tell parents what to do because my job would be in jeopardy, but I could let them know they could do something. If you have a sympathetic teacher with whom you've established a relationship, listen very carefully to what they "really" might be saying.

If your child is not present, communicate their fears about the process to the team. If there will be changes, you can share probable reactions of your child. If your child is present, be sure to facilitate the child's communication with the team. Help members of the team speak to your child, and help your child speak with them. Be sure to redirect some questions that you know that your child can answer. You are an advocate for your child and representing them as well as yourself at the IEP meeting. You should encourage your child to self-advocate as much as possible and insist that other grown-ups listen.

Remember that if you have any questions about the IEP, you can take a few days to sign it. You do not have to sign it right then and there, and you should not feel pressured to do so. However, even if you do sign the paperwork, you are not necessarily agreeing with the conclusions of the IEP team. You have the right to convene the team again if you have concerns or questions.

After the IEP Meeting: Working With Your Child's Teachers

Perhaps the best thing you can do for your child is to become involved with and reinforce their experiences at school. If you and your child's teachers are on the same page, your child can make tremendous progress.

Here are some general strategies for working well with your child's teacher:

- ◆ Give your child's teacher some time to get to know your child. The beginning of any school year is a crazy time for all teachers. Give everyone time to settle into a normal routine before you appear on the scene. You should try to give the teacher at least two weeks before you make an appointment to talk to them.
- ◆ Introduce yourself and share something positive about the teacher that you've learned. You might have to really reach, but generally there will be something (ask your child if there is anything in particular they really like about their teacher or what they are learning—this usually is helpful when building compliments).

◆ State that you would like to reinforce the activities and strategies that are taking place within the classroom. Ask the teacher to share some of the activities or ideas for parents with you. Let them know that you are a fellow team member and that you are willing to help as well.

◆ Offer some specific help to the teacher. For example, you can offer to read to a small group of children every Friday afternoon. When I was teaching, the parent I had the best working relationship with offered to help with art activities every Monday at 1 p.m. If you have a skill of your own, offer to share it with the teacher. If you can write, draw, or even weave, offer to teach the children. My husband brought in stuff from his time growing up in Greece during one memorable academic unit. If you can't be in the classroom, offer to help with the newsletter, advertise the Book Fair on social media, or contact other parents for activities. There is a tremendous amount of work that can be done to help the teacher!

◆ If your first interaction with a teacher is a negative one in which they are calling to complain about your child's behavior, you should listen carefully and validate the teacher's anger or frustration. Then, you can make suggestions that you have found helpful from other teachers or situations. You also should state that you would like to check in with the teacher within the week to see if the strategies you suggested are effective.

◆ If something changes in your home environment, you should communicate that to the teacher that day if possible. You don't want the teacher to think that changes in your child's behavior are due to their resistance to school, and you want the teacher to be proactive and avoid escalating situations if your child is already fragile.

◆ Offer to design a form that can be quickly used that lists your child's IEP goals and activities associated with them.

When I was a teacher, I had a checklist for each child that listed IEP goals, and every day I documented which goals we worked on. If the teacher doesn't do that, the creation of a form can be a real headache. Offer to help with various paperwork regarding your child.

◆ If your child has a teacher who is difficult, poorly trained, or overwhelmed, be sympathetic and offer suggestions that you have found helpful. Give the relationship between the two of you some time to work. Also, realize that even though you may not like the teacher, the key thing to focus on is your child's relationship and progress. I found one of my son's teachers to be incredibly brusque and rude to parents. But I watched her classroom and talked to my son enough to know that the children loved her. Ray stayed because he was benefitting. I didn't have to like her—just her effect on my child. But know that you might have to request a change in placement or program. Ultimately, it is your child whose growth you have to advocate for.

Whatever your choice for education is, remember that every choice can be changed. Most parents end up doing an amalgam of educational placements, from private to homeschooling to public, in different combinations. As your child grows, their needs change, and the effectiveness of the educational placement can change. Stay on top of things and be an active member of the team that are all working to help your child. Trust them—but be cautious.

And be prepared for everything to change from elementary to middle and high school...

References

Alsante, C. A. (2017, June 1). Supreme Court decision special ed decision leaves questions unanswered. *Special Needs Alliance*. https://www

.specialneedsalliance.org/blog/supreme-court-special-ed-decision
-leaves-questions-unanswered

American Psychiatric Association. (2013). *Diagnostic and statistical manual of mental disorders* (5th ed.). https://doi.org/10.1176/appi.books .9780890425596

Assouline, S. G., Colangelo, N., VanTassel-Baska, J., & Lupkowski-Shoplik, A. (Eds.). (2015). *A nation empowered: Evidence trumps the excuses holding back America's brightest students* (Vol. 2). The University of Iowa, The Connie Belin & Jacqueline N. Blank International Center for Gifted Education and Talent Development.

Colangelo, N., Assouline, S. G., & Gross, M. U. M. (Eds.). (2004). *A nation deceived: How schools hold back America's brightest students* (Vol. 2). The University of Iowa, The Connie Belin & Jacqueline N. Blank International Center for Gifted Education and Talent Development.

Griffith, M. (2018). Is the federal government shortchanging special education students? *Ed Note Education Policy Blog.* https://ednote .ecs.org/is-the-federal-government-short-changing-special -education-students/

Hughes, C. E. (2017). Focusing on strengths: Twice-exceptional students. In W. W. Murawski & K. Lynn Scott (Eds.), *What really works with exceptional learners* (pp. 302–318). Corwin.

Kranowitz, C. (2003). *The out-of-sync child has fun: Activities for kids with sensory integration dysfunction.* Perigee Trade Books.

Beck, C. (2018, April 10). How to create a sensory diet. *The OT Toolbox.* https://www.theottoolbox.com/how-to-create-sensory-diet

Individuals With Disabilities Education Act, 20 U.S.C. §1401 *et seq.* (1990). https://sites.ed.gov/idea/statuteregulations

Keefe, E. S. (2017). *Licensed but unprepared: Special educators' preparation to teach autistic students* (Publication no. 10687296) [Doctoral dissertation, Boston College]. ProQuest Dissertations and Theses Global.

Learning Disabilities Association of America. (2004). *Principles of IDEA.* http://www.ldanatl.org/aboutld/parents/special_ed/print_ principles.asp

Samuels, C. A. (2019, February 26). Survey offers front-line view into special education. *Education Week.* https://www.edweek.org /teaching-learning/survey-offers-front-line-view-into-special -education/2019/02

Senator, S. (2005). *Making peace with autism: One family's story of struggle, discovery, and unexpected gifts.* Trumpeter.

7

Detours and Bumps

Middle School, High School, and Beyond

Autism, Giftedness, or Middle School?

No two ways around it—middle school is hard. It's hard for kids going through it, and it's hard for parents who are both watching their child turn into a being who bears limited resemblance to the relatively sweet baby they were in elementary and trying to help their child navigate the byzantine rules and tortured social traps of middle school. It's hard for typical kids, gifted kids, and autistic kids. It's especially hard for smart kids with autism. Middle school is just hard. I am not going to share much of our specific experiences in middle school. Privacy and respect for kids' struggles at such transition times are critical in a family. As a former middle school educator, I can identify issues and strategies that can help families. But the stories of my own children in middle school are theirs to tell, not mine.

That being said, it's important to focus on the issues your child is facing. I find that trying to explain situations (i.e., "It's because they're gifted/autistic/a girl") is less important than just trying to cope with a situation. Yes, being gifted, autistic, or twice-exceptional makes a complicated situation even more complicated, but most parents are going through some sort of change with their child, and most families are struggling during

DOI: 10.4324/9781003237006-7

middle school. Your battles have a different flavor, but you have lots of company. It is important to reach out for help during this time. Help is not reserved for "those" people who are struggling "more" than others—it's there for anyone who is struggling and wants strategies to help things get better.

Physical Changes, Hormones, and Other Roller Coasters

Right in front of your eyes, your baby will sprout. You worry when they sprout too late, and you worry when they grow too early. Menstrual cramps in fifth grade and being small in eighth grade can be traumatic to kids. Newly surging hormones can play havoc on already stressed systems, and emotional regulation is difficult. Added to this, middle school children move into a psychological state where they believe that they are the main character of a play and everyone is watching them—and judging. The emotional centers of their brains are rapidly developing, and getting new hormones adds to the mix. Add in a neurology where hormones are arriving right on time, but social skills are delayed, and you have a child who is living asynchronously.

It is very important to discuss physical changes with your child and explain when and where they should share this information. A teacher friend of mine found herself explaining the use of pads to a very stressed autistic fifth-grade girl who had started her period and was convinced that she was going to bleed to death. Her parents had not discussed this with her, and her anxiety was off the charts as she dealt with this new information. The teacher had to convince her that she needed to carry on with her regular schedule and that the change in her body did not mean that she could miss her science class. My teacher friend knew that if she let the child skip her science class on this first day, this child would be asking to skip science every month. Similarly, it is very, very important to teach your sons when and where they can discuss their physical responses to sexual desires. The danger is particularly high among young men who can be accused of sexual harassment if they do not understand the limits they must put on their sharing to the objects of their desire.

At the same time that hormones are beginning to flow, the adolescent brain is restructuring itself. During a time that is reminiscent of the brain development phase when a child is two and learning language, the brain is realigning, pruning itself, and creating new paths and synapses. Because the brain is restructuring and pruning itself to operate more efficiently, a joke I tell in workshops is, "Adolescents and two-year-olds are literally losing their minds—and so will you if you don't understand what is happening."

Such energy in the middle portion of their brains decreases activity to the prefrontal cortex that is responsible for decision-making and to other centers responsible for motivation. Clear thinking and focused behavior may decline. Children sometimes seek "drama" because the intensity breaks through the brain fog created by the emotional overexcitability and becomes a way to help middle schoolers focus their attention (McDonald, 2010). Procrastination and other avoidance behaviors become coping strategies that help adolescents gain access to their "thinking brain" when the level of panic or the intensity of a response to a parent's nagging sets in. Think of panic or elevated annoyance as a bulldozer that provides access through the emotional marsh and random thoughts to the decision-making capabilities of the prefrontal cortex. Even typical kids turn into sensory-seeking beings who are looking for heightened sensations so that they can find ways to regulate themselves.

One of the biggest challenges that some parents face is that as their child gets physically larger, the parents' previous skills of containing or soothing their child do not work anymore. When a middle schooler with autism is lashing out, the physical threat can increase. When children are small, some parents use strategies of wrapping their child in a bear hug or physically removing them from situations. These strategies will not work for a middle schooler and definitely not for a high schooler. If physical touch or removal was your go-to, be sure you talk to a counselor and have a plan of action *before* anything happens. It can be incredibly distressing when your child initiates a confrontation and you realize that your old ways of managing a situation aren't going to work.

As a parent of a smart kid with autism in the middle and high school years, it is important to know five things:

1. You have been navigating this dance of emotional regulation for a long time. Your child has been having meltdowns as a way of finding their calm for years, and the strategies you used when they are small can still work—but you do need to adapt them. Instead of offering a stuffed animal to hold onto during a meltdown, a cozy bed pillow might be just the thing. Instead of a quick trip to the park to swing, a visit to a trampoline park or a swing chair on the porch might work. If your child "bolts," find the nearest track for them to run on. Help them access their frontal lobe by soothing the misfiring emotional brain. It is important that they, and you, understand that learning self-control is understanding that "only you control only you"—a lesson we discussed often.

2. As your child gets older, it is critically important that you learn the skills of de-escalation. De-escalation is understanding that when a child is heading for a meltdown, ANYTHING you do—yelling, talking, touching, is going to aggravate the situation. You want to: a) intervene as quickly as you start to see dysregulated behavior; b) provide a safe, isolated, quiet space for any meltdowns that might happen; c) provide support for your child afterward. Meltdowns are exhausting and humiliating for children and as they get older, the social consequences become more significant. Kerry Chillemi (2020) has what she calls the "3 Rs"—Regulate, Relate, Reason. As a child or young adult becomes agitated, you want to help them use self-regulation strategies. If those don't work, you need to work on reaching them emotionally and being non-judgmental. Once the emotional storm has passed and you have established the sense of collaboration, you can use reasoning to address either the cause or the reaction of the behavior.

3. This sensory-seeking and anxiety-driven behavior may be new to other parents, but you should still seek and offer advice. Sharing the skills that you have learned over the years is helpful, but just as every kid is convinced that they are going through this alone, parents are convinced that this

path is unique and challenging. Middle school can be incredibly lonely for parents—schools don't invite you in as much, and your child doesn't want you around as much. It's harder to meet up with other parents, and you don't get the same friendly teacher communication that you got in elementary school. But your child will need you when they need you, so you have to be close by.

4. Your smart child with autism may not follow the same pattern of behavior that typical children do. Just as your child has always followed their own trajectory, they may be on their own path during middle school. I knew one autistic middle school girl in the gifted program who was incredibly popular for the single reason that she *didn't* create drama among the other girls. She didn't understand the changing rules among the other seventh-grade girls, and so was "an island of calm." She would offer a game or an activity to do, and the other girls absolutely enjoyed being around her. Her difficulty reading social cues was ironically an advantage because she was so much less engaged in the emotional storms and eddies around her.

5. It is very important during this time to help your child find friends and others who are like them. Middle school and then high school are a set of changing expectations and circles of friendships and it is very important that they begin to identify with a peer group.

Changing Passengers, Changing Friends

Because kids are changing so fast in middle school, it is very possible that the friends your child had in elementary school will change when they get to middle school. This can be traumatic and lead to many (many, many!) evenings of tears, distress, and obsessive thinking. As a parent, you might be frustrated that the friendships that you mediated and navigated so much in elementary school are now tossed aside. I grieved the loss of some of my kids' friends—they had been like bonus kids to me—who ran all over the neighborhood, in and out of each other's houses. My kids were part of this pack and were accepted. In middle school, they were tossed into a larger group that quickly established a different pecking order.

Bullies, Mean Girls, and Queen Bees

Because social dynamics are changing so much, kids will quickly sort themselves into groups. Middle school is all about groups. What was "cool" before no longer is. Your child who may have loved Barbies, Minecraft, or even Blue's Clues will be rejected now for their "baby" ways. Unfortunately, one of the most critical issues you will have to deal with in middle school are bullies. Whether there is physical bullying, Queen Bee power struggles, or Mean Girl cliques, power struggles are a factor in middle school. Autistic kids are three times more likely to be bullied than their typical peers (Verrett, 2021), and up to 90% of children with autism are bullied at some point (Maïano et al., 2016). Their difficulties with social cues or "reading the room," feelings of inadequacy, finding the right words at the right times, and more limited support and contact with teachers can all lead other kids to identify them as an easy target.

Perhaps one of the most insidious cautions is to beware of adults bullying kids with autism. Because autistic kids don't have visible disabilities and there is so much misunderstanding about autism among the general population, adults may expect a certain level of behavior from children (Young, 2019). Other parents, even teachers, can misunderstand a situation as a power challenge and feel it necessary to enforce their power.

Perhaps one of the more challenging aspects of having a bright child with autism is that they can be more easily triggered and "tend to consider a broader range of behavior offensive" (Sohn, 2020, para. 5), where they misunderstand intent and feel that they were singled out when they were not. Bantering becomes interpreted as bullying when it may have been lighthearted teasing and inclusion, rather than exclusion. This continual interpretation of intent and social cues can cause tremendous stress and anxiety, which can then make social issues worse. Attempts to help reframe these kids' perceptions can be a form of gaslighting. It is important to remember that the feelings of being bullied are valid feelings and should be acknowledged and dealt with. Whether your child's feelings of being bullied are the result of actual actions or misinterpretations of actions is something else to be determined.

Although less common, autistic kids are also at risk of being accused of being a bully. Autistic kids' hurtful and offensive comments, inability to take the perspective of others, focus on what they want with little regard for others, and difficulty with social groups can lead others to feel uncomfortable and report them for bullying (Wells, 2016). Smart kids with autism are often rule followers, and if others are not following the rules, they can badger and harass other children over this perceived slight.

Tips and Strategies for Handling the Bullied and the Bullying

As a parent, you can help your child process their feelings, emotions, and determinations of bullying. Some of the things that you can encourage them to do include:

♦ **Identify what bullying looks like:** Bullying is much more than words. Actions like not being invited to a social activity, body language that indicates rejection, having conversations behind one's back—actions and body language are much more important in determining intent of bullying than words are. I teach students I work with to use a visual of a Venn Diagram in their mind's eye— comparing what is being *said*, what is *intended*, and what is being *done*. I also provide explicit instruction in body language interpretation and tone (e.g., using the phrase "oh yeah" to share the wide range of tonal implications). You might need to encourage your child to choose to be around people who are nice. This interpretation process can be exhausting and stressful, which leads to the need for a safe place.

♦ **Have a safe place available:** Whether it is their bedroom, a trusted teacher's room, or a hammock under a tree, there should be a place where there is silence, peace, and a lack of social engagement. It can be even better if it has your child's favorite sensory things, such as a soft pillow, sounds that are muted, and a sense of peace. Pets are often used in safe places because pets can provide sensory information as well as companionship that is undemanding. Having a safe place allows them time and limited demands to move past the jangled emotional storm and find their calm.

◆ **Strategize how to self-advocate:** You can teach your child about "mini-disclosures." Mini-disclosures are ways your child can share with others an explanation for their behavior from their point of view without sharing the entirety of their label (Oswald, 2019). Mini-disclosures comprise three parts: (a) identifying the behavior that has been noticed; (b) explaining why they do this (e.g., "because it helps me…"); (c) asking for support or a behavior from another. An example might be: "Oh, I'm so sorry I didn't answer you. When I'm focused on something, I find it really hard to see or hear other things. When you see me ignoring you, it helps to gently touch my shoulder to get my attention."

◆ **Make sure they are healthy and well-rested:** Sensitivity increases when children are tired, and they are apt to have a lower threshold of acceptance when they are already physically depleted and stressed.

◆ **Ask questions:** When they aren't sure how they feel about being bullies or if they are even bullying there are some questions that they can ask themselves to help themselves process the experience. Lisa Gardner (2013) proposed five questions that can be used as a metacognitive support to help become more empowered:
  ◆ Was it intentional?
  ◆ What am I feeling?
  ◆ Is there anything else that is going on here—either inside of me or in this circumstance?
  ◆ What will bring relief?
  ◆ How can I prevent this from happening again?

◆ **Ask for help from someone you trust:** Although parents often teach children in elementary school to go find an adult, this advice is less helpful in middle school and high school, where many adults expect children to solve problems for themselves. Asking for help can often lead to bullying by clueless adults. In middle and high school, kids often feel that they cannot reach out to adults because of this pressure to "handle it," and they can feel very alone. Help your child keep a mental list of people they can talk to who understand them and care about them.

◆ **Determine if your child is the one being the bully:** If your child is doing the bullying, it can help to determine if they are the initiator or the responder (Stichter, 2016).

　　If they are accused of bullying because of the ways they initiate social conversations, it is very helpful to seek professional help in learning how to initiate more socially acceptable conversations.

　　If they are accused of bullying because of the way they respond to others, they may need instruction on appropriate ways to respond that would not be considered bullying.

◆ **Address the culture of bullying:** If the bullying is significant and/or physical, you must contact the school and adults that are empowering the activities. I would suggest the antibullying toolkit from Bully Free World (see https://bullyfreeworld-bully.nationbuilder.com/toolkit) as a means of building a set of conversations to address a culture that tolerates such actions.

There is one huge piece of advice I have for you: *Get your child involved in something—anything*. Middle school kids define themselves and others by who they hang out with and what they do. The best thing you can do is get your child involved in theater, dance troupe, sports, band, chess club, Beta Club, volunteer activities, or church youth groups—something that gives them a structured, formal place to engage in activities. Clubs and extracurriculars provide opportunities for parallel activities where social interactions and engagements are framed around the goal of the activity. Even if my children changed their minds, lost interest, or weren't very good at an activity, I always required that they be involved in something. They were not allowed to quit without having something else to do in its place. Academics in middle school are not enough to fill the social void, and no one expects kids to be good at anything yet. My son tried multiple sports, band, and art clubs. My daughter stuck with competitive cheerleading and gymnastics for years. A good friend of ours had a son who learned the trumpet and played at weddings. Outside activities are also a place for your smart kid with autism to shine—a place where their particular passion and interest can be appreciated and valued. If they know every Broadway hit, then they can find a group with the theater kids. If they know every fact about the New England Patriots, then football or announcing the football games can be a place for them to start. It is even more critical that they find a group to identify with in high school, and middle school is where they can learn the basics. High school activities require skills that kids start to learn in middle school.

The one area I would warn you about is limiting socializing with screens. There are two competing issues at play here:

1. Kids are not exaggerating when they say that every kid has a phone. They are also not exaggerating when they insist that not having a phone or gaming system is social death. Although most elementary school kids are on various screens, the use of social media takes a dramatic rise in middle school. Kids talk, communicate, play, gossip, and share information on their apps and screens. You are going to spend your time trying to monitor and keep up with their social media usage, and they are going to spend their time trying to outsmart you. This is the dance of increasing independence when their brains are not yet capable of handling the greater outside world. You need to find the balance of monitoring without constricting. You also need to take the approach of teaching kids how to handle it when feelings get hurt, when they make a misstep, and when emotions get the better of them. I knew a kid who got in serious trouble when, after an online heated argument with a friend, he managed to "dox" his friend's house and had the power turned off. Luckily, the parents of the friend were relatively understanding, and the problem

was resolved with everyone a lot wiser. But it could have led to serious legal and financial issues.

2. Although phones and screens are essential features of kids' social encounters today, as parents we have to insist that they interact with others in ways other than on screens. Some schools will have "gamer clubs," and although these certainly harness common interests, I know of way too many parents whose children, most often sons, are addicted to these games. Many of these families now have young adults who are depressed, unable to work, and only want to play games. I have seen families who had to have their child hospitalized because their child was unable to function and would use violence when attempts were made to separate them from the screens. Obviously, depression and addiction are not limited to screen activities. But screens do offer a siren call that can be difficult to break. Screen addiction is a symptom of deeper problems and you should seek therapy as soon as you see problems beginning. Finding the balance between creating a space for your child to learn how to make and keep new friends after elementary school and protecting them from their own emotions and bad choices is difficult enough in middle school—and having a smart kid with autism makes it even more complex to manage.

High School and Beyond

High school is a very strange experience—a place between the freedoms and responsibilities of adulthood and the limitations and care of childhood. Children in high school *look* like adults, they may *talk* like adults, but they do NOT *think* like adults. And there is a bright line that happens on their 18th birthday.

Changing Legal Supports
Revisit the legal supports that are supporting your child. At age 16, as required by the federal Department of Education (and sometimes by age 14 in many states), if a child is on an IEP, there

must be a statement of transition or specific planning about what a child's future is going to look like. There need to be discussions about college or career preparations, independent living possibilities, and how to access social and interest activities...because when your child graduates high school, all of those lovely requirements of the IEP end. It's called "the cliff" of services and it can mean the end of speech, counseling, and occupational therapies through the school, and you are dependent on services set up through Medicare—if you qualify. In some states, there are waitlists as long as 14 years (yes, you read that correctly—*years*) for services such as supported independent living and applied behavioral analysis therapies. This discussion about future needs and educational approaches needs to happen as soon as a child enters high school because there is a very thin support system after high school.

College and Adulthood

Colleges must follow the same nondiscriminatory rules that all work places have to follow. Your child may already "be on a 504," and this protection does not end when they transition to college. Colleges have to follow the Americans with Disabilities Act of 1990 and Section 504 of the Rehabilitation Act of 1973, both of which require that schools provide "access" to individuals with disabilities. Access means that although these places may have to modify the environment, such as physical access, test-taking environments, or provide a notetaker, they are not expected to provide instruction or to materially change what they do. That means that your child will not get an individualized education plan and that colleges do not have to amend rules for your young adult. Many colleges, because of the influx of young adults with autism over the last 20 years, will provide some services, but it is on a campus-by-campus basis. Definitely ask about the mental health supports that a college provides!

Another important change from high school to college is that colleges are held to a level of privacy that is not found in high schools. The Family Educational Rights and Privacy Act dictates that students have to give permission for their parents to access any information about them—their grades, their emails, and even their financial standing. And students have the right to take away their parents' permission at any time. For "snowplow" parents who are used to smoothing the way for their children, this legal roadblock can lead to great frustration. It is very important to teach your child to take an active role in their own lives.

Gender Identity and Sexuality

During this time of growth and identity formation, it is important to recognize that gender diversity is much greater among kids with autism (Dattaro, 2020). Adults who are gender-diverse are more likely to be autistic, and autistic adults are more likely to be gender-diverse. Gender identity is a person's "internal sense of their own gender" (Dattaro, 2020, para. 4). Those people who identify with the gender they were assigned at birth are called "cisgender," while those who are not as tied to this identity can be transgender, gender fluid, or nonbinary. Some experts suggest that as many as 25% of gender-diverse individuals are also autistic (Strang et al., 2018).

In addition to gender identity, sexual diversity can be greater among autistic individuals. A study of 247 young autistic women found that although 50% of them identified as cisgender, only 8% strongly identified as heterosexual, while more than half identified as asexual (Bush et al., 2021). Those who reported being asexual had lower sexual desire but greater sexual satisfaction and lower generalized anxiety.

Experts suggest that because of their decreased influence by social norms, autistic people may be more inclined to be their authentic selves (Strang et al., 2018). However, they also note that although there is an uptick in gender and sexuality exploration among middle and high school students, there is still considerable pressure to conform to a social norm. If a child on the spectrum is experiencing stress and anxiety about their gender identity or sexuality, efforts should be made to find a counselor who is trained in multiple aspects of diversity.

As parents, you should also seek counseling if you are struggling with your child's identity or sexuality. The child of a friend of mine came out as nonbinary at age 14 after having been raised as a daughter. My friend was surprised to find herself the most upset, not at supporting her child in their identity, but at their change of name. Their original name had been a family name, and when they rejected the name, my friend felt that they were rejecting their family. Just as you are allowed to grieve the "trip to Italy" that you lost when you had a child with autism, you are also allowed to grieve the loss of your dream of the stereotypic family. It doesn't mean that you love your child any less, but you do have to be careful to make sure that they understand that you love and value them exactly for who they are.

Interests Become Careers: Talent Trajectories

It is essential that three things happen in high school and early college:

1. Your child needs to have experiences that are broadening their horizons. These are the years in which their abilities *must* be recognized and developed so that they can explore their myriad interests. If the entirety of a school experience focuses on a child's *dis*ability, their ability becomes less important to their self-concept.
2. Simultaneously, they should be experiencing a deepening of their specific talents and abilities. Although they may be caught up in social activities and worried about friends, their pursuits of their interests are the most likely to impact their life choices.
3. It is important that the roadblocks created by characteristics of their autism are mediated, so that education does not focus on the remediation or improvement of autism characteristics, but rather on how to live with, and even capitalize on, autistic characteristics.

Work as an Essential for Happiness

There is a concept of "autistic joy," or the single-minded joy that comes from an autistic individual doing the thing that they love to do. It's the joy an autistic person feels when they become engrossed in watching bubbles or when they come across a multiple of seven (Bascom, 2015). It is a sense of complete peace—being perfectly in the moment that is free of stress. Autistic behaviors that bring joy are often excluded from the artistic and creative conceptions of joy (White-Johnson, 2019), so it is important to recognize them as joy, not as a demonstration of disability. It is no small wonder that autistic people, who are often impacted by anxiety in a social world of language and interactions, can escape by finding an experience. This focus on experience is one that has been coopted by the mindfulness movement for reduction of stress and anxiety. The difference, of course, is the degree to which someone can emerge from this transitory place of joy to function again in the "real world." However, the joy that a child feels in that moment cannot be reduced to a minor thing or, worse, denigrated and stifled. When the adults around an autistic teenager can recognize that Blue's Clues, singing, or listening to police scanners (things that create happy places for three friends of mine) is creating joy within that child, those activities should not be looked down upon, but encouraged and celebrated with them.

A longitudinal study (Helles et al., 2015) of male adults who had been identified as having Asperger's syndrome found that although typical people defined happiness as being involved in social relationships, many autistics stated that they were happy even when they were not in numerous relationships. Many were leading a "restricted life" with two or more close friends, and very few were in romantic relationships. A very bright autistic adult I know related that there is a cycle that as he accumulated negative social experiences, he developed more severe social anxieties, which led to more maladaptive behavior patterns, which led to more negative social experiences.

Their level of intelligence and their pursuit of a career they value appeared to be significant factors in the level of happiness of bright autistic adults (Wright, 2016). Joely Williams (2019) shared,

> We can be enabled to be the best we can by people who nurture our interests and talents, who support us unconditionally and who make an effort to learn to understand us, as individual human beings—every autistic person does not display the same.
>
> (para. 9)

As I tell my own children, "All you need are a small number of friends and a big sense of purpose." That is why it is so important for smart autistic young adults in high school and college to begin to focus on their sense of direction and purpose—to harness their sense of passion and joy and develop it into a career trajectory.

One approach to help guide your child's exploration of their career interests is to follow the guidelines of Jaime Casap (2020), Google's "Education Evangelist," who recommended that we do *not* ask children "What do you want to be when you grow up?" but rather:

1. What problem do you want to solve?
2. How do you want to solve it?
3. What do you need to know to solve that problem?

Archetypes

There is no single best profession that bright children with autism should go into, despite the stereotype of Silicon Valley computer "geeks" or "egghead" mathematicians. While STEM areas are certainly one area in which they may excel, there are many others. Jake Michaelson (2021) described the various "archetypes" of bright autistic individuals as falling into six distinct areas. While they do sound like characters from a Dungeons and Dragons game, all of these archetypes capture the ability of the bright, autistic person to focus on details and make unusual connections between relationships. They include:

1. The engineer, or the designer who is aware of details and materials;
2. The polymath—often seen in many STEM areas;
3. The bard, or artist;
4. The performer—often seen in theater or marketing;
5. The writer—or the master of words;
6. The "non-geek" who seeks to fit in.

The various strength areas are less related to a person's autism but are much more tied to their personality and thinking skills.

For example, someone's need to withdraw, or introversion, is highly positively correlated with being a writer, while withdrawal is highly negatively correlated with being a performer. The only area, according to Jake Michaelson that is negatively affected by the ability to pay attention is the area of "non-geek." The better attention someone can pay to a subject, the less likely they are to be a "non-geek" and the more likely they are to be one of the other archetypes. I have introduced the Japanese concept of *ikigai* to my children and to others working with smart autistic young adults as a way of helping them target something that will bring a sense of purpose to their lives. *Ikigai* means "reason for living" with an implicit sense of balance, and it is the intersection between those things that you care deeply about, those skills you have that you are good at, actions that help improve the world, and actions that will be paid (Figure 7.1).

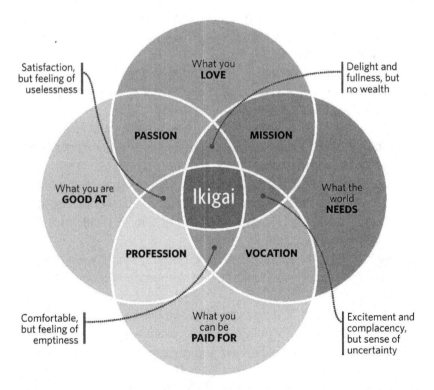

FIGURE 7.1 Finding *ikigai*. This Photo by Unknown Author is Licensed under CC BY-SA-NC

Finding *ikigai* is a lifelong process that requires support, encouragement, self-understanding, and awareness of the world around your child. It can also be the recipe for deep happiness.

References

Bascom, J. (2015). *The obsessive joy of autism*. Kingsley Publishers.

Bush, H. H., Williams, L. W., & Mendes, E. (2021). Brief report: Asexuality and young women on the autism spectrum. *Journal of Autism and Developmental Disorders, 51*(2), 725–733. https://doi.org/10.1007/s10803-020-04565-6

Casap, J. (2020, January 8). What problem do you want to solve? *Arizona State University News*. https://news.asu.edu/20200108-creativity-asu-thrive-what-problem-do-you-want-solve

Chillemi, K. (2020). The GPS Method: De-escalating autistic meltdowns. *Psychology Today*. https://www.psychologytoday.com/us/blog/functional-legacy-mindset/202003/the-gps-method-de-escalating-autistic-meltdowns

Dattaro, L. (2020, September 18). Gender and sexuality in autism, explained. *Spectrum News*. https://www.spectrumnews.org/news/gender-and-sexuality-in-autism-explained

Gardner, L. (2013). Five ways to deal with emotional oversensitivity. *Tiny Buddha*. https://tinybuddha.com/blog/5-ways-to-deal-with-emotional-oversensitivity

Helles, A., Gillberg, C. I., Billberg, C., & Billstedt, E. (2015). Asperger syndrome in males over two decades: Stability and predictors of diagnosis. *Journal of Child Psychology and Psychiatry, 56*(6), 711–718. https://doi.org/10.1111/jcpp.12334

McDonald, E. S. (2010, January/February). Ten to teen. *Principal*. https://www.naesp.org/sites/default/files/resources/2/Principal/2010/J-Fp46.pdf

Maïano, C., Normand, C. L., Salvas, M.-C., Moullec, G., Aimé, A. (2016). Prevalence of school bullying among youth with autism spectrum disorders: A systematic review and meta-analysis. *Autism Research, 9*(6), 601–615.

Michaelson, J. (2021, May). The plural of anecdote is data. Summit on the Neurology of Twice-Exceptionality, University of Iowa.

Oswald, T. (2019, December 23). Social skills in the workplace: The power of hyperfocus. *Open Doors Therapy*. https://opendoorstherapy.com/workplace-social-skills-hyperfocus

Sohn, E. (2020, February 5). How abuse mars the lives of autistic people. *Spectrum News*. https://www.spectrumnews.org/features/deep-dive/how-abuse-mars-the-lives-of-autistic-people

Strang, J. F., Janssen, A., Tishelman, A., Leibowitz, S. F., Kenworthy, L., McGuire, J. K., Edwards-Leeper, L., Mazefski, C. A., Rofey, D., Bascom, J., Caplan, R., Gomez-Lobo, V., Berg, D., Zaks, Z., Wallace, G. L., Wimms, H., Pine-Twaddell, E., Shumer, D., Register-Brown, K., Sadikova, E., & Anthony, L. A. (2018). Revisiting the link: Evidence of the rates of autism in studies of gender diverse individuals. *Journal of American Academic Child Adolescent Psychiatry*, *57*(11), 885–887. https://doi.org/10.1016/j.jaac.2018.04.023

Stichter, J. (2016, October 14). Help! Our son with autism just laughs when others bully and tease. *Autism Speaks*. https://www.autismspeaks.org/expert-opinion/help-our-son-autism-just-laughs-when-others-bully-and-tease

Verrett, G. (2021). Bullying and autism spectrum disorder (ASD): How to help your child. *Children's Hospital of Los Angeles*. https://www.chla.org/blog/rn-remedies/bullying-and-autism-spectrum-disorder-asd-how-help-your-child

Wells, D. (2016). To bully or be bullied, that is the question. *Autism Society of North Carolina*. https://www.autismsociety-nc.org/to-bully-or-be-bullied-that-is-the-question

White-Johnson, J. (2019, October 25). Autistic joy as an act of resistance. *Thinking Person's Guide to Autism*. http://www.thinkingautismguide.com/2019/10/autistic-joy-as-act-of-resistance.html

Williams, J. (2019). Autism and gaslighting. *All Thing Autism*. https://www.psychreg.org/autism-gaslighting/

Wright, J. (2016, August 4). Never mind statistics: Adults with autism may be happy. *Spectrum News*. https://www.spectrumnews.org/news/never-mind-statistics-adults-autism-may-happy

Young, R. (2019, January 29). Kids with disabilities can be at risk of bullying by adults. *WBUR*. https://www.wbur.org/hereandnow/2019/01/29/kids-autism-bullying-adults

8

Parental Rest Stops and Self-Care

Although there are no Olympic competitions for stress and exhaustion, it is important to understand that having a child with differences can create a unique set of stressors. Christine Miserandino (2003), in her article about living with chronic illness, described her "spoon theory," which is very easy to apply to the mental health of those with disabilities and perhaps those caring for those with disabilities. Typical families "have the luxury of a life without choices" (Miserandino, 2003, para. 6) because they do not have ongoing limits they have to consider. When there is a physical or emotional disability, there are a certain number of "spoons" that you start the day off with. The more sleep you get and the better you eat, the more spoons you might get, but there is still a limit. Everything you do—everything you choose to do—removes a number of spoons from this limited supply. A tantrum will remove a spoon. A picky eater at breakfast will remove a spoon. Making an appointment removes a spoon, while going to an appointment takes several spoons. Once you are out of spoons, you are done—really and truly done. Chaos, illness, and disintegration happen.

DOI: 10.4324/9781003237006-8

While "autism burnout" (Raymaker et al., 2020) describes the exhaustion, loss of skills, and the reduced tolerance to stimuli of an autistic person, caring for an autistic child can result in similar characteristics. Self-care isn't an indulgence—it's a way of making sure that you have enough energy and focus to help you, your child, and anyone else who might depend on you. So, at the beginning of every day and the creation of every to-do list, there are conscious choices to be made: How many spoons will this cost, and how many spoons do I have left?

Tired...So Very, Very Tired

Children, particularly bright, autistic children are exhausting. Being a parent of an infant is exhausting. Being a parent of a middle school child is exhausting. Add unrelenting crying, vague fussiness, trying to figure out *what* is causing the problem, having glimpses of skills that then disappear, trying to find the right type of therapy, researching until late in the night, not sleeping, vague worry that something's really wrong, and frustration that no one seems to know how to help you...and, well, you're tired. You're tired for a long time.

Tiredness is the demon my family fought constantly. When the children were tired, their challenges were so much worse— many more tears, sensitivities, and lost words. And when I was tired, my sense of control slipped, and I ended up shrieking at the children. There is an interesting link between sleep disorders and autism. I don't know which comes first; it's a chicken-and-egg argument. Does lack of sleep exacerbate autism, or does autism create sleep disorders? A 2007 study by Dr. Nicholas and colleagues from the University of Wales found that there is a genetic interruption in the genes that regulate a child's internal clock and sense of sleep rhythms, and this appears to be related to autistic behaviors. I do know that generally I have been blessed with good sleepers. When we all sleep, we can all cope so much better. And when we don't...oh Lordy!

In our house, getting to sleep when the children were little was a two-hour ritual. We had the bath, the book reading, the rocking, the last drink of water, the singing, and the white noise machine. My son had me kiss him in a particular order. First the kiss on each cheek, then the touching of cheek to cheek with a hug. Then, two air kisses and two air hugs, and then, and only then, could he settle down and go to sleep. My kids also *needed* a lot of sleep. I was the "mean" mommy who hauled her kids in for bed at 8 p.m. not to get up until 7:30 a.m.

It didn't help that we had two sets of circadian rhythms in our house. My husband and daughter would put themselves to sleep at "reasonable" hours. I was the lucky mom whose toddler would announce that she was tired and would go put herself to bed. But she did not sleep well. When Elizabeth was little, she would spin in her bed and wind up with her head on the other side of the bed. She needed bedrails until she was almost ten because she would fall out of bed when she spun. Her anxieties would keep her awake during the night, and she often woke up with the characteristic dark eye circles of exhaustion and allergies. She has learned to regulate herself through the use of melatonin, blackout curtains, and a white noise machine, but even these strategies are limited during times of significant stress.

Although my daughter and husband fall asleep easily, my son and I both fight sleep. We have ADHD, and sleep is difficult to fall into. I well remember the vague sense of fear when I was little that I would die in my sleep—my body fought the drop off to sleep so badly. People with ADHD have less GABA, a neurotransmitter that is related to surrendering into sleep, and a delay in the production of melatonin (Olivardia, 2021). We can also focus better in the evenings, another typical symptom of ADHD (most of this book was written after 8 p.m.). Both my son and I will lose hours reading and playing on the computer or our phones before we can fall asleep. He will text me in the middle of the night, and often, I am awake enough to chat with him.

It's a vicious circle. You can't sleep because you're anxious, and then you're anxious because you can't sleep. Good solid sleep becomes this Holy Grail that we pursue. An awful lot of people turn to various legal and illegal drugs to help them achieve a balance where they can function. But then they can't actually function without the medication, and the vicious circle continues.

I have found a few things that have helped. They don't help all of the time, but they do help some of the time:

- ◆ **Do a "sleep assessment":** Gather data about your actual sleep habits. When do you go to bed versus when you fall asleep? How often do you nap? What do you drink and eat after 4 p.m.? What phone apps are "time sucks" for you when you're trying to relax? What medication do you take, and when do you take it? Don't judge yourself—just gather data. Observe your own habits.
- ◆ **Think baby steps:** You're not going to fix everything all at once. But you can try to fix one thing at a time. Small improvements add up. Sometimes, I focus on getting through one day, one evening, or one hour at a time.
- ◆ **Try to exercise a little bit every day:** I have found that the days that I don't get a brisk walk in are the days that I don't sleep well.
- ◆ **Try to find something that is creative but that will take a long time to finish:** I crochet, and I prefer to crochet blankets. I'm not trying to finish them in one go, but I find that I sleep better the nights that I crochet a row or two. It's monotonous and yet creative.
- ◆ **Learn to say no:** This is way easier to say than do because I struggle with perfectionism and the internal voice that says, "You should be able to do that if you could get more efficient at XYZ." The best way I have learned to say no is "I'm so sorry. I can't do this as well as it deserves to be done. I'm going to pass on this for now." Saying no reduces the anxiety jabber in my head that reviews all of the things that need doing.
- ◆ **Recognize the internal lies you create:** Recognize internal lies such as "With all of this stress I'm feeling, I need

to relax, and this one computer game/pint of Ben and Jerry's/glass of wine will help me do that." I try to use the 20-minute rule: If I still want it in 20 minutes, I can go ahead and do it. But I try to wait it out for 20 minutes.

It's easy enough from the pages of this book to say, "Make time for yourself. Relax. Find your calm." These self-help statements are everywhere, and I remember thinking, "If I could do that, I wouldn't be feeling the way I am. I just don't have the time/ support system/resources/situation to do any of these things." A month-long trip to Hawaii sounds like a perfect solution, but it was not a solution that was available to my family.

Missing the Old Map—"Oughtism"

"Oughtism" rears its ugly head at most major transitions and developmental points, and sometimes completely out of the blue. I remember going home and crying when I was at a park one day with my children when they were two and three, looking for manatees in the canals. I was excited, and they were much less so—more interested in the swings than peering into the murky waters below the bridge. A younger child, who I found out was 20 months old, toddled over to me and asked, "What are you doing?" I explained that I was looking for manatees, and he proceeded to tell me about his fish and the moon he had seen last night and how the moon wasn't really made of cheese, and on and on. When his mother rushed over full of apologies for his "bothering me," I told her that her baby was quite advanced in language. I turned away from my own silent daughter with tears in my eyes, knowing that I would never apologize for her chattiness.

Oughtism is part of the grieving process, and it is important to recognize that we grieve at different points in different ways for incredibly long times. Elizabeth Kubler-Ross (1969) noted that grieving follows a cycle, and professionals often note that parents of children with special needs follow the same cycle. However, not everyone follows the same order or the same length of time. It can become important for spouses to understand that their partners may be in quite a different stage of grieving and that it is important to remain connected and communicative. Also, if any of these stages become too intense, please seek therapy. Therapists are trained to help people move toward healthy ways of dealing with grief. Their expertise—and sometimes medication—may be necessary for you to be able to help your child.

First, there is anger. You might be angry at God, the professionals for not helping early enough, or the "mistakes" that you made. Anger provides initiative, but it often quickly moves to denial. Denial is part of the process as parents wonder if everyone was wrong and this child really is fine. Often, after diagnosis, parents will be frozen in denial, not certain how to go about getting started, and not wanting to get started. This stasis can happen when a parent just can't follow through on professional recommendations or read the materials that are given to them.

I felt the pulls of oughtism and depression deeply during this phase. Denial also happens when parents jump on a bandwagon of a strategy that "everyone" is trying. They tend to look for immediate consequences and actions, rather than really focusing on the needs of their individual child. A new therapy has the promise of fixing everything, so parents join up, thinking that this will fix it and that all will be well soon. Finally, denial can lead to parents not being able to process all of the information that they need to. They can hear only portions of the information and ignore or discard the rest. If you know that you are in this stage, or it feels too overwhelming, remind the professionals that you will need to hear important information again.

Bargaining often is the next stage. This is when parents start gathering as much information as possible on the issues surrounding autism. There is the feeling that if we just learn enough, we can beat this thing, or if we do the right thing, we will come through this. Parents bargain and search and become completely absorbed by this issue that they are determined will not get the best of them. It is during this time that parents can ignore their own needs and other needs of their family as well. Also, because they are learning so many different things, they may bombard their child with a variety of different therapies, minimizing the effectiveness of any one of them.

Accompanying each of these stages is depression. "What-ifs" and "maybes" attack at night and interrupt your sleep. Second thoughts, blame, and tiredness all mix together to create a person that you and your spouse may not recognize anymore.

The final stage is acceptance, which occurs when you realize that there is a "new normal" in your life. You can see and celebrate your child for who they are. Things have gotten better, and you have accommodated. The acceptance stage doesn't last forever, and the full cycle of grief can be triggered again by a birthday, your friend's child getting a driver's license, a wedding you attend—any event in which you see the differences between the life you anticipated and the life you got. Grief doesn't make you a bad mom; all of us have dreams of when we "grow up," and having a child with a disability rarely figures into that dream. But the periods of normality will get longer, and the periods of grief and fighting will get shorter and less intense. And you can live with grief instead of fighting it.

Grief, Depression, and Resilience

It is important to recognize the toll that having a child with autism can have on your mental health. Yes, it is helpful to be positive and to recognize that autism is who they are and that, of course, you love them absolutely. But when positivity results in the "denial, minimization, and invalidation of the authentic human emotional experience" (Quintero & Long, 2019, para. 4), it can become toxic. Parents must acknowledge that having a child who is both bright and autistic places them in a strange place that can be full of simultaneous sorrow and pride. Toxic positivity does not allow space to explore complex emotions, and parents can fall into an emotional state where they feel disconnected from themselves and others.

Nurturing connections to others is perhaps the most important thing you can do for yourself and your child. A 2019 study by Akram and others found that mothers of children with autism had higher levels of suicidal ideation, but their degree of perceived social support was the most significant moderator of these suicidal levels. Whether it is through Facebook groups, face-to-face support groups, or a family you can lean on, having an emotional support group can literally be the difference between life and death.

Grief and depression are emotions that are never far away as you watch your child struggle and you try to help them navigate their way, while at the same time taking care of your other children, your partner, your family, your job, your finances, your house, and, oh yeah—yourself. Parents are grieving the loss of their dreams, of the images of the life that they wanted. Part of that grief is a shared grief by all families. All families begin to realize that this is not the life that they set out to make. But having a bright child with autism provides its own flavor of grief. You grieve when you hand down the Barbie house you had been saving for your daughter and she has no interest. You grieve when you cannot go to your child's game because you have to take your other child to occupational therapy. You grieve when your child does not go to prom, and you grieve when your child goes to community college instead of the selective schools all of their friends are going to. There are so many moments of grief.

It was a beautiful day in May, and my family was scheduled to spend the afternoon at the speech therapist working on yet another day of pronouns and word identification. My daughter and son and I were in the car, preparing to turn right to go to the office. Instead, I turned the car left, towards the beach. I announced in a happy tone that we were going to be spending the afternoon looking for seashells. For a blissful hour, we were a normal happy family searching for seashells on the seashore. Elizabeth had shoes on, so she could walk on the beach with us. I taught them the rhyme of "She Sells Seashells Down by the Seashore," and we had a wonderful time in the afternoon and came home slightly sunburned. Of course, at the end of that golden hour, Elizabeth started shaking her hands and wailing about the sand on the shells, and Ray got hungry and cranky. The next day, when I was chided about missing a therapy session, I mumbled a brief apology and cried in the car afterward that all I had wanted to do was enjoy a brief hour of being normal.

Lucy Hone (2020) has the most amazing TED Talk about resilience that focuses on living with grief. In the video, she takes an active role and focuses on what you can do. She acknowledges that emotions can be crippling but also talks about how humans try to fix things and often need ideas. She makes three points about finding your way through the loss of grief, including:

1. **Finding acceptance:** This is not "acceptance" as in a meek, passive giving up, but an active process in which you understand that life isn't fair, life has struggle, and sometimes things are just hard. It's accepting that things happen to everyone and that this—whatever "this" is—is not personal. You didn't cause it, and you can't fix it. You can only get through it. It's acknowledging that having a bright child with autism isn't what you would have chosen, but it did happen, and you can deal with it.

2. **Choosing to find positives:** This doesn't mean toxic rejection of the human feelings of sorrow, but it does mean shifting your attention to looking for the silver lining and understanding that both feelings can live side by side. No, your child doesn't want to go to prom. But they do want to spend time at the climbing wall, and they are really very good at the climbing wall, so they have found a place of calm for themselves. Finding positives means looking for and paying attention to what might be good.

3. **Intentionally making choices:** This involves deciding if an action is going to help or harm you. There are some things that will help in the short run—that glass of wine, that pint of Ben and Jerry's—but it is important to choose them intentionally, knowing that a glass every hour or a pint every night is going to end up being negative for you in the long run. There isn't judgment associated with these choices. The key is to make them consciously. By making choices one at a time, you can evaluate your progress and your mental state.

Redefining Success

"Success" is one of those celebratory terms because it means that you have achieved something. Parents celebrate the first word, the first step, the good grades, and the milestones of their children. Parents of typical children celebrate with each other and keep track of their child's development against each other. When my son wasn't walking at 12 months, I had to check his progress against other parents' reports—"Is this typical? Is this something I should seek help on? Should I be worried?" When the answer was "This is typical," and he started walking at 13 months, my family celebrated with other families who had toddlers who were also starting to walk. We acknowledged that this was a milestone. No longer did we have babies; they were now toddlers. There was a shared growth moment. When my daughter hadn't started talking at 15 months, I did the same thing: "Is this typical? Is this something I should seek help on? Should I be worried?" When the answer was "This is not typical," and she started talking at age three, we celebrated her progress with her therapists, our family, and with very close friends. We celebrated her highest GPA and her science fair win with our family and on social media, but our best celebrations were with other families of bright children with autism who knew what was involved in both the milestone and the achievements. We didn't celebrate the level of achievement; we celebrated the level of effort. It is so important and critical to redefine success for your child on their own terms.

Redefining success means that you do not use the "typical" yardstick of developmental success against your child. "Comparison is the thief of joy" is a phrase long attributed to Theodore Roosevelt, and it is important to understand what kind of success you are celebrating. There are going to be some achievements that are defined by autism and there are going to be some achievements because of the talents. There are some achievements that will be competitive against other people and some achievements that will be personal bests. In all of these, it is important to celebrate with your child. Help your child make the connection between their efforts and their successes.

Perhaps one of the most significant ways you are going to change your definition of success is in the area of milestones. You will begin to realize how many cultural expectations there are for events like birthday parties, sports, holidays, driver's licenses, prom, graduation, going to college…and you will begin to realize just how those expectations are changed because of your child's needs and interests. When you focus on the gap between where your child is and where typical expectations are, you may feel grief. But when you focus on how far your child has come and the wholeness of their gifts and struggles, you can feel gratitude. It's OK to grieve, but don't get stuck there.

Flipping the Narrative: Should Versus Could

One of the greatest stressors on parents is the tyranny of the word *should*. You will hear it a lot: "Your child *should* behave, score higher, be talking, have more friends, calm down…" The list is endless, and you will hear this expectation of *should* from strangers, teachers, family, friends, your own head, and saddest of all, your child. *Should* is an example of the "modals of lost opportunity" (Everyday Grammar, 2018, para. 3). It implies that something is supposed to happen that we wish would happen but might not happen. There is an implied directiveness and judgmental opinion in the word, but it is a passive observation about someone else's actions. *Should* emphasizes the gap between reality and expectation and is part of the language of depression and oppression.

Could on the other hand is loaded with possibilities. *Could* leaves the future up to the person (Sevastopoulos, 2021). The word *could* offers possibilities and power, especially when paired with the word *if*. When you, your child, or your family start saying *should* statements, there is a powerlessness and a frustration that is being expressed: "I should be able to read/be less anxious/ make friends…" When you replace *should* with *could*, there is a power given in the follow-up clause of *if*. For example, "I could be able to read if…" or "I could be less anxious if…" When you notice your child, your partner, or yourself using the word *should*

Look for Purpose

FIGURE 8.1 Moving From "Should" to "Could"

frequently, you could (see what I did there?) make an intentional effort to flip the story (Figure 8.1).

Look for Purpose

Not that you need one more thing to do, but one of the most effective strategies to help your mental health is by helping others who are struggling. Mental health issues often occur when parents compare themselves to where they think they should be (notice that word again!). Whether that expectation is provided to by their friends, social media, family, or their own ambitions, the gap between reality and expectation will be filled in with depression, anxiety, frustration, or anger. You can choose to dwell here for a while, or you can seek to change things. There is a big gap between surviving and thriving, called *striving*.

When you are striving to make things better, one of the most powerful interventions is to help others (Titova & Sheldon, 2021). Whether that involves volunteering, donating money, or mentoring, there is a powerful feeling when you can reach out and lift someone else. There are a number of social media boards where parents of bright kids with autism are helping other parents navigate these waters, providing advice and resources. By doing this, they are providing a very valuable service for others—and for themselves. You can help on an organizational basis through a church or an organization that means something to you, or on a personal basis by directly volunteering services or making a personal connection.

One of the benefits of helping others is that you become more willing to accept help yourself. You realize the importance to the giver when they are able to help, which will, in turn, help you be more willing to ask for and receive help yourself. It's a wonderful twist of giving—by reaching out, you are helping someone, which helps you. By accepting help, you understand that you are also helping the helper. By providing and accepting help, you build relationships, build support, and change things for yourself and for others.

List of Strategies

The National Alliance on Mental Illness Minnesota (Abderholden, 2020) and the University Health Service of the University of Michigan (2021) both offer lists of things that you can do to help your own mental health. They include:

- ◆ **Control what you can, and let the rest go:** Limit the news, limit information, create a routine, and recognize what you cannot control.
- ◆ **Break the monotony:** Create a routine and plan small deviations from it. The goal is not to create stress, but to create enough small changes that you and your child can get used to larger ones.
- ◆ **Move every day:** Help your physical body in some manner. Get out into nature as often as you can and take big, large movements that reduce stress.
- ◆ **Quiet your mind:** Try strategies like mindfulness, meditating, or prayer. Practicing quieting your mind during calmer times will allow you to find quiet during times of unusual anxiety and stress.
- ◆ **Try to eat food that is good for you:** Nutrition is key to good mental health. If your child is a picky eater, it is OK to make food just for you. Good food is necessary fuel for your mind and your body.
- ◆ **Connect with others:** Go on social media and visit websites. Try to find other families who are experiencing what you are experiencing. You are reading this book, so you're already taken a big step forward. You are not alone. You just have to find someone who understands or cares.

- **Value yourself:** Monitor your own thoughts and be aware when you start thinking negatively. Try to have a plan when you start having thoughts that are not helpful to you and your child.
- **Give of yourself:** Volunteer time or energy to help someone else. It can help you feel better when you help others.
- **Think the best of people:** Many autistic people ask that you "presume competence" when working with them. That may mean believing that children are acting out for a reason and that professionals are often dealing with their own stressors as well. If you go looking for the points of contact and connection, you are very likely to find them.
- **Get help when you need it:** Therapy and treatment are meant not only to "fix" things, but also to stop them from breaking in the first place—and treatment works.

References

Abderholden, S. (2020). 5 things you can do for your mental health. *National Alliance on Mental Illness Minnesota.* https://namimn.org/five-thing-you-can-do-for-your-mental-health

Akram, B., Batool, M., & Bibi, A. (2019). Burden of care and suicidal ideation among mothers of children with Autism Spectrum Disorder: Perceived social support as a moderator. *Journal of the Pakistani Medical Association, 69*(4), 504–508.

Everyday Grammar. (2018, February 8). Could have, would have, and should have. *VOA Learning English.* https://learningenglish.voanews.com/a/everyday-grammar-could-have-should-have-would-have/3391128.html

Hone, L. (2020). 3 secrets of resilient people [Video]. *TED.* https://www.ted.com/talks/lucy_hone_3_secrets_of_resilient_people

Kubler-Ross, E. (1969). *On death and dying.* Scribner.

Miserandino, C. (2003). *The spoon theory.* https://cdn.totalcomputersusa.com/butyoudontlooksick.com/uploads/2010/02/BYDLS-TheSpoonTheory.pdf

Nicholas, B., Rudrashingham, V., Nash, S., Kirov, G., Owen, M. J., & Wimpory, D. C. (2007). Association of Per1 and Npas2 with autistic disorder:

Support for the clock genes/social timing hypothesis. *Molecular Psychiatry, 12*(6), 581–592. https://doi.org/10.1038/sj.mp.4001953

Olivardia, R. (2021, May 5). How to fall asleep with a rowdy, racing ADHD brain. *ADDitude.* https://www.additudemag.com/how-to-fall -asleep-adhd

Quintero, S., & Long, J. (2019). Toxic positivity: The dark side of positive vibes. *The Psychology Group.* https://thepsychologygroup.com/ toxic-positivity/

Raymaker, D. M., Teo, A. R., Steckler, N. A., Lentz, B., Scharer, M., Santos, A. D., Kapp, S. K., Huner, M., Joyce, A., & Nicolaidis, C. (2020). "Having all of your internal resources exhausted beyond measure and being left with no cleanup crew": Defining autistic burnout. *Autism in Adulthood, 2*(2), 132–143. https://www.liebertpub.com/doi/pdfplus /10.1089/aut.2019.0079

Sevastopoulos, J. (2021). Could vs. should. *Grammar-Quizzes.com.* https:// www.grammar-quizzes.com/modal5b.html

Titova, M., & Sheldon, K. (2021). Happiness comes from trying to make others feel good, rather than oneself. *Journal of Positive Psychology.* https://doi.org/10.1080/17439760.2021.1897867

University Health Service of the University of Michigan. (2021). *Ten things you can do for your mental health.* https://uhs.umich.edu/tenthings

9

Siblings, Spouses, and Other Passengers

Siblings

Having two or more children can enrich and complicate a family dynamic. As Valerie Nazarian (2010) said,

> Siblings fight, pull each other's hair, steal stuff, and accuse each other indiscriminately. But siblings also know the undeniable fact that they are the same blood, share the same origins, and are family. Even when they hate each other. And that tends to put all things in perspective.
>
> (p. 46)

For some families, there is concern about having another child once they have one with autism. It is important to know that you do have a statistically slightly higher chance of having another child with autism if you already have one. And if there is more than one child with autism in a household, they often are very different from each other. However, many parents feel that their family is not complete, and they want their child with autism to have a sibling so, hopefully, they can be family support for each other for the rest of their lives. The best advice generally is to be prepared for your next child to have issues, including different

DOI: 10.4324/9781003237006-9

sibling issues than are typical. But if you are prepared to love another child, no matter what, and are prepared for the challenges of raising two, then you should not be afraid. Plus, you already have an idea of the landscape of autism. But you should *not* think of having another child as a chance to get the child you "should" have gotten the first time.

Introductions and Comparisons

My family was lucky: Elizabeth welcomed Ray with open arms. She was *thrilled* to have another little person in the house. Not all children with autism are like this. A new infant and mom's catatonic state are significant changes in routine. Perhaps it was because she was so little when Ray was born that she didn't really remember life without him. But whatever the reason, my two are remarkably close and have found a sense of stability and peace with each other. Do they fight and push each other's buttons? Of course. But they have been remarkably "there" for each other and understand each other at a very deep level. We call them the "twins" because they are so much alike, look so much alike, and are so close in age.

Other families may not have this same dynamic. Many bright children with autism will reject the new baby, and many typical siblings will not understand their sibling who has autism. And as they grow up, the differences can become more significant, causing them to drift apart.

Child With Autism as the Older Sibling

If your autistic child is older, you should carefully prepare them for the change in schedule when the new baby comes home. Be prepared for regression. *All* children will regress when a new baby comes into the picture, and a child with autism will feel the change in schedule in an extraordinarily strong manner. Regression for a child with autism can be pretty dramatic, and it might mean going back to the diapers they just grew out of, increased thumb sucking, or a greater pulling away from the environment as they want you to come and pull them back into the world.

You can talk to them about the baby and bring in a baby doll to model behavior. Do not be surprised if your autistic child does not necessarily recognize the new baby as something other than a really noisy doll. I knew a family whose son with autism tried to put his baby sister in the garbage can because he wanted to get rid of the doll.

If you have pets, you can put your child in charge of helping the animal adjust to the baby. We found that our pets were invaluable in helping our children adjust to new settings, and Elizabeth and Ray both clung to our dog whenever they were anxious about something. By reassuring the pet, children can sometimes work out their own issues. It's important to have the right animal, however. Ray frequently hauled around our cat Chrissie, who was amazingly tolerant of his need for snuggling. Our other cat, Nellie...not so much.

Books also are helpful because they provide visuals about having a baby around. Susan Senator (2005) made a crisis book for her child to view before the arrival of a sibling, but there are many already-published books on the topic such as *The Berenstain Bears' New Baby* by Stan and Jan Berenstain. You should emphasize that love is something that grows the more there is. You might grow a seedling plant for a few weeks to show your child that the longer a plant grows, the bigger it gets, just like love does. The bigger a family is, the more love there is. One more person will add to the love, not divide what is there.

If the hospital will allow it, let the child visit the hospital where you will give birth. Do trial runs where your caretaker stays over at your house with your child so that your child is not confused when you disappear.

Stick to your old routine as much as possible when the new baby comes. You may not be as coherent as you would like, but if your child has swim class, bundle up the new baby as soon as possible and head out to the pool. I was very aware of the differences between the wonderful "cocooning" I got to do when Elizabeth was born (where we shut out the world and I got to live on her schedule), and the way that Ray had to fit himself into Elizabeth's preexisting life. Ray was fed in many more cars and on the run much more than Elizabeth. Such is the life of a younger sibling, with or without autism.

Child With Autism as the Younger Sibling

Your older, perhaps typical child may not understand why you are so absorbed with the issues of the new little one. It's hard enough for an older sibling to lose their place as "baby," much less understand why that new baby is so very demanding in terms of your time, energy, and worries.

It is impossible to give the same amount and type of attention and energy to two children—even typical children. And siblings are masters at pointing out how unfair this is. You also may be aware of the unequal distribution of time and energy you can provide your two children and feel bad about this. The best piece of advice I ever got was to remind the child that you are absolutely there to give them exactly what they *need*, and that if they were in the other child's situation, you would be doing the exact same thing for them as well. Do not try to make it up to the other child, but do try to focus on what it is that they might need. This might be trips away without everyone else. This might be going to their soccer games. This might mean an extra cuddle before bed. This also might be teaching them how to wash the dishes or clean their room when they are six so that you can be relieved of a household task. Independence is a worthwhile goal, but you need to couple it with appreciation and value for that child.

"Not Fair"

It is difficult to explain to your child who does not have autism why their sibling is the way they are. A friend of mine was asked by her typical son why his brother was "so weird." She explained to her son without autism that everyone is different; everyone has parts of their brains that work differently from the way we might expect them to. Then she tickled him, telling him that his feet must be weird because they were really smelly.

Many children who have an older autistic sibling are at risk for behavioral issues themselves. Behavioral interventions should start early, and therapy for the family is a good idea if this occurs. Clearly, there needs to be good communication between the parent and the child that they are to help their sibling, but not feel responsible for their sibling's actions.

When I teach the concept of fairness to teachers (and to kids), I use an analogy. I hand out "issues" on little slips of paper. They include things such as paper cut, shark bite, diphtheria, cancer, depression, broken leg, sunburn, etc. I notice who I give the slip that has "paper cut" on it. I then ask them to read their issue aloud. When they say, "Paper cut," I respond, "Oh my gosh! I can help you! Here is a bandage!" and give them a bandage. I then have the next person read their issue. When they read theirs— "shark bite" for example—I carefully explain that we certainly don't want to treat others any differently because that would not be fair, and I hand them a bandage. I go around the class, handing out bandages to fix everything. We then have a great discussion about how one way of working with a child doesn't work for everyone, and if we do treat everyone the same, that's really *not* fair. If the participants are children, I have them put their bandages on their desks so that they can see them as a visual reminder. This quickly ends the "That's not fair" whine!

Having a sibling with a disability doesn't have to be a bad thing. Sandra Harris and Beth Glasberg (2012), authors of *Siblings of Children With Autism: A Guide for Families*, noted that typical siblings of children with disabilities are more responsible, more caring, and more tolerant of differences than other children. They learn early that they play a very important role in the family and often move into a caretaker role. If they are younger, they can learn self-confidence because they sometimes move beyond their older sibling. If they are older, they can learn how to be responsible and compassionate—a lesson that many children need to learn.

"Dusted" With Autism—Comparisons

Many siblings of children with autism, although not exhibiting classic or severe autistic behaviors themselves, appear to be "dusted" with autism (Senator, 2005). When Ray started babbling right on cue at 14 months, I wanted to celebrate. When he didn't start walking until 13 months, I worried until I read that he was right on track. I relaxed. I hauled him around to all of Elizabeth's speech therapy sessions and all of her occupational therapy sessions. I put him into the same Montessori school she was in. He started to talk, and she started to talk to him. I was deeply grateful that not only did we have a speech therapist to teach her to talk, we had another little person learning and leading the way right next to her! Research has found that autistic children who have siblings with strong verbal and social skills have better verbal and social skills than those who do not (Ben-Itzchak et al., 2019).

I was thinking that perhaps we had a typical—and perhaps gifted—child, until Ray started showing strange behaviors of his own. Ray gained not an ounce between age one and age two. Not. A. Single. Ounce. In a most apologetic manner, the pediatrician noted that she had to make a report to Social Services because he was showing signs of "failure to thrive" and they had to make sure that we were not at fault. I couldn't help but wonder: if we were poor and from a different culture, would we have gotten the same apologetic tone? It was not the first and certainly not the last time I saw that my husband and I were treated differently because of our educational background.

When Ray turned two, which happened to coincide at the same time my daughter was fully involved with speech and occupational therapy, he was tested for everything gastric. He was tested for Crohn's disease, celiac disease, some form of allergies, and diabetes. On one particularly hellish day, I took him to the doctor's office in the morning, where they injected him with something (I was so overwhelmed at that point that I was losing track of what was being done to whom), then he had to wait an hour and get hot, and then go back and have his sweat tested. We lived in Florida, so I dug out his snowsuit we used when we visited the grandmothers in colder climates and had him play on the playground for an hour. He cried and fussed and tried to take it off. I fought with him and tried to keep my daughter occupied as well. She was happily playing on the playground and didn't want to go walking around the complex. Ray wanted to go for a walk and wanted nothing to do with the playground. I figured that in fighting with me, he was at least working up a sweat. We then went back to the doctor's where they had to tie him down to test his sweat and get blood drawn. Then, we had to take Elizabeth to speech therapy, and then I left to teach an evening class. I cried—*a lot*—that night.

The tests all came back negative, of course. I remember the doctor looking at Ray and saying, "Look little man. Either you eat, or you'll be put into the hospital where you'll be tied down and have tubes put into your arms to make you eat." Ray gained two ounces over the next two weeks and developed a fear of doctors. For his five-year checkup, he hid under the table, and I had to drag him out and hold him while the doctor took his vitals. She remarked dryly that his lungs were working just fine.

Ray has always been a great talker and can carry on a conversation for hours on end with people he knows. At 14 months, Ray used a 12-word sentence, "I want to go to the store to get a new truck." We were excited to see not only language, but gifted language! However, for years, he would respond to "How are you?" from strangers with grunts or by hiding behind a parent. He loved getting dirty and playing with water. He was quite popular with his friends at school. But he always cried when I sang (and I don't sing *that* badly!) and hated it when I read him a story with an accent. He hated wearing shoes. When he was tired, he put his hands over his ears and was comforted by petting our cats. On the spectrum? Oh yes. But not enough for a diagnosis.

Interactions

All children will push each other's buttons on purpose just to aggravate the other. My friend Rachel has a story that describes this process of how siblings can use the characteristics of autism to "get" to each other:

> We were riding in the car and there was this discussion going on in the backseat about dinosaurs. They were three and four at the time, and the conversation was similar to what you would expect for their age: basic dinosaur facts. Then the discussion started to heat up when it came to color. I am not even sure how it escalated, but Ben, my son with ASD, was telling Robert that dinosaurs were green, which is apparently mostly true, but Robert kept

saying that they were white. Now Robert is a really smart kid, and even at three, he knew that most dinosaurs were green, but he also knew that it would get Ben going. Back and forth they went...

Ben: "Green. Dinosaurs are green."

Robert: "White...they're white."

Ben: "Green!"

Robert: "White."

Ben: "GREEN!"

Robert: (pause) "White."

I finally had to intervene. "Stop it, just stop it, the two of you!"

Then, as things calmed down and all was quiet, this tiny voice whispered, "Dinosaurs are white."

"MOM!!!!!!!!! Robert says dinosaurs are white! MOMMMM!!!" The tears started flowing and the rage was full blown.

Perhaps one of the more interesting research findings is that the sibling relationship isn't just impacted by autism, but "disability is actually part of the relationship" (Laber-Warren, 2020, para. 5). The relationships between siblings tend to be transformative in both of their lives, especially if there is shared closeness. Siblings of autistic children tend to have a stronger empathy for others through perspective taking and tend to be more mature than other children their age. They also see things that parents often miss. One of my friends has an older typical daughter who helped her mom see that cheerleading would be perfect for her younger autistic daughter, not despite her autism but because of it. The little sister's use of echolalia where she gets others to script along with her is perfect for cheers and chants. It was the older sister who realized that this skill would be well within the younger sister's capabilities and encouraged her mom to have the younger sister try out.

However, there are some unique challenges. Because autism tends to impact emotional and social closeness, typical siblings often have a more difficult time than siblings of typical children in developing relationships of their own (Shivers et al., 2019).

Conversely, the autistic child with a typical sibling tends to have a stronger ability to form relationships than autistic only children. Additional issues such as poverty, violence in the home, and other family stressors can put additional pressures on a typical sibling.

It is very important that siblings of autistic children also get interventions and therapy for their own coping. Those who get support from other adults tend to be more secure than those who feel the family dynamics are exclusively driven by their autistic sibling (Tomeny et al., 2019). A metaanalysis of studies of siblings of children with ASD found that the siblings struggled with depression and anxiety far more than siblings of typical children, even when compared to siblings of children with intellectual disabilities (Shivers et al., 2019). There are a number of support groups for siblings of children with autism, both online and through advocacy associations. I also would recommend therapy when or if a sibling appears to have a hard time dealing with their brother's or sister's issues. As children grow up, their needs change, so the happy little brother who went along with watching Disney videos might get frustrated at the child with autism's tantrums when he is older or might express significant anger at some of the damage that the child with autism can inflict. If this happens, I highly recommend family therapy. Behaviors change, and so do family dynamics.

Spouses and Partners

Let's be honest here: the person reading this book is probably a mother. A lot has changed over ten years since I wrote the first edition of this book, but still, most of the time the person doing the research, running kids around from place to place, and taking care of the day-to-day stuff is the mom. Every now and then a partner will be the "carrying parent" (the one who takes the responsibility of the "work" of having a child with autism), but it's rare. Sadly enough, there appears to be a *tremendous* rate of divorce among parents with a child with autism. The general number cited on multiple websites is 80%–85%, but there appear to be no solid statistics on this. A well-designed study of families with ASD and typical families found that the rate of divorce among ASD families was 23.5%, while it was 13.8% among typical families (Hartley et al., 2010). However, the divorce rate was similar compared to typical families until the youngest child was eight. There is a tremendous amount of stress on a marriage the first few years of having children. After eight, however, families with ASD continued to divorce, while families of typical older children tended to stay together. It is undeniable that autism places tremendous stress upon a marriage and continues to place a stress on marriage as children age. For marriages that are challenged in the first place, autism may be the very wedge that serves to drive couples apart over time. For marriages that are strong and parents who are willing to do what's necessary, there is a good chance of survival.

When a child is diagnosed with autism, or any disability, both parents grieve the loss of their "perfect" child. Men often try to be the strong one for their wife and family, often feeling that their concerns and fears are more trivial than those of their child and their child's mother, which can lead to feelings of isolation and burnout (Burrell et al., 2017). Mothers can either over-rely on their spouse to listen or can become so invested in the search for help that they stop listening or sharing with their spouse. Families with non-traditional family makeups often find themselves falling into traditional roles with the resultant stressors because one parent tends to take on a primary carer role, although there is some research that gay and lesbian families tend to be slightly more buffered by these expectations (Holden, 2010). Successful collaborations happen when both parents begin working together to solve the various problems that come up, rather than one solving and one reassuring. If you can form an "us vs. this issue" mentality, there's great hope of a successful parenting experience. Susan Senator (2005) discussed how she and her husband worked together with what they called a "Sweetie Treaty" (which essentially was an agreement "not to feel bad about feeling bad") and helped each other focus on making one small change at a time, rather than trying to fix all of the things that were going wrong.

It is very, *very* important for families, and especially children, to understand that parents don't divorce because of the child, or even because the child is autistic. Parents can divorce because sharing a life with someone is hard and having a child with additional issues can place additional stressors on a marriage, on a budget, and on well-being. But it is important to clarify that it is not the child that is the cause of parental stress—it is the response of the parents that brings a marriage to a breaking point. The child should never, ever feel that they are the source of their parents' divorce.

My husband, James, was very encouraging and patient throughout this ordeal. A second cousin of his, Christos, had been born with a subgaleal hematoma that resulted in long-term growth trauma that impacted his speech and hearing. Having grown up with Christos resulted in James becoming more understanding of personal challenges from a very early age.

Having an autistic child also forces you to look back in your family tree and identify traits that would probably have been identified as being on the spectrum in these times. I would have undoubtedly been identified as ADHD, and James definitely exhibits some ASD characteristics. Bipolar disorder and depression run in my family, and OCD runs in his. We are also both very bright. As my mom said about our children, "They didn't stand a chance." However, we discovered through our work with our children that we were able to reframe our idiosyncrasies, not as willful and intentional behaviors, but as demonstrations of differences and disabilities. We found that the more we learned about our children, the more we learned about each other—and the more we learned about each other, the more we were able to forgive each other our various responses to stressors.

James is very spiritual, and that sense of self and family kept him very grounded and anchored in how he engaged with me and with the children. According to my husband, a deeper truth helps us weather the currents of emotion that pass through us during very personal challenges, like a child being diagnosed with autism. Maintaining a healthy resolve and taking a positive stance on everything that may appear insurmountable makes the journey more tolerable and keeps things more focused and directed. His positive outlook tended to bring my anxieties back to reality, or at least helped me see things in a different light.

But not everyone has a companion who can balance out their needs. Divorce can have tremendous impacts on any child, and can have very significant, but different impacts on a child with autism. The biggest stressor for the child will be both the removal of the person and the change in the routine. If the other parent was very loving, that will be a significant change. But even if the other parent was abusive, the structure and routine of that cycle will be difficult for the child with autism to release. In addition, the tension that can be found within a relationship that is deteriorating can be felt very acutely by a child with autism who may shut it, and the rest of the world, out, or act out. If divorce is something that cannot be avoided, you should seek therapy for you and for your child. The various autism support networks have significant resources available for parents who are divorcing. The presence of disability also can impact the divorce process and child support issues. Check with your state and your lawyer for specifics.

I know that my own marriage suffered—we didn't even understand the depths of our challenges until years after Elizabeth's diagnosis. So much was put on the back burner that wasn't dealt with. We were in crisis mode for years and years dealing with the challenge of two children with issues, lack of family nearby, and financial stress. However, James and I problem solved everything tremendously well. I did the research; he listened to me and gave me feedback. I paid the bills; he worked full-time. I ran the children from doctor to doctor, and he kept track of them on his calendar. We are both only children, so we turned to each other every night to cry and plan the next step.

Throughout it all, he was strong, steady, and focused on Elizabeth and Ray's needs—to the point that so many of our own were neglected. He, and I, let him be the strong one for so long that he didn't feel he had anyone to talk to or to share his day's events with. When we got away for the first time together, we had no idea what to say to each other that didn't involve the children.

Trying to take care of each other was very difficult. I gained weight from lack of exercise and eating too much. Ice cream really helps calm that panicky feeling in your stomach when you don't know what is coming up. I consumed pint after pint of ice cream. He found solace in work—completely absorbed by various problems and projects. Both of us suffered in our friendships because we were unable to make commitments to meet friends and we felt that we were boring our friends with our stresses. Heck, we were boring ourselves.

And oh, the financial stress—that in itself seriously strained our marriage. We borrowed *lots* of money on credit cards and then even more money from my mother. She helped pay for therapy, new clothes, doctors' bills, electricity, and private school. I couldn't work full time for several years and was constantly trying to juggle consulting and various adjunct teaching jobs at several universities. I would have to go to conferences to make the connections to get more consulting gigs, but the conferences themselves would be expensive. I was heartbroken the day we closed the sale on our first house we ever owned. It was a lovely house in Florida that we had purchased right before Ray was born and months before all hell broke loose in trying to juggle everything. We had our fantasy house for two years and ended up losing it. Yet another dream deferred.

Therapy helps tremendously. For years, there was no therapy—no money, no time, and no energy for one more thing. When the children were in elementary school and things settled down, therapy helped us remember who we were when we weren't in crisis mode—but it took ten years of crisis to get to that point. If you have no time or energy for therapy, and are married to a stranger, my best advice for both of you is to wait it out. I had a policy of waiting six months to see if things got better. If at the end of six months, things were not better, I could think of doing something. For a girlfriend of mine, things were not better, and so she made changes. But at the end of six months, they always were better for us.

There *will* be a time when there is a "normal" to your days and you can deal with things. James and I stayed married given our deep love for one another and innate sense of family, not "for the sake of the children" as in the martyr-laden old days, but because the realization that our anchored love and the family unit are for us at the core of our beings. We were both willing to get past the hurt we had done to each other, the years of anxiety and stress, and remember why we were together in the first place. But it came whisper close…and had we been different, had we been less lucky and less privileged, things would have been different. We are now stronger together in the same way that a scar is strong. There was damage done, but the result is stronger than it was before.

Angels

Recently, Tina, a friend of mine, was wondering what were the factors that "cured" her son Brandon, who no longer qualified for services through the school system. She knew that he had made tremendous strides, and even marveled that of her three children, he was now the easiest one to understand and manage! She credited her actions and some of her ex-husband's, but she noted that "Jen" had made some of the most significant impacts on her son's development. "Who is Jen?" I asked. Jen was the teenage nanny who helped Tina for several years and took great pride and enjoyment in working with Brandon. "Jen was our angel," Tina said fervently.

You will find the right people at just the right times in your life. They will pass through your life, and you may have to eventually say goodbye to them, but they will leave tremendous growth behind them. Although you can't guarantee an angel, you can appreciate all of those who come into your life to help you.

We asked a lot of our angels. They had to handle tantrums, sibling fights, fussy eaters, and stimming behaviors, *and* come up with ideas to help the children manage themselves and track the changes. We came up with the idea of crisis books from Irene, who wrote cute little books for the children about major events that were coming up. We learned to sneak vegetables into Ray's muffins from Emmy. We had an opportunity to teach the children the effects of their behavior one day when Elizabeth was being particularly awful to Miss Lori, who seriously thought about leaving us as our babysitter. We all had a long talk about how actions have consequences and friends can love you but not want to be around you if you do not treat them nicely. Miss Nicki would take the kids to Six Flags for stimulating activity when I was too overwhelmed to face a roller coaster. (OK, maybe that wasn't asking too much of her on that one, but it was more than I could do.)

Advertising works. We found four of our nannies, including Irene, our first nanny and first angel, by running an ad at the local university. I can recommend future special education teachers as a source for nannies. You can go to the university's career placement office, or their newspaper's classified section, or the college department, and often they will run an ad for childcare for free.

Our angels tended to be young and on the way to a great profession. They cared about children, were flexible in their work schedules and demands, and were willing to communicate with us and celebrate our child's growth almost as much as we did. They became part of our family for a year or two until their lives took them somewhere else. In each case, it was very hard to explain to my little tender souls why they had to leave. Our children still love them and talk about them. Irene (Nanny Vene), Miss Molly, Emmy, Miss Lori, Miss Nicki, Miss Amberly, and Zach all enriched our lives tremendously.

The Real Drivers

It is important to note that, even with all of the help of our angels, my help, my husband's help, the school's help…the most important people in this process have been Elizabeth and Ray. It takes great courage in the face of what appears to be overwhelming fear and anxiety to keep going. I have tremendous respect for my children when I see one of them take a deep breath and step into something that must be terrifying. I remember when they first moved to a new house and they were anxious about going to the playground right outside. Boxes were everywhere, the smells were new, the humidity was new, and there was a group of children already playing outside. To get their bikes and join a new group of children who had routines and social rules that they didn't know was terrifying for them. And they did it: they rode around and around and gradually joined the pick-up game of soccer that was going on. Elizabeth came in after about an hour and hid in her closet to regroup. I knew exactly how she felt and, after a while, joined her in there. It was a lovely moment of calm in an otherwise chaotic time.

I also appreciate their ability to forgive me. I have screamed at them, I have been irritable, and I have been deeply angry at them. On one memorable day when things were just so stressful that I was snappy and hot, Elizabeth got in my face and used a line from the Disney movie *The Game Plan* where the little girl asks her father, "Is that why you never smile?" We all laughed, my bad mood vanished, and we got popcorn to go and watch a favorite movie. I thank God that I have my children and that they are the people that they are. Being bright and autistic is a map for us, and we live with it, understand its power, and work on all of us becoming the best people that we can be. Even though we all have a ways to go, it's good to know that we're all in the process together.

Gifts From Autism

Even though most of the time we are working against the negative effects of autism, I am reminded every now and then of its gifts. There was a time when my family was unpacking, and I was getting frustrated because I couldn't find the forks. Why I had separated the forks from the spoons and knives in the boxes was beyond me. I was banging around, trying to remember what I could have done with them. Elizabeth came in and very calmly said, "Here they are, Mommy," as she pulled out the forks buried in the inner recesses of a box that had been opened but not unpacked. How she could remember the box that the forks were in was an ability I was in awe of. There are gifts that autism brings not only to Elizabeth and Ray, but to us, their family.

Ability to Focus

So many careers require an ability to focus in the midst of chaos. With today's rapidly changing technology, people have to learn to sift through reams of information to synthesize new ideas. Both Elizabeth and Ray have intense, long periods where they can focus. If the topic or task is interesting to them, they will maintain fixed attention spans. Of course, if the topic is not of interest to them, their attention span is like a butterfly, lightly landing, only to flit off again. However, I know that whatever they find to do with their lives, they will be able to give it the attention it needs in order for them to succeed. They do not play the "game" of social engagement well, but neither are they distracted by social activity.

Superb Memory for Events and Details

While writing the original edition of this book, I could not remember the line from the Disney movie I just discussed, and so I called my children over to ask them. "Is that why you never smile?" said my daughter, craning her face to look in mine, reenacting the scene in the movie. They have phenomenal memories for events, lines, and random pieces of information. Once, while recounting a challenging test, Elizabeth said "My photographic memory got a little blurry on that part of the page." Because her memory is for visual things, and rarely for social interactions, I am always amazed at the level of detail that she can use to describe a past event. For a very long time when he was a toddler, my son insisted that he could remember being born and he would relate small, unusual details. I wasn't quite sure what to make of that, but I had to believe him when his memory for other events was so strong.

Unique Perspective

Because they watch human behavior with such focus, my children tend to have phenomenal insight into people. They know when someone is trustworthy, when someone is lying, and when someone is pretending to be happy. They don't always know how to engage with other people, but they have a remarkable sensitivity to others' needs and moods. Ray, in particular, is our barometer and reflects the tensions and joys around him.

I know that most of the very successful people in life were the ones who saw a new or unusual way of doing things. They aren't always the most content, but they are driven by an innate need to know or to find out.

Precision

When Ray starts something, he has to finish it. When Elizabeth is working on an activity, she has to get it just right. Such a drive for perfection can lead to tears, but it also can lead to excellence. When precision is not reached, I want my children to look at their actions in the big picture and to understand why things can't be just so right *now*. And when precision is reached, I want them to celebrate the feeling of accomplishment. Such skills are noted in many aspects of life, and although I want my children to have a sense of forgiveness, I do want them to keep trying to improve things around them.

Passion

What my children feel, they feel intensely. When Ray is hugging me good night, he holds on so tight that I *know* that I am loved. When Elizabeth removes herself from the activities around her, I know that she is processing it in order to deal with it. When my children study a subject that is of interest, they are captivated. Although great emotions can overwhelm, they also can inspire. I want them to feel the warmth of the flame of passion without being burned.

Because I have a double background in gifted education and special education, I recognize that what is a strength to one person can appear as a disability to another. We have given up defining so much of "This is autism"/"This is giftedness" and we just accept it as "them." We offer help when it is needed, and we focus forward. Our goal for both of them is to learn to understand themselves and to have skills to help themselves move forward—no matter what.

I have been on a parent panel at a national conference for parents of twice-exceptional children twice—once when my children were preschoolers and once when they were young adults. During the first one, I remember being highly anxious as other mothers of twice-exceptional girls looked at me and said "It gets better. You will be amazed at how strong her abilities are and how she will find her way. It won't be easy, but it will be ok." Eighteen years later, I sat on a panel convened by a mother of a twice-exceptional boy who was in early elementary, and I looked at her and said, "It gets better. You will be amazed at how strong his abilities are and how he will find his way. It won't be easy, but it will be ok."

I want my children, my marriage, and my family to make their way with strength and a deep knowledge that they can make it through—no matter what life gives them. I hope that the map in this book helps you in your journey also.

References

Ben-Itzchak, E., Nachson, N., & Zachor, D. A. (2019). Having siblings is associated with better social functioning in autism spectrum disorder. *Journal of Abnormal Child Psychology, 47*(5), 921–931. https://doi.org/10.1007/s10802-018-0473-z

Burrell, A., Ives, J., & Unwin, G. (2017). The experiences of fathers who have offspring with autism spectrum disorder. *Journal of Autism and Developmental Disorders, 47*(4), 1135–1147.

Harris, S. L., & Glasberg, B. A. (2012). *Siblings of children with autism: A guide for families* (3rd ed.). Woodbine House.

Hartley, S. L., Barker, E. T., Seltzer, M. M., Floyd, F., Greenberg, J., Orsmond, G., & Bolt, D. (2010). The relative risk and timing of divorce in families of children with an autism spectrum disorder. *Journal of Family Psychology, 24*(4), 449–457. https://doi.org/10.1037/a0019847

Holden, G. W. (2010). *Parenting: A dynamic perspective.* Sage Publishing.

Laber-Warren, E. (2020). How autism shapes sibling relationships. *Spectrum News.* https://www.spectrumnews.org/features/deep-dive/how-autism-shapes-sibling-relationships/

Nazarian, V. (2010). *The perpetual calendar of inspiration.* Spirit Books.

Senator, S. (2005). *Making peace with autism: One family's story of struggle, discovery, and unexpected gifts.* Trumpeter.

Shivers, C. L., Jackson, J. B., & McGregor, C. M. (2019). Functioning among typically developing siblings of individuals with autism spectrum disorders: A meta-analysis. *Clinical Children and Family Psychological Review, 22*(2), 172–196. https://doi.org/10.1007/s10567-018-0269-2

Tomeny, T. S., Rankin, J. A., Baker, L. K., Eldred, S. W., & Barry, T. D. (2019). Discrepancy in perceived social support among typically developing siblings of youth with autism spectrum disorder. *Autism, 23*(3), 594–606. https://doi.org/10.1177/1362361318763973

Essential Resources

This section is a brief listing of some of the major sites and books that provide support, resources, and information about bright children with autism. There are many, many sites, books, and information out there. This list should simply get you started…

Name/Title	Location	Description
Advocacy and Support Organizations for Families and Individuals With Autism		
Autistic Self Advocacy Network (ASAN)	https://autisticadvocacy.org	Highlights neurodiversity and self-empowerment; motto is "Nothing About Us Without Us"
Autism Speaks	https://www.autismspeaks.org	Provides research and information; well-funded and well-known, but some very problematic messages
Autistic Women and Nonbinary Network	https://awnnetwork.org	Community, support, and resources for autistic women, girls, nonbinary individuals, and all marginalized genders
National Autistic Society	https://www.autism.org.uk	UK-based, up-to-date information with a broad view of neurodiversity and pathological demand avoidance
Pathological Demand Avoidance Society	https://www.pdasociety.org.uk	Provides information and support for those with PDA
Advocacy and Support Organizations for Twice-Exceptional Children		
Council for Exceptional Children	https://exceptionalchildren.org	Special education advocacy group; has connections with national and state organizations
Council for Exceptional Children–The Association for the Gifted	https://cectag.com	Advocacy organization division focused on the needs of twice-exceptional and other diverse learners
Supporting Emotional Needs of the Gifted	https://www.sengifted.org	Resources and information about twice-exceptional students and supportive community

---

Autistic Voices and Neurodiversity

Amanda (Mel) Baggs: "In My Language"	https://www.youtube.com/watch?v=JnylM1hI2jc	An amazing video using AAC about how Baggs sees the world
Jim Sinclair: "Why I Dislike Person-First Language"	http://www.larry-arnold.net/Autonomy/index.php/autonomy/article/view/OP1/html_1	One of the foundational texts of the neurodiversity movement
ASAN Book List	https://autisticadvocacy.org/resources/books	List of books written for autistic people by autistic people
Not an Autism Mom: "100-ish books on Autism and Neurodiversity"	https://notanautismmom.com/2020/07/20/autism-books	List of books that support neurodiversity; parenting with a dash of awareness
Thinking Person's Guide to Autism	http://www.thinkingautismguide.com	Autism news and resources from autistic people, professionals, and parents

---

Ideas and Strategies

All Kinds of Minds	https://www.allkindsofminds.org	Advice on how to use a neurodevelopmental framework for teaching
Brain Balance Achievement Centers	https://www.brainbalancecenters.com	Brain-based learning and support plans
Bright and Quirky	https://brightandquirky.com	Experts and programs for helping your bright child with challenges thrive
Special Needs Antibullying Toolkit	https://bullyfreeworld-bully.nationbuilder.com/toolkit	Guidance on what to do when your child is being bullied or is the bully
Lives in the Balance	https://www.livesinthebalance.org	Ross Greene's website of ideas and strategies; collaborative and proactive solutions for behaviorally challenging kids
Social Thinking	https://www.socialthinking.com	Great ideas for how to help someone think through social situations
The OT Toolbox: "How to Create a Sensory Diet"	https://www.theottoolbox.com/how-to-create-sensory-diet	Things you can do to create a sensory diet
2e Twice-Exceptional Books List	https://www.hoagiesgifted.org/2e_books.htm	Hoagie's Gifted Education Page's list of 2e books

---

Identification and Assessment Tools and Resources for Autism/Twice-Exceptionality

The Amend Group	https://theamendgroup.com	Comprehensive psychological services specializing in 2e
Autism Navigator: ASD Video Glossary	https://autismnavigator.com/asd-video-glossary	Videos to compare typical toddlers with toddlers with possible ASD

Belin-Blank Assessment and Counseling Clinic	https://belinblank.education .uiowa.edu/clinic	Comprehensive evaluations and counseling clinic
Gifted Development Center	https://www .gifteddevelopment.org	Assessment, advocacy, and scholarly contributions
The Gifted Resource Center of New England	http://www.grcne.com	Resource specializing in different minds
Face Memory Test	https://facememory.psy.uwa .edu.au	A good way to evaluate the degree of prosopagnosia someone has
M-CHAT: Modified Checklist for Autism in Toddlers	https://mchatscreen.com	At-home screener you can share with your pediatrician
Summit Center	https://summitcenter.us	Assessment, consultation, and counseling services to help 2e children reach their potential

Legal Rights and Information

Center for Parent Information and Resources	https://www .parentcenterhub.org	Provides answers to many legal questions
Wrightslaw	https://www.wrightslaw.com	The best website for special education law questions
U.S. Department of Education, Office of Special Education and Rehabilitative Services	https://www2.ed.gov/about /offices/list/osers/osep/ index.html	The original law and parent information

Films and Television Shows

2e: Twice-Exceptional (2019)	https://vimeo.com/ ondemand/2emovie	Film about being a twice-exceptional kid
2e2: Teaching the Twice-Exceptional (2019)	https://vimeo.com/ ondemand/2e2movieoc	Film about teaching twice-exceptional kids
The Good Doctor (2017–)	https://abc.com/shows/the -good-doctor	Television show about a doctor who is gifted and autistic
Temple Grandin (2010)	https://www.hbo.com/ movies/temple-grandin	Film about Temple Grandin
Family Friendly Autism Movies	https://www.autism.org/ autism-movies/#Family -Friendly-Autism-Movies	A list of family-friendly movies about autism from Autism Research Institute. (*Note.* Not all are supportive of neurodiversity—one has Elvis curing autism…)

Research-Based Strategies

National Association for Gifted Children: Gifted Education Strategies	https://www.nagc.org/ resources-publications /gifted-education -practices	Evidence-based practices for gifted kids

National Autism Center: National Standards Project	https://www.nationalautismcenter.org/national-standards-project/phase-2	A list of strategies that have been researched to be effective
The National Clearinghouse on Autism Evidence and Practice	https://ncaep.fpg.unc.edu	Evidence-based practices for kids with autism
A Nation Deceived and *A Nation Empowered*	https://www.accelerationinstitute.org/nation_deceived	Evidence for acceleration

Research/Program/Information Sites

2e News	https://www.2enews.com	News resource for all things 2e; great starting point
Belin Blank Center at the University of Iowa	https://belinblank.education.uiowa.edu	2e research
The University of North Carolina TEACHH Autism Program	https://teacch.com/research	TEACCH program information
Hoagies' Gifted Education: Twice-Exceptional ·	https://www.hoagiesgifted.org/twice_exceptional.htm	Gifted education page with resources about 2e
National Autism Center at May Institute	https://www.nationalautismcenter.org	Major center for curriculum and resources for autism
SPARK (Simons Foundation Powering Autism Research)	https://sparkforautism.org	Medical and genetic information and research
Vanderbilt University Treatment and Research Institute for Autism Spectrum Disorders (TRIAD)	https://vkc.vumc.org/vkc/triad/home	Treatment and research information

Schools/Programs

Bridges Academy	https://www.bridges.edu	School in Los Angeles for 2e kids; also runs a graduate program and the 2e Newsletter
Colorado Department of Education: Twice-Exceptional	https://www.cde.state.co.us/gt/twice-exceptional	Parent and professional development resources
Montgomery County Public Schools Twice-Exceptional Program	https://www.montgomeryschoolsmd.org/curriculum/enriched/gtld	Includes an amazing list of resources for parents and teachers
Top Schools for 2e Kids in the U.S.	https://www.youngwonks.com/blog/Top-Schools-for-2e-Kids-in-the-US	Not an endorsement, but a good way to find a school/program near you

Schools and Programs for 2e Students in the United States	https://www.2enewsletter.com/topic_resources_schools-programs.html	2e Newsletter list, including state public school information
Hechinger Report: "Twice exceptional, doubly disadvantaged? How schools struggle to serve gifted students with disabilities"	https://hechingerreport.org/twice-exceptional-doubly-disadvantaged-how-schools-struggle-to-serve-gifted-students-with-disabilities	Useful article about challenges finding a school setting

Support Groups for Parents and Families

Gifted Homeschoolers Forum	https://ghflearners.org	Support for parents homeschooling their children, including 2e children
Raising Poppies	https://www.facebook.com/groups/RaisingPoppies	Private Facebook group devoted to parents of gifted and twice-exceptional kids
Parents of Twice-Exceptional (2E)	https://www.facebook.com/groups/parentsof2e	Private Facebook group devoted to parents of twice-exceptional kids
Twice-Exceptional/2E Network International	https://www.facebook.com/groups/2E.Network.LA	Private Facebook group providing support, resources, and more to 2e individuals and families
Washington State Fathers Network	https://www.fathersnetwork.org	Provides support and information for fathers
With Understanding Comes Calm	https://www.withunderstandingcomescalm.com/	Counseling support for families and individuals

Books About Autistic and Twice-Exceptional Children

Ballou, E. P., daVanport, S., & Onaiwu, M. G. (2021). *Sincerely, your autistic child: What people on the autism spectrum wish their parents knew about growing up, acceptance, and identity.* Beacon Press.

Kircher-Morris, E. (2021). *Raising twice-exceptional children: A handbook for parents of neurodivergent gifted kids.* Taylor & Francis.

Prizant, B. M. (with Fields-Meyer, T.). (2015). *Uniquely human: A different way of seeing autism.* Simon & Schuster.

Reber, D. (2018). *Differently wired: A parent's guide to raising an atypical child with confidence and hope.* Workman.

Silberman, S. (2015). *Neurotribes: The legacy of autism and the future of the neurodiversity.* Avery.

Trail, B. (2010). *Twice-exceptional gifted children: Understanding, teaching, and counseling gifted students*. Prufrock Press.

Webb, J. T., Amend, E. R., Beljan, P., Webb, N. E., Kuzujanakis, M., Olenchak, F. R., & Goerss, J. (2016). *Misdiagnosis and dual diagnosis of gifted children: ADHD, bipolar, OCD, Asperger's, depression, and other disorders* (2nd ed.). Great Potential Press.

About the Author

Claire E. Hughes-Lynch, Ph.D., is Professor of Elementary and Special Education at the College of Coastal Georgia. A Fulbright Scholar to Greece, she has taught in twice-exceptional programs and lives her life in twos—two cats, two dogs, two children (but one husband) across two countries.

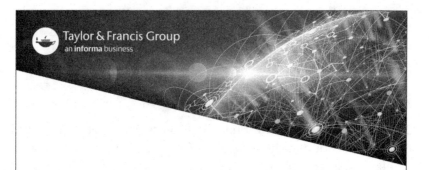

Printed in the United States
by Baker & Taylor Publisher Services